150

Sunseekers'

GREEK ISLANDS

The only Greek Islands' Guide to include ... re you can sunbathe and swim without clothe...

CW01662224

Sunseeker Publications

Compiled, designed and published by
Sunseeker Publications, Congleton,
Cheshire, CW12 3RB, England.

First published 1982.
Reprinted, revised and updated 1983 and 1985.

© Sunseeker Publications 1985
ISBN 0 9508885 1 6

All rights reserved. Without written permission
from the publisher this volume, or any part of it,
may not be reproduced by any means or in any form.

Printed and bound in Great Britain by
Harvest Printers Ltd
Park Street, Macclesfield
Cheshire SK11 6SR

Acknowledgements

Thanks to the following for their help and assistance in the preparation of this edition:

J. Alfred Brown, W.R.R. Bruce, L.A. Davies, D. Deyes, David Eagle, P.R. Frances, John Harris, Dennis Jeffery, Colin Hutchinson, Jonathan Lister Smith, Robin Major, Ron Merrett, Duncan Paterson, Derek Peckham, Jeff Piner, John Preston, P.D. Reddick, Joachim Saffert, H.G. Schnittger, Steve and Lyn Spiers, Timsway Holidays Ltd., Phil Vallack, G.P. Warneford, B.J. Whittaker and P.G. Wardle.

Although great care has been taken to ensure accuracy, the publishers cannot accept any responsibility for errors or omissions or for any consequential loss arising therefrom.

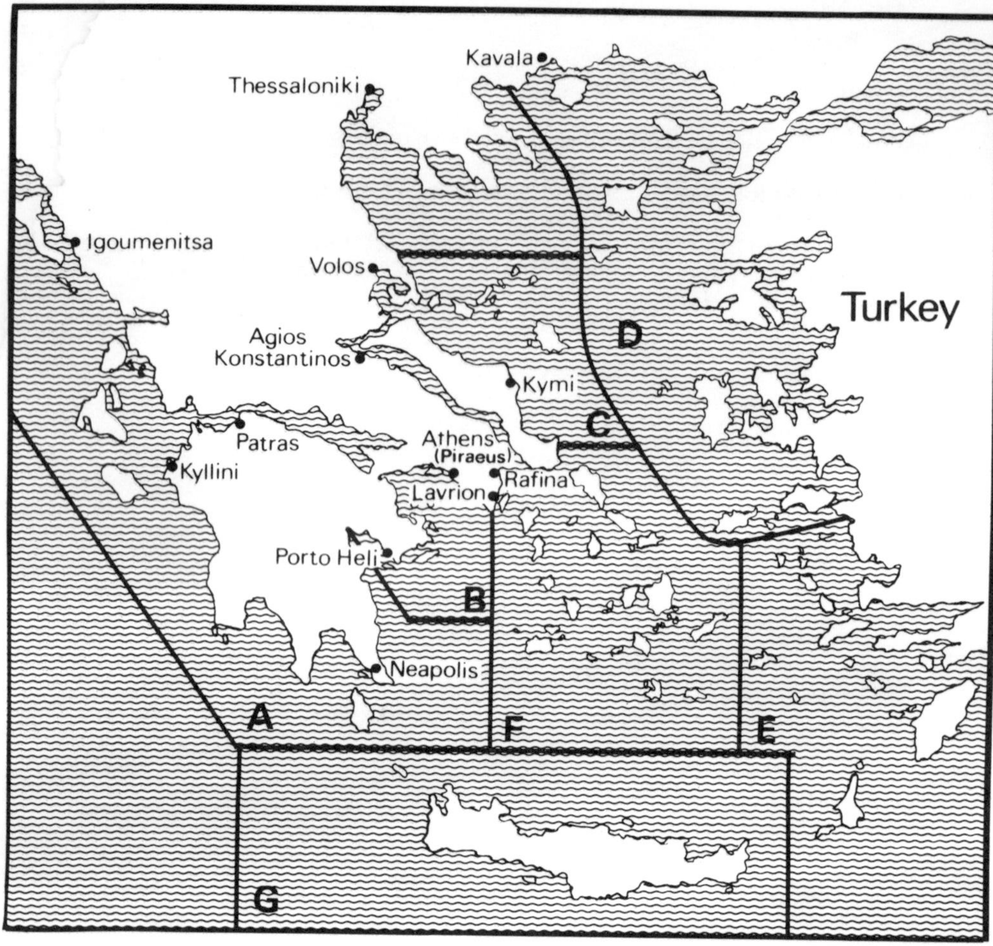

A IONIAN ISLANDS

B SARONIC ISLANDS

C SPORADES

D NORTH-EASTERN AEGEAN ISLANDS

E DODECANESE

F CYCLADES

G CRETE

CONTENTS

PRELIMINARIES

About the Factfile

Beach nudity is a pleasure so enjoyable that, once experienced, most of us become devotees unwilling to accept less. However, when choosing a holiday destination the availability of nudist beaches is only one of a number of considerations. Different people look for different things from their holidays and it makes sense to try to ensure that the destination which you choose matches your expectations as closely as possible. Worthwhile information is, however, difficult to come by. Holiday brochures usually provide only a minimum of information and what they do say isn't always objective. For those of us who enjoy sunbathing and swimming without clothes the problem is even more acute and the **Sunseekers' Guide** is designed to identify those places which are suitable for nudism while at the same time giving factual information about such things as air and sea connections, availability of accommodation, etc.

Although great care is taken to ensure accuracy, things can change quickly and if you think that we've got something wrong, or if you have any additional information, please let us know. In the next edition we will again be acknowledging readers' contributions which are used.

'Nudist' or 'Naturist'?

In the following pages we refer to 'nudists' and 'nudism' as well as 'naturists' and 'naturism'. We recognise, however, that there are many who strip off on the beach who consider themselves to be neither nudists nor naturists although, for the sake of convenience, we have used the terms in this book to describe all those who enjoy sunbathing and swimming without clothes.

Nudity and the Law

Nudism is not uncommon on most Greek islands. In fact, the writer has enjoyed sunbathing and swimming naked on every island that he has ever visited and has never encountered any problem either with the authorities or with the local people. It has, however, to be said that, in the past, there have been examples of harsh treatment of those arrested for nudity including stiff fines and even jailings. This often depended on local whim. The Cretan authorities, for example, had a 'hard-line' reputation a few years ago while, at the same time and by way of complete contrast, beach nudity was so widely practised and accepted on the island of Mykonos that, on most beaches, it had become the norm. In 1983 legislation was enacted which made possible the creation of officially recognised nudist beaches and there are now several of these with more expected to be designated in the not too distant future. Although elsewhere nudity is still technically illegal, the passing of the Act gave official impetus to already changing attitudes and nudists are now unlikely to experience any problem provided sensible discretion is used. It is, however, important to bear in mind that tourism is relatively new to some of the islands, many of which still retain strong customs and traditions, and we should be careful not to cause gratuitous offence. Those insensitive enough to strip-off on town beaches or in other unsuitable places can expect trouble.

Environmental Issues

The Greeks have, in the past, been guilty of a notoriously indifferent attitude to pollution and in some places the problem has reached enormous proportions. They are, however, now expending a great deal of time and money in an attempt to improve the situation (particularly with regard to oil pollution) but the task facing them is a huge one.

Sadly, much of the problem is due to the uncaring or unthinking attitudes of many of Greece's foreign visitors. Backpackers in particular, attracted to the islands by the generally relaxed attitude towards camping, bear a large part of the responsibility. The more isolated beaches (which are also frequently the better ones) where unofficial camping takes place are now often littered with empty bottles, tin cans, plastic cartons and toilet tissues (which at least are biodegradable). As with all freedoms there are always those who will abuse the privilege and in many places the law, which prohibits camping outside official sites, is now rigorously enforced.

It cannot be true that people actually relish the prospect of lying on dirty beaches surrounded by piles of rubbish. However this is, ultimately, the inevitable consequence of an uncaring attitude to litter pollution. The very least that we can do is not to add to the litter already there although, in some places, the problem is so bad that even if no further litter is deposited, the beaches would remain permanently scarred. What is required, therefore, is a more positive approach. If we really want to do something to improve the situation let us, in addition to taking away our own litter, also remove some of the existing stuff, particularly those items which are not easily biodegradable such as plastic, glass bottles and tin cans. Please help in this. If we all, say, take away a couple of somebody else's empty bottles or tin cans every time we use a beach we will be making a worthwhile contribution to improving matters. Naturism, above all else, is about the enjoyment of things natural. Let us express our appreciation of this enjoyment by cherishing and protecting the environment which gives us so much pleasure.

When to Travel

If possible you should avoid high season – mid July to about mid September. Not only do many of the islands become unpleasantly busy but also the character of many of the beaches changes. Beaches which are used for nudism earlier and later in the season become so overrun with clothed sunbathers that naturists are squeezed out. If you are obliged to travel at this time of year consider visiting one of those islands with beaches where nudity is the norm at any time such as Mykonos or Skiathos (Banana Beach).

The best time to travel is either late spring (May-June) or autumn (September- October). During these periods you'll not only miss the crowds and the hottest temperatures but also the *meltemi*. This strong wind, which blows periodically from about mid-July and throughout August, can make lying on the beach unpleasant if not impossible and often results in the cancellation of all but the largest inter-island ferries (sometimes for days on end). Even in midsummer, evenings can sometimes be chilly and it is advisable to take a warm sweater or similar garment. The period November-February can be both chilly and wet while in March and April the weather is unpredictable with warm sunny days interspersed with cool, windy weather. The following table shows monthly average temperatures:-

	J	F	M	A	M	J	J	A	S	O	N	D
Air temperatures												
C	11	11	13	16	20	24	26	26	24	20	16	13
F	52	52	56	60	68	76	79	79	76	68	60	56
Sea temperatures												
C	14	14	15	17	21	25	26	25	24	19	17	15
F	57	57	59	63	70	77	79	77	75	66	63	59

Accuracy

Although we have tried to ensure accuracy, please note that bus times and things like museum opening times can change from year to year. You are advised to check timings before travelling if the non-arrival of a particular bus is likely to cause you a great deal of inconvenience.

BEGINNERS PLEASE!

The Psychological Barrier

There is a tremendous psychological barrier which inhibits people from removing their clothing except in limited and very specific circumstances. Generally, people shower or take a bath naked, most people (although by no means all) make love in the nude and some even go so far as to sleep in the nude. In the past nudism has often been thought of as a somewhat abnormal pastime but doesn't it strike you as odd (even bizarre?) that most people spend practically every minute of their lives from cradle to grave wrapped in restrictive and sometimes positively unhealthy clothing. Of course, no one is suggesting that we should walk around naked all day but in those situations where there is no logical need to wear clothing why do we continue to do so? What is the reason for this reluctance to strip-off? Could it be anything to do with the fact that we live in a society where so much emphasis is put on nakedness in a sexual sense? If our only experience of shared nudity is in the context of sexual activity is it surprising that our minds and bodies have become conditioned to equate nudity with sex? This conditioning is exploited and further reinforced by films, 'girlie' magazines, advertising and the media generally. However, nakedness is obsessive only because it is unusual; put someone on a beach full of naked people and it is amazing how quickly they will accept nudity as the 'norm' – psychologically nakedness and carnality become no longer synonymous. This is not to say that those who enjoy beach nudity are asexual – merely that nudism encourages more mature and balanced attitudes to sexuality. This allows men and women to enjoy each other's company in a relaxed way without the sexual pressures and innuendos so common in clothed situations. There can be other benefits. Those who become devotees often begin to take more care of their personal appearance – encouraging sensible eating habits and regular exercise. Others find naturism an almost transcendental experience. The removal of every last vestige of clothing enables them to come closer to nature and, in so doing, to restore some equilibrium and inner-calmness to a psyche battered and bruised by the demands of modern living. The finer appreciation of things natural also encourages an awareness of the need to protect our environment from pollution and despoilment.

Taking the Plunge

As with many unfamiliar things people find it hard to take the first step but visualise, if you can, a Greek island beach. The fine, golden sand shimmering in the heat haze, a clear blue sky, the deeper blue of the sea. Just imagine stepping out of your swimming costume, feeling the gentle breeze caressing your naked body, running into the warm sea, swimming naked and unrestricted – at one with nature. Drying off back on the beach – no soggy swimming costumes, no more weals of white flesh to mar otherwise perfect tans – just the wonderful, exhilarating feeling of the warm sun and fresh air on your naked body. It's as easy as that – once you've done it you'll wonder what all the fuss was about. One thing is certain – you're unlikely to ever want to wear clothes on a beach again.

Beach Etiquette

The best beaches are those where clothed sunbathers and nudists talk and mix together, quite unconcerned about their state of dress or undress, each respecting the other's right to choose as he or she pleases. However, until this situation becomes more widespread, the reader may find the following 'code' useful. It is based on the premise that, while naturists have just as much right to enjoy a beach as anyone else, we do not have the right to deny that enjoyment to others who may, however misguidedly, find our nakedness offensive:-

- We should be careful not to give gratuitous offence to local people. The islands themselves vary between cosmopolitan and sophisticated ones like Mykonos, where almost anything goes, to less visited places where customs and traditions have hardly changed in hundreds of years and where it would obviously be inappropriate to strip-off within the public gaze.

- Some beaches, which at other times are suitable for nudism, are used by conservative Greek families at week-ends. Father will often wear less than brief swimming trunks and mother rarely goes topless. It may be that there is enough room for you to strip-off without the risk of giving offence but, if not, you should remember that you are a guest in a foreign land and it is best to concede the beach and find somewhere else.

- On less busy beaches it is often the first to arrive who sets the tenor. If someone else comes onto the beach it is perfectly reasonable for you to stand your ground and ignore them. They will either join you, move away to a different part of the beach or find somewhere else.

- On the longer beaches there will usually be enough room to allow happy co-existence between nudists and non-nudists. Most people stay at the end of the beach nearest to the point of access. If you walk to the far end of the beach and there are still clothed sunbathers it is reasonable for you to strip-off anyway, provided that you leave a distance of say 20-30 yards between you and the next person. The rationale for this is that, on a long beach, there is no reason why clothed bathers should hog the whole of the area and, if they take offence, they can always distance themselves allowing everyone to enjoy the beach in their own way. Newcomers to nudism may find this approach difficult at first but the more seasoned among us will be less inhibited.

BEACH CLASSIFICATION

In order to give readers some ideas of what to expect, we have classified the beaches mentioned in this book as follows:-

☆ Beach which is considered to be suitable for nudism (perhaps because of its isolated position or because it is large enough for everyone to do their 'own thing'). It is possible that you will be the only naked person there and you should be prepared to have the courage of your convictions.

☆☆ Beach known to be frequented by nudists to some degree.

☆☆☆ Well used and accepted nudist beach.

PACKAGE HOLIDAY ACCOMMODATION

To assist in planning your holiday we have, for most islands, included details of the accommodation offered by various tour operators and, wherever possible, these details are given in respect of places to stay which are close to naturist beaches. The following abbreviations have been used:-

H – Hotel

P – Pension

R – Room only (i.e. accommodation without self-catering facilities).

S – Self-catering

T – Taverna

In some cases brochure descriptions are confusing (often, for example, there is no clear distinction between pension and room-only accommodation) and readers should satisfy themselves as to what is being offered before booking.

At the back of the Guide is an alphabetical list of tour operators together with the telephone numbers which can be used to obtain brochures.

GETTING TO THE ISLANDS

Greek island hopping sounds romantic but in reality it can often be frustrating, time consuming and boring.

The easiest way is to fly direct and quite a number of the smaller islands have been opened up to direct flights in recent years. Even although there may be no direct flights many of the islands are, nevertheless, connected with Athens by air.

The cheapest method of travel is by ferryboat. The majority of these start from Piraeus and serve the Saronic islands, the Dodecanese, the Cyclades and some of the Eastern Aegean islands. Other islands are reached from the ports of Rafina, Lavrion, Agios Konstantinos and Volos. The Saronic islands and Kythera are also served by hydrofoils ('Flying Dolphins') from Piraeus. These are quicker but get very full and are more expensive.

For those islands which are near to the mainland a boat trip can be very pleasant but many will find the longer journeys tedious especially as, by the time they board the boat, they may already have been travelling for many hours. It is a common misconception that the Aegean is always as flat as a millpond. Even in summer the sea can be rough when the *meltemi* is blowing, making extended journeys extremely unpleasant.

BY AIR

		Duration of Trip	Approximate Single Fare £
ATHENS to	Chania (Hania), Crete	45 mins.	17.50
	Chios (Hios)	40 mins.	14.50
	Corfu (Kerkyra)	50 mins.	24.00
	Iraklion, Crete	50 mins.	21.00
	Karpathos (via Rhodes)	2 hours 30 mins. or 3 hours 30 mins.	41.00
	Kefalonia (Argostoli)	45 mins. or 1 hour 45 mins.	16.50
	Kos	50 mins.	20.00
	Kythira	50 mins.	14.00
	Leros	1 hour 5 mins. or 1 hour 20 mins.	32.50
	Lesbos (Mytilini)	45 mins.	16.50
	Limnos	45 mins. or 1 hour 20 mins.	15.00
	Milos	45 mins.	13.50
	Mykonos	50 mins.	16.00
	Paros	45 mins.	18.00
	Rhodes (Rodos)	55 mins.	26.50
	Samos	45 mins.	16.50
	Santorini (Thira)	40 mins.	19.00
	Skiathos	50 mins.	16.00
	Skyros	50 mins.	24.00
	Zakynthos (Zante)	45 mins. or 1 hour 45 mins.	16.50
IRAKLION, Crete to	Athens	45 mins.	21.00
	Mykonos	1 hour 10 mins. or 1 hour 40 mins.	21.00
	Paros	45 mins.	24.00
	Rhodes (Rodos)	40 mins.	20.50
	Santorini (Thira)	40 mins.	14.50

		Duration of Trip	Approximate Single Fare £
KARPATHOS to	Athens (via Rhodes)	2 hours 30 mins. or 3 hours 30 mins.	41.00
	Rhodes (Rodos)	50 mins.	14.50
	Sitia (Crete)	35 mins. or 1 hour 5 mins.	14.50
KEFALONIA (Argostoli) to	Athens	40 mins. or 1 hour 40 mins.	16.50
	Zakynthos (Zante)	20 mins.	5.00
KOS to	Athens	45 mins.	20.00
	Leros	15 mins.	6.00
	Rhodes (Rodos)	40 mins.	13.00
LEROS to	Athens	1 hour 5 mins. or 1 hour 20 mins.	32.50
	Kos	15 mins.	6.00
	Rhodes (Rodos)	1 hour 25 mins.	18.50
LESBOS (Mytilini) to	Athens	45 mins.	16.50
	Limnos	50 mins.	15.00
LIMNOS to	Athens	45 mins. or 1 hour 20 mins.	15.00
	Lesbos (Mytilini)	50 mins.	15.00
MYKONOS to	Athens	50 mins.	16.00
	Iraklion, Crete	1 hour 10 mins. or 1 hour 40 mins.	21.00
	Rhodes (Rodos)	1 hour 10 mins. or 2 hours 0 mins.	23.00
	Santorini (Thira)	40 mins.	12.50
PAROS to	Athens	45 mins.	18.00
	Iraklion, Crete	45 mins.	24.00
	Rhodes (Rodos)	1 hour 10 mins.	27.50
RHODES (Rodos) to	Athens	55 mins.	26.50
	Iraklion, Crete	40 mins.	20.50
	Karpathos	45 mins.	14.50
	Kos	35 mins.	13.00
	Leros	1 hour 20 mins.	18.50
	Mykonos	1 hour 10 mins. or 2 hours 0 mins.	23.00
	Paros	1 hour 10 mins.	27.50
	Santorini (Thira)	1 hour 0 mins.	21.00
	Sitia (Crete)	55 mins. or 2 hours 10 mins.	27.50
SANTORINI (Thira) to	Athens	40 mins.	19.00
	Iraklion, Crete	40 mins.	14.50
	Mykonos	40 mins.	12.50
	Rhodes (Rodos)	1 hour 0 mins.	21.00
SITIA, Crete to	Karpathos	35 mins. or 1 hour 5 mins.	14.50
	Rhodes (Rodos)	55 mins. or 2 hours 20 mins.	27.50
ZAKYNTHOS (Zante) to	Athens	40 mins.	16.50
	Kefalonia (Argostoli)	20 mins.	5.00

If you decide to fly to the islands from Athens you are advised to book several months in advance through Olympic Airways in the U.K. as island planes are often small and seats are much in demand. Olympic Airway's London office is at 141 New Bond Street (tel. 01-493 7267). It is not unusual for U.K. flights to be delayed and you should bear this in mind when you book your internal flight.

Another point to watch is that Ellinikon Airport in Athens is divided into two. The East Terminal is for international flights and is where you will usually arrive. The West Terminal is used by Olympic Airways for both international and domestic flights. The trip between the two terminals takes about ten minutes by bus or taxi. Allow time for possible delays. It is better to spend a few hours hanging around Athens airport than to miss your internal flight because you are unlikely, in season, to be able to transfer to another. If you do happen to miss your internal flight you will probably have to stay in Athens overnight and go by boat next morning (most of the ferries leave at around 8.00 a.m.). A refund can be obtained from Olympic when you return to the U.K.

Buses to the East Terminal leave from 4 Amalias (off Sintagma Square) in Athens every twenty minutes between 06.00 and 00.20. The journey takes twenty-five minutes. Buses to the West Terminal leave from outside Olympic's office on Syngrou Avenue every twenty minutes between 06.00 and 23.20. The journey takes twenty minutes.

The East Terminal is connected to Piraeus by bus number 185 which leaves from Theotoki and Sofokleous Streets in Piraeus.

BY SEA

		Duration of Trip	Approximate Price Range (in Drachmas)
PIRAEUS to	Aegina	1 hour 30 mins.	265 – 352
	Amorgos	11 hours 15 mins.	950 – 1291
	Astipalea	13 hours 0 mins.	1147 – 1962
	Chios (Hios)	10 hours 0 mins.	992 – 1853
	Crete, Agios Nikolaos	12 hours 0 mins.	1655 – 2925
	Crete, Chania (Hania)	11 hours 0 mins.	1172 – 2201
	Crete, Iraklion	12 hours 0 mins.	1246 – 2285
	Folegandros	12 hours 0 mins.	1093 – 1853
	Hydra	4 hours 10 mins.	427 – 572
	Ikaria	12 hours 30 mins.	891 – 1591
	Ios	10 hours 0 mins.	1093 – 1672
	Kalymnos	14 hours 0 mins.	1147 – 1962
	Kimolos	6 hours 0 mins.	887 – 1358
	Kos	20 hours 30 mins.	1388 – 2440
	Kythera	9 hours 45 mins.	1147 – 1811
	Kythnos	4 hours 0 mins.	576 – 992

From	To	Duration of Trip	Approximate Price Range (in Drachmas)
	Leros	11 hours 30 mins.	1147 – 1962
	Lesbos (Mytilini)	14 hours 0 mins.	1246 – 2114
	Milos	8 hours 30 mins.	887 – 1358
	Mykonos	6 hours 15 mins.	853 – 1337
	Naxos	8 hours 10 mins.	887 – 1358
	Paros	6 hours 20 mins.	772 – 1183
	Patmos	8 hours 0 mins.	1147 – 1962
	Poros	3 hours 40 mins.	386 – 521
	Rhodes (Rodos)	20 hours 0 mins.	1545 – 2668
	Samos (Karlovassi)	14 hours 30 mins.	1117 – 1940
	Samos (Vathi)	16 hours 0 mins.	1192 – 2114
	Santorini (Thira)	12 hours 0 mins.	1093 – 1672
	Serifos	5 hours 0 mins.	650 – 1112
	Sifnos	5 hours 30 mins.	806 – 1226
	Sikinos	10 hours 30 mins.	1288 – 2207
	Spetses	5 hours 25 mins.	560 – 728
	Symi	26 hours 30 mins.	1388 – 2440
	Syros	4 hours 30 mins.	768 – 1121
	Tinos	5 hours 30 mins.	853 – 1254
AGIOS KONSTANTINOS to	Alonissos	6 hours 0 mins.	1042 – 1565
	Kavala	16 hours 30 mins.	2014 – 2565
	Limnos	10 hours 30 mins.	688 – 1136
	Skiathos	3 hours 15 mins.	787 – 1139
	Skopelos	5 hours 25 mins.	934 – 1424
	Volos	9 hours 30 mins.	625 – 1064
KAVALA to	Agios Konstantinos	11 hours 0 mins.	2014 – 2565
	Lesbos (Mytilini)	12 hours 0 mins.	1764 – 2848
	Limnos	5 hours 0 mins.	1065 – 1424
	Samothrace	4 hours 0 mins.	742 – 1139
	Skiathos	13 hours 0 mins.	1424 – 2136
	Skopelos	12 hours 0 mins.	1427 – 2136
KYMI (Evia) to	Alonissos	2 hours 54 mins.	1034 – 1424
	Kavala	12 hours 20 mins.	1588 – 2136
	Samothrace	16 hours 45 mins.	1588 – 2565
	Skiathos	5 hours 30 mins.	1350 – 1851
	Skopelos	3 hours 30 mins.	1129 – 1566
	Skyros	1 hour 45 mins.	522 – 777
	Volos	8 hours 0 mins.	1948 – 2415
LAVRION to	Kea	2 hours 30 mins.	364
	Kythnos	4 hours 0 mins.	544
PATRAS to	Corfu (Kerkyra)	10 hours 15 mins.	1205
	Ithaca	5 hours 0 mins.	709
	Kefalonia (Argostoli)	3 hours 30 mins.	684
	Paxos (Paxi)	9 hours 0 mins.	1205
RAFINA to	Andros	3 hours 0 mins.	450 – 675
	Ios	8 hours 30 mins.	948
	Kythnos	6 hours 30 mins.	485 – 510
	Mykonos	5 hours 0 mins.	884 – 1324
	Naxos	6 hours 30 mins.	940 – 1570
	Paros	5 hours 0 mins.	804 – 1530

		Duration of Trip	Approximate Price Range (in Drachmas)
	Syros	3 hours 30 mins.	749 – 1120
	Tinos	4 hours 0 mins.	749 – 1120
VOLOS to	Agios Konstantinos	9 hours 30 mins.	625 – 1064
	Alonissos	5 hours 0 mins.	833 – 1149
	Kymi (Evia)	8 hours 0 mins.	1948 – 2415
	Skiathos	3 hours 0 mins.	581 – 926
	Skopelos	4 hours 30 mins.	730 – 1068
	Skyros	11 hours 0 mins.	1673 – 2350

The price within the range is dependant on class and Greek boats have a bewildering classification system. There are often up to four classes. 'A' or 1st class is the dearest. 'D' or deck class is the cheapest. Deck class (which is sometimes also called 'tourist') is always pretty crowded with people lying on the upper deck (it is easy to get badly sunburned this way) or on the covered deck where there are usually some wooden benches. Package tour operators send their clients deck class although it is possible to pay extra to transfer to a better class (see the purser once you are on board). 1st class costs about twice as much as deck class and allows you to sit in reasonable comfort in a lounge with waiter service.

The National Tourist Organisation (NTOG) publishes a weekly list of ship departures and this is available from the NTOG desk in the National Bank of Greece in Sintagma Square. The daily newspaper 'E Navtemporike' also publishes weekly schedules or you can confirm times by telephoning the following numbers:-

Piraeus	4511311
Agios Konstantinos	4178084
Kavala	4178084
Kymi	4178084
Lavrion	0292-25249
Patras	8236012
Rafina	0294-23300
Volos	0421-23400

Ferry timetables are also available in the U.K. from the Greek National Tourist Organisation, 195-197 Regent Street, London (tel. 01-734 5997).

Athens Airport (East Terminal) is connected to Piraeus by bus number 185 which leaves from Theotoki and Sofokleous in Piraeus.

Frequent buses from Athens to Piraeus (bus number 040) leave from Sintagma Square (Fillelinon Street) but the easiest way is by the Metro from Omonia Square or Monastiraki. The journey takes about twenty-five minutes.

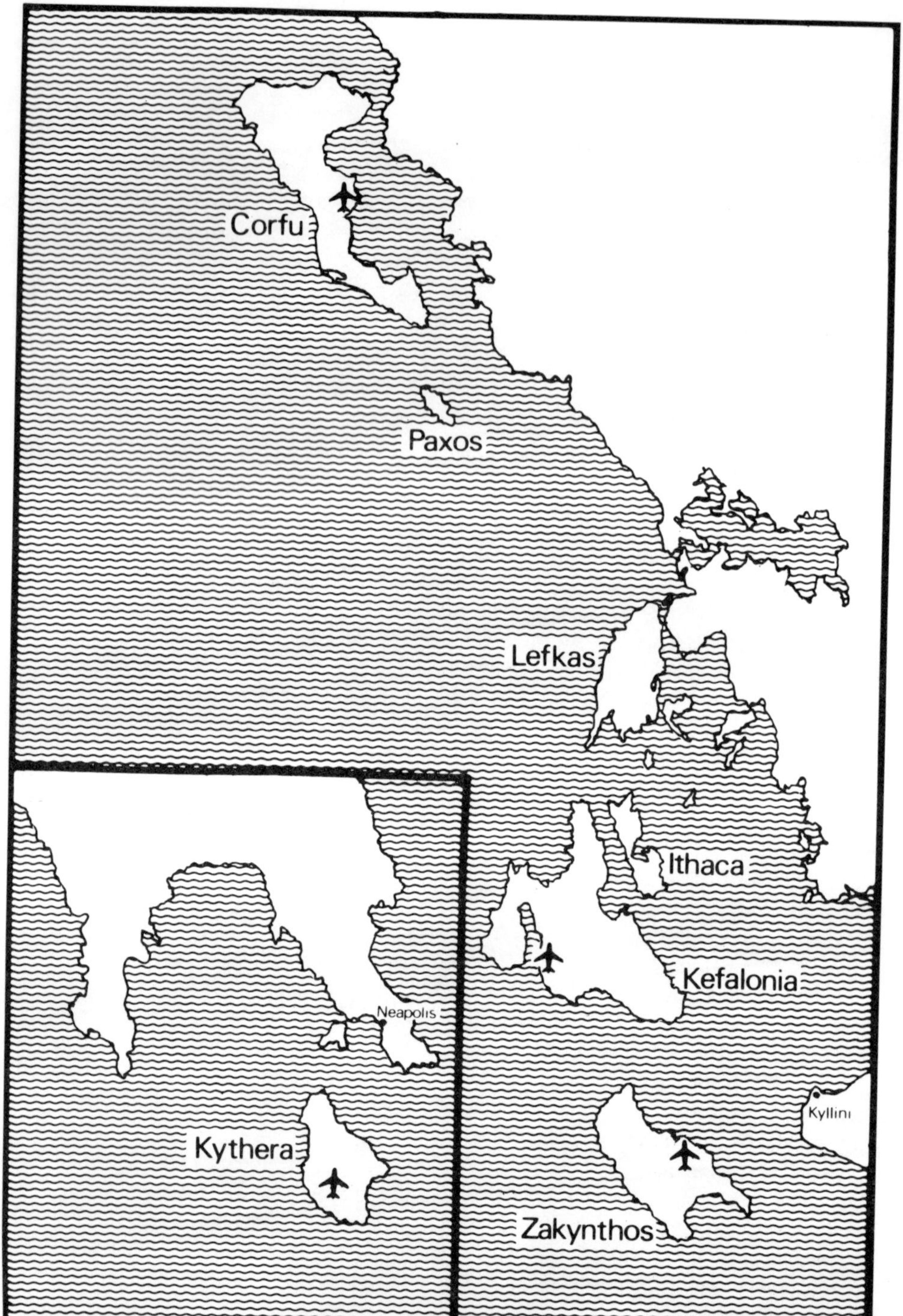
Corfu
Paxos
Lefkas
Ithaca
Kefalonia
Neapolis
Kythera
Kyllini
Zakynthos

THE IONIAN ISLANDS

The Ionians are situated off the west coast of Greece. They enjoy a sheltered position and are less subject to the strong winds which sometimes affect the other island groups. Heavy winter rainfall (avoid the period October – April) makes them green and lush even throughout the long hot summer. They are linked by ferries to the mainland ports rather than to one another. However, the 'Ionis' sails every two days between Brindisi (Italy) and Patras (June – September) and calls at Corfu (8 hours), Paxos (10 hours), Ithaca (13½ hours) and Kefalonia (14¾ hours). The 'Kefallinia' sails once a week from Patras to Sami and Fiscardo on Kefalonia and on to Paxos and Corfu; returning by the same route.

CORFU (KERKYRA)

Corfu, approximately 35 miles long and 18 miles across at its widest points, is a beautiful island rich in vegetation and luxuriously green. It is by far the most popular Greek island and this popularity has resulted in apparently unrestrained development and not a few concrete eye-sores. However, in spite of the worst excesses of mass tourism, the island has undoubted charm and it is not difficult to enjoy peace and tranquillity – although you may have to travel a little to find it. The inhabitants are amongst the friendliest people to be found anywhere and have a particular fondness for the British.

In winter Corfu is wet and this explains the greenness of the island. The average number of rainy days in April are 9, 6 in May, 4 in June, 1 in July, 1 in August, 5 in September and 11 in October.

The National Tourist Office is situated in the new government building (Dikitirion) next to the post office on Samara Street. Open 15th May to 15th October, 07.00-14.30 and 18.00-20.00 Monday to Friday and 09.00-12.00 on Saturday. Out of season open 07.30-15.00 Monday to Friday only. Telephone 0661 39730.

The tourist police for Corfu town are on Arseniou Street. Telephone 0661 30265. For elsewhere on the island contact the tourist police at 4 Polychroniou Konstanta. Telephone 0661 30669.

The island's two youth hostels are located outside town. One is at Agios Ioannes, 6 miles from town (0661 30468) and the other is at Kontokali, 4 miles from town (0661 91202). There are also six official camping sites, two at Kontokali and the rest at Dassia, Ipsos, Corfu town (Kerkyra Camping, tel. 0661 93246) and Korakiana.

Connections: Direct flights from most U.K. airports. Up to five flights a day from Athens. Bus connections three times a day with Athens and once a day with Thessaloniki. Ferryboats every two hours from Igoumenitsa (2 hour crossing). At least one boat daily from Patras (10 hours). Many of the ferryboats between Italy and Greece call at Corfu (especially those from Brindisi).

Centres: The majority of package holidays are to the resorts of Paliokastritsa, Glyfada, Kavos, Benitses, Perama, Kontokali, Gouvia, Dassia, Ipsos, Pyrgi, Nissaki, Kassiopi, Roda and Sidari.

PALIOKASTRITSA, probably the most famous beauty spot on the island is, in the opinion of the writer, overrated and overcrowded. Years ago, no doubt, it was all that is claimed for it but mass tourism has taken its toll. Although there are good pebble and sandy beaches there are no nudist beaches close by.

GLYFADA is similar. Although it has a beautiful beach (not nudist) the bay is totally dominated by a massive hotel and apartment block. KAVOS, in the far south of the island at the end of a long and, in places, extremely bad road, is isolated. It does, however, have a very nice, sandy beach. BENITSES, often described as a fishing village, gets full to overflowing in season and displays some of the less attractive features of 'package tour' resorts. PERAMA, nearer to Corfu town, is less frantic with a good choice of restaurants and some nice self-catering 'villas', many of which are hidden amongst the trees. This stretch of coast consists of shingle beaches and the closeness of the main road and the built-up nature of this part of the island makes them unsuitable for nudism. The first 12 miles of coastline to the north of Corfu town has been remorselessly developed and the resorts of KONTOKALI, GOUVIA, DASSIA, IPSOS and PYRGI get horrendously busy with people vying for a few square feet along the usually narrow strip of shingle which serves as the beach. NISSAKI is quieter with a lovely, although stony, beach.

For an all-over tan you should consider staying at Kassiopi, Acharavi, Sidari, Agios Stefanos, Arillas, Agios Georgiou or Agios Georgios. However, with the exception of Kassiopi, these are quieter places and you may need to consider hiring transport for at least part of your stay.

KASSIOPI, 22 miles from Corfu town, is a pretty fishing village built around a picturesque harbour. It is a fairly well developed tourist resort with tavernas, cafes, bars, shops and discos. Accommodation is mainly on a self-catering basis although there are a few small pensions and also some tavernas which offer rooms. Much of the available accommodation is contracted to tour operators. On either side of the harbour are rocky headlands and paths lead over these to reveal small coves of shingle or pebble backed by low cliffs. The main bay consists of pebbles and is about 15 minutes' walk from the village. Here you will find all the usual facilities including waterskiing, windsurfing and paragliding. Nightimes are lively and this is not an early-to-bed place (try Kassiopi by Night, a disco-bar built around the oldest olive-press in the region). There is a good bus service between Kassiopi and Corfu town and taxis are also available. Cars, jeeps and motorcycles can be hired in the village as well as self-drive motorboats.

The original village of ACHARAVI, 28 miles from Corfu town, is some 800 yards inland from the new resort which has taken the same name. The resort

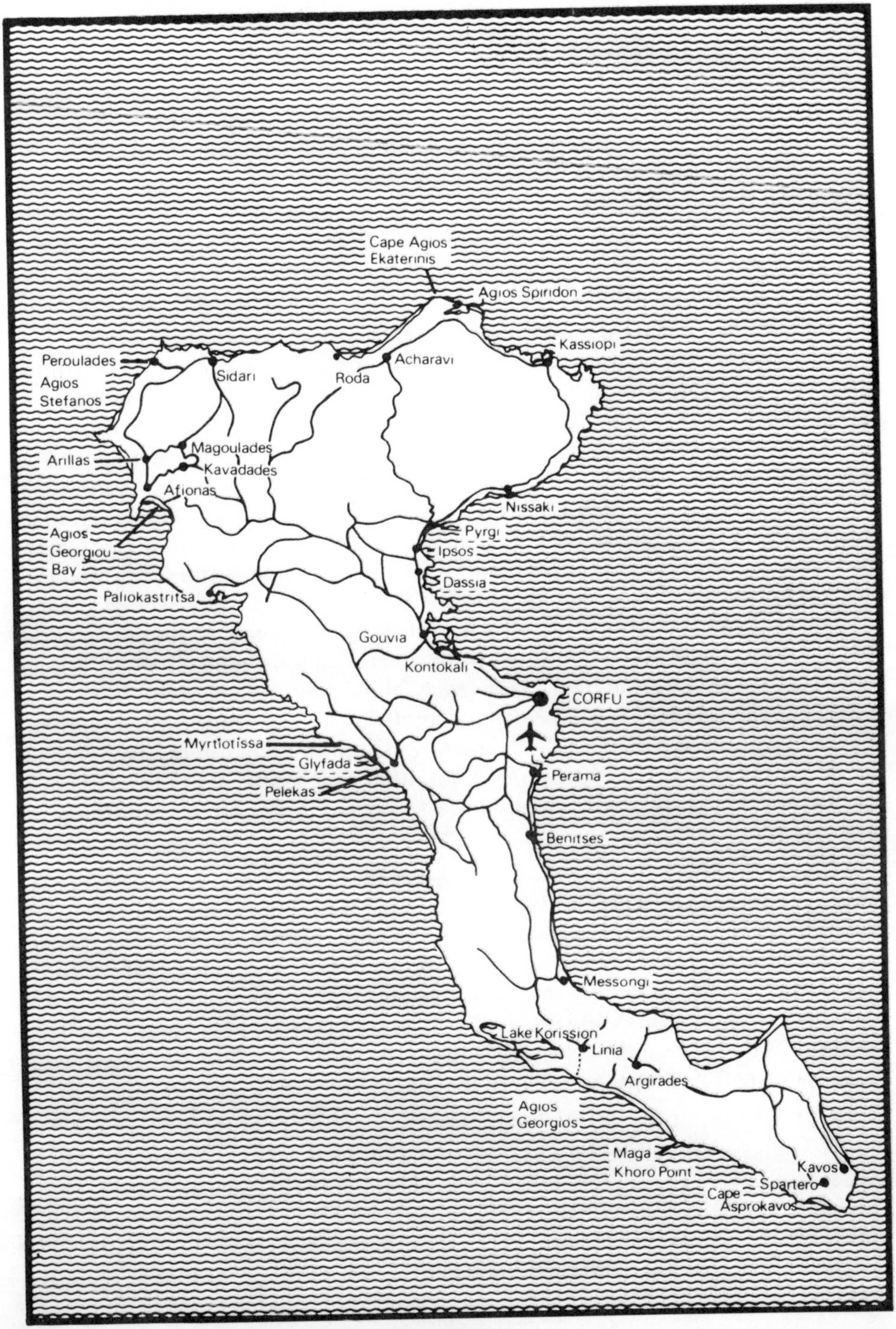
Cape Agios Ekaterinis
Agios Spiridon
Kassiopi
Peroulades
Agios Stefanos
Sidari
Roda
Acharavi
Magoulades
Arillas
Kavadades
Afionas
Agios Georgiou Bay
Nissaki
Pyrgi
Ipsos
Dassia
Paliokastritsa
Gouvia
Kontokali
CORFU
Myrtiotissa
Glyfada
Pelekas
Perama
Benitses
Messongi
Lake Korission
Linia
Argirades
Agios Georgios
Maga Khoro Point
Kavos
Spartero
Cape Asprokavos

area consists almost entirely of spasmodically placed villas, although there is one hotel, the 'B' class Pringipissa Ioniou (Ionian Princess Hotel). There are also a few tavernas, a mini-market and a couple of shops. Acharavi's main attraction, however, is the sandy beach which stretches for about 2 miles to Roda, another small resort. Waterskiing and windsurfing are usually available and at the Roda end of the beach there is paragliding and boat hire. Nightlife consists of the Skondros Cocktail Bar, Barn Bar and one disco on the main road. In view of the isolated location and few amenities, some will feel that transport is essential and car and scooter hire are available in Acharavi.

The main bay at SIDARI (23 miles from Corfu town) stretches for a couple of miles and consists of fine, golden sand. In parts, the beach is broken up by unusual outcrops which form a series of sandy coves. Narrow tracks run across the tops of these cliffs offering lovely views and good walking. The water stays shallow for some distance offshore and the sandy bottom makes sea temperatures gloriously warm. On the main beach there are sun umbrellas, canoes, pedeloes and windsurfers for hire. There is also paragliding and waterskiing but, because of the shallowness of the water, these have to be undertaken from a large platform anchored 100 yards offshore and, even here, the water is still only waist deep. Sidari has grown considerably in recent years and, while it is still only small, there is a good choice of self-catering accommodation as well as a number of small hotels including the Astoria (0663 31315), the Mimosa (0663 31361) and the Three Brothers (0663 31242) – all 'C' class. Nightlife centres around the tavernas, several bars and two discos – 'Legends', 10 minutes' walk out of town and, at the far end of the beach, the Canal d'Amour Disco. There is a reasonable bus service and taxis are also available as well as car, jeep, scooter and bicycle hire.

AGIOS STEFANOS, on the north-western coast, is a long, wide, sandy bay which is enclosed by a green hillside sprinkled with houses, small hotels and tavernas. There is no main street, hardly any shops and nothing in the way of sophisticated nightlife. There are some rooms to rent and two small 'C' class hotels, the Nafsika (0663 31254) and the Saint Stefanos. Canoes, pedeloes, windsurfers and waterskiing are available and mopeds and scooters can also be hired in the village. Lovely walks along the cliff-tops. This place will suit those looking for complete relaxation.

ARILLAS, 24 miles from Corfu town, is another small village which remains completely unspoilt and uncommercialised. It is set in a green valley which gently slopes down to a bay of sand and shingle (see 'Beaches'). Here you can hire pedeloes, windsurfers, sunbeds and umbrellas. There are only four tavernas (three of these are on the beach) and two small 'C' class hotels, the Arilla Beach (0663 31401) and the Marina Beach (0663 31400), both with very good restaurants. There are three local shops for the purchase of essential provisions. Other than the tavernas, there is nothing in the way of nightlife. One early morning bus a day leaves for Corfu town and returns in the afternoon (the journey takes about two hours!).

AGIOS GEORGIOU, not to be confused with Agios Gordis (further south) and Agios Georgios (further south still), could not be described as a resort and doesn't even really qualify as a village. Here you will find a mile long stretch of wide, golden sand backed by wooded hills and flanked by rocky headlands. There are a handful of tavernas, the small 'D' class St. Georgio Hotel and a campsite (a 10 minute walk up the hill) which is mainly frequented by Germans. On the beach you can hire pedeloes and windsurfers and there is also paragliding and waterskiing. The nearest bus service is from the village of Pagi (about 3 miles away).

AGIOS GEORGIOS, in the south of the island, is about 20 miles from Corfu town. Although it is only a small resort it extends for about a mile along the huge bay of yellow sand. There are the usual tavernas as well as a couple of mini-markets and a souvenir shop. Accommodation is in tavernas, a couple of pensions and self-catering rooms and 'villas'. Pedeloes, canoes and windsurfers can be hired and there are also a couple of beachside showers. This resort attracts mainly young people and night-time entertainment, although unsophisticated, can get very lively. There is no public transport although scooters can be hired here.

Beaches: The best sandy beaches are on the northern and western coasts although, surprisingly, the majority of tourist development has taken place along the mainly shingle beaches to the east and these are often very crowded. Nudists prefer the sandy, unspoiled, quieter beaches elsewhere on the island and car or scooter hire is recommended. To find these beaches you will need to buy a good map of the island such as the Clyde Leisure Map (obtainable from good bookshops in the U.K. as well as on the island or, in case of difficulty, contact Clyde Surveys Ltd., Reform Road, Maidenhead, Berkshire). Many of the locally produced maps are misleading if not completely inaccurate.

There are a couple of nudist beaches close to the busy resort of KASSIOPI**. One can be reached by taking the footpath which starts at one end of the waterfront (to the left as you face the sea). The path leads through bushy scrubland passing an old castle on the way. After about 10 minutes' walk you will come to three small coves. The furthest of these is used almost exclusively by nudists. The beach consists of sand and shingle and swimming is good here although the sea gets rough on windy days. There is a very good taverna near-by. The other naturist beach is a couple of miles to the east and is reached by leaving Kassiopi on the Corfu town road. You will pass the turn-off to Roda. Shortly after leaving behind the last house the road enters an olive grove. Look out for a wide track branching off to the left (it is about 1½ miles

Kassiopi

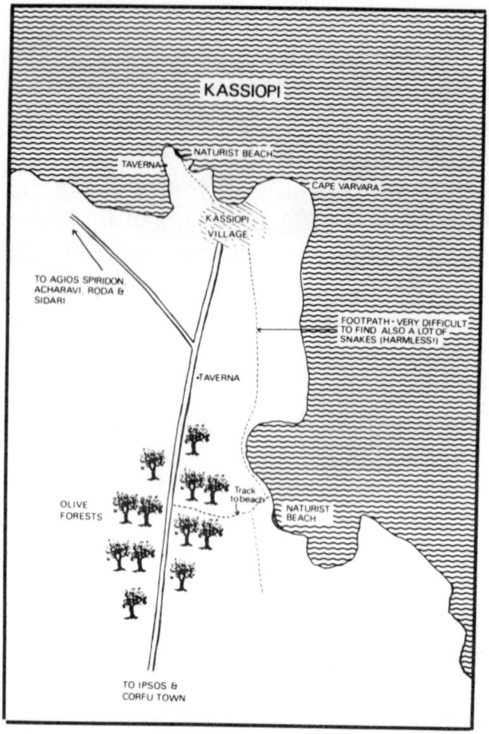

Sidari (West)

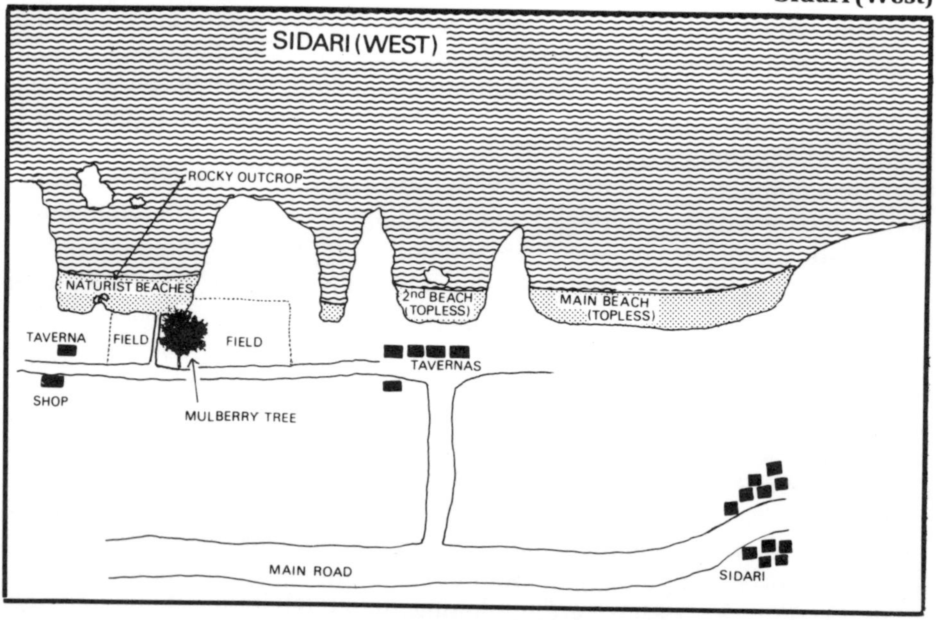

from Kassiopi to here). If you have transport you should park here. Follow this track for half a mile through olive groves and a cherry orchard to a farmhouse. The farmhouse is by-passed by a footpath and from here it is 100 yards to the beach. There are a few holiday cottages where the path joins the beach and a boat landing stage. Turn south along the beach until you are prevented from going further by rocks. This delightful cove of crystal clear water has a beach of shingle and loose rocks and is used mainly by nudists.

AGIOS SPIRIDON** is situated about halfway between Kassiopi and Roda. This is a small sandy beach reached by means of a rough road off the main road. The beach is usually quiet and is used for nudism. However, a large chalet-type holiday complex has recently been built and its opening could result in the loss of this beach to naturists. There is a good taverna here.

ACHARAVI*. The main part of the beach (near the tavernas) is only topless. However, the beach stretches eastwards for miles and it should always be possible to enjoy nudism here. Access to this part of the beach is by means of a track off the main road about 1 mile north-east of Acharavi. The beach from here to Cape Agios Ekaterinis consists of sand and fine shingle with rocks at the waterline which run into the sea for 10-15 feet. At intervals it is possible to find a way through these rocks onto the hard sand beyond. Here the beach is virtually deserted and can be enjoyed for nude sunning and swimming although it is used by locals at week-ends and gets busier.

SIDARI (WEST)***. Sidari has a good sandy beach which extends for over a mile. The main beach is generally crowded and is not nudist. However, if you follow the Canal d'Amour road (turn right by the Hawaii Taverna) for about 15-20 minutes to the west, you will come to a large isolated mulberry tree on the right-hand side of the road. A little way past this tree is a track leading across the fields to the cliff-top. The cliff is not very high and rough steps lead to the sandy nudist beach at the bottom. Beyond a rocky outcrop is another smaller beach which is also used for nudism. The water in this bay is very shallow and, in fact, you can wade almost all the way to a small rocky island which is about 200 yards offshore and where rocky ledges are used for nude sunning. There are no facilities and no natural shade although there is a taverna and a shop about 5 minutes' walk away.

PEROULADES**. There is a good sandy beach situated about 2½ miles to the west of Sidari and reached through the village of Peroulades. It is well used by naturists but, because it is backed by cliffs, there is no sun until the afternoon.

AGIOS STEFANOS* is a long stretch of hard, flat sand which makes it possible to drive along the beach. It can get busy at week-ends and is not much used by nudists. When it is not too busy, the northern end of the beach under the cliffs is the most suitable place for an all-over tan.

ARILLAS*. The beach at Arillas consists of shingle with sand towards the waterline. We are told that the beach changes shape during the course of the summer and that in the early part of the season there is not as much sand as later on. One report, from a reader who visited Arillas in May, describes the beach as shingle with sand below the waterline. However, we understand that in July and August the water level drops – revealing a good width of fine sand. Our information is that the beach is used for nudism at both ends but that, at week-ends, the northern end can get crowded with Greek families. There are three tavernas on the beach and pedeloes and windsurfers can be hired here.

AGIOS GEORGIOU* – easy access by means of a rough road off the surfaced road which joins Magoulades and Afionas via Kavadades. This long beach of coarse, golden sand is clothing optional at its northern end. There are tavernas here, pedeloes and windsurfers for hire as well as paragliding and waterskiing.

MYRTIOTISSA*** can be reached from the village of Pelekas. Leave Pelekas on the Glyfada Beach road and take the first right turn which is signposted to Ermones. Follow this road for about 2 miles and look out for a track on the left which leads off into the trees. It is possible to follow this track by car or scooter although the going becomes progressively worse and you would probably be wise to leave your transport in the trees part of the way along and complete the last section on foot. This spectacularly situated beach which is backed by high cliffs is described in the Berlitz Guide as one of the world's loveliest. When the writer first visited Myrtiotissa in 1980 it was an idyllic naturist beach. Recent reports describe it as being overcrowded and filthy. How can people be so utterly selfish and unthinking that they can enjoy the beauty of a place like Myrtiotissa while at the same time denying that enjoyment to those who will follow them by defiling it with litter?

PELEKAS BEACH*** is reached by a rough track which runs from the hairpin bend on the road below the village of Pelekas. The track winds down an almost sheer cliff with a drop of 800 feet or so and, although it is possible to drive down, you may have difficulty getting back up if you are on a moped or a scooter. The walk down takes 10-15 minutes (a lot longer coming back). Pelekas is a beautiful beach in spectacular surroundings. It rarely gets crowded and there is plenty of room in which to spread out. Nudists are to be found at the southern end of the beach away from the tavernas. There is no natural shade on the beach. The sea is relatively shallow for some way out making it safe for children.

LAKE KORISSION** (sometimes called Korissia Lagoon) is probably one of the best beaches on the island on which to enjoy nude sunning. Follow the track leading off to the right from the little village of Linia. The going is rough but the track can be negotiated on two wheels with care and the trip to the beach is well worth the effort. This excellent sandy beach, which is backed by sand dunes, stretches for miles. Behind the dunes is the lake. Swimming in the sea is delightful. The bottom is sandy and the water is little more than waist high for a long distance offshore making the sea luxuriously warm. Here you can experience total solitude but go prepared as there is no natural shade and no facilities. The nearest taverna is on Agios Georgios beach, a long walk away, so take something to drink.

AGIOS GEORGIOS* is a long beach of coarse, golden sand with a developing resort which, although small, straggles for about a mile along the beach. There is no natural shade on the beach although there are tavernas as well as pedeloes, canoes and windsurfers for hire and waterskiing and paragliding. There are reports of nudism at the northern end (towards Lake Korission) and it should also be possible to strip-off at the other end of the enormous beach (towards Maga Khoro Point).

CAPE ASPROKAVOS*. This lovely deserted beach can be reached from Kavos by following the unsurfaced road to Spartero. After the village and about 250 yards, look out for a newly made track on the left (just before the Bar Metaxa). This track crosses a shallow valley and zigzags down to the sea. The beach is wide, clean and mainly sandy and is backed by cliffs. There are no facilities here and no shade. Swimming and diving are safe and good. Walking time from Kavos is about 1 hour.

Things To Do: Go to Pelekas to see the spectacular sunset. The sunsets here are famous for their beauty, especially from mid-July onwards. So much so that a special bus leaves San Rocco Square in town at 18.00 each day returning at about 20.00. The trip takes about half an hour followed by a 15 minute walk to the taverna from the terrace of which the view can best be enjoyed.

There are no archaeological sites on Corfu but if you get desperate to traipse around somewhere you could always visit the Achilleion Palace near Benitses. It is spectacularly situated and was built by the Empress Elisabeth of Austria. When she was assassinated Wilhelm II (better known as Kaiser Bill) bought the Achilleion. In 1963 it became a museum and the island's casino. It was a location in the James Bond film 'For Your Eyes Only', much of which was filmed in Corfu. The Achilleion is open Monday to Saturday, 08.00-19.00 and on Sunday between 09.00 and 17.00.

Boat trips around the island, to Paxos and to the mainland.

Getting Around: Buses to Pelekas leave from San Rocco Square in Corfu town at 06.30, 10.00, 14.15, 17.00 and 19.30. Buses return at 19.00, 20.00 (in high season) and 21.00. Buses to Perama, Benitses, Kontokali and Dassia also leave from San Rocco. Buses to the following places run from New Fortress Square:- Ipsos, Nissaki, Kassiopi, Roda, Sidari, Paliokastritsa, Messongi, Agios Georgios (a 20 minutes' walk from the main road) and Kavos. Schedules are chalked up on a board outside the bus company office here. Bus schedules are also available from the National Tourist Office.

Car and scooter hire in Corfu town and many other places.

Tour Operators:

KASSIOPI: Aspro (R,S); Beach Villas (S); Club 18-30 (H,P); C.V. Travel (S); Falcon (R,S); Global (R,S); Grecian (S); Intasun – Main Brochure (S); Intasun – 'Plain and Simple' Brochure (S,T); Kypros (R,S); Leisure Villas (R,S); Sigma (S); Sunmed (P,R,S,T); Sunstart (R,S); Twentys (T); Ventura (R,S); Villa Seekers (S); Zeus (R,S).

AGIOS SPIRIDON: Beach Villas (S).

ACHARAVI: Beach Villas (S); C.V. Travel (S); Ellerman (H); Grecian (S); Leisure Villas (S); Martyn (S); O.S.L. (S); Sigma (S); Sunmed (H,R,S,T).

SIDARI: Club 18-30 (H); Corfiot (S); Ellerman (H); Grecian (R,S); Kypros (H,S); Manos (H,R,S); Olympic – Main Brochure (H,S,T); Olympic – 'A Touch of Greece' Brochure (R,S,T); O.S.L. (S); Sun Club (P,S); Sunmed (H,P,R,S); Thomson – 'Small and Friendly' Brochure (H,R,T); Thomson – 'Villas and Apartments' Brochure (S).

AGIOS STEFANOS: Corfiot (H,S); Corfu Trust (S); Greek Connection (S,T); Ilios (S); Sun Club (H,S).

ARILLAS: Corfu Trust (S); Kypros (S,T); Timsway – 'Original Holidays in Greece' Brochure (H,S).

AGIOS GEORGIOU: Manos (H,R,S,T); Sunmed (H,P,R,S).

AGIOS GEORGIOS: Airlink (T – Marathias); Sigma (S); Sunmed (P,R,S,T).

PAXOS (PAXI)

Paxos, 7 miles long by 3 miles wide, is a charming, unspoilt island situated 10 miles south of Corfu. It resembles a vast garden planted with olive trees (there are over 300,000 of them), tall pines and a profusion of wild flowers. What the island lacks in sophistication it makes up for in peace and tranquillity, natural beauty and the warmth of its people.

Connections: Daily ferries from Corfu in season (3 hour crossing). However, in order to board them, you must have already booked accommodation on the island for a minimum of two days – a sensible precaution on the part of the islanders who have no wish to see Paxos overrun by people with nowhere to sleep.

Centres: GAIOS is the main port and village. It is beautifully situated around a natural harbour and attracts visiting yachts from all over the Mediterranean. These moor alongside the little village square with its church and pink and white oleanders and give a cosmopolitan air to the island's capital. The village has a strong Venetian influence and is a maze of narrow flagstoned streets from which cars are barred. There is a good selection of bars and tavernas, two discotheques as well as several mini-markets. Gaios has no hotels and few places to stay and rooms to rent are difficult to find. There is a selection of attractive bays and coves including a sandy beach near to the village.

On the north-east coast is the tiny fishing village of LONGOS (also sometimes referred to as LOGGOS). It consists of just thirty houses clustered around a picturesque harbour. There are a number of good tavernas, a few shops and numerous beaches on either side of the village (the nearest is about 5 minutes' walk away).

LAKKA, on the north coast, is another small fishing village built around the almost perfect semi-circle which forms the harbour. Here you will find a good selection of shops, waterfront tavernas and bars as well as an open-air discotheque which is located on the outskirts of the village. There are three beaches within the bay itself and, for those who enjoy sailing, the Greek Islands Sailing Centre is situated on a sand beach at the entrance to the harbour. Windsurfing and waterskiing are also available at Lakka.

It should be noted that much of the available accommodation in all these places is contracted to tour operators and you are advised to book before leaving the U.K.

Beaches: Beaches are mainly pebble, (sand is a rarity on Paxos). There are, however, over thirty of these and most of them are deserted so that acquiring an all-over tan isn't a problem. The most convenient way of getting to them is by boat (see Getting Around). The larger beaches, however, tend to be busier and the degree of undress often depends on the tenor set by those who arrive there first. While sensible discretion should be exercised on these busier beaches there is generally a relaxed attitude to nudism on the part of both the locals and also those who prefer to retain some vestige of clothing.

ANTIPAXOS, just one mile off the southern tip of Paxos, has some of the loveliest sandy beaches in the Mediterranean. This and the fact that it is virtually uninhabited (just thirty people during the holiday season) make it ideal for naturism and about half of those using the main beach are usually naked.

Things To Do: Daily boat trips to Antipaxos and Parga (on the mainland). Otherwise very little – except to relax!

Getting Around: Bus times are fairly 'hit and miss' but buses are supposed to run between Gaios and Longos at 09.30 and 11.30 and between Gaios and Lakka at 10.30, 13.15 and 21.30. Taxis are available and, although they are in short supply, are cheap. Every morning caiques depart from the square in Gaios for Antiparos. There is also a caique service from here to the fine, sandy beach on the islet of Mogonissi. It runs almost hourly from morning until dusk and the trip takes 40 minutes. Unfortunately, this beach can get crowded and is not nudist. There is a taverna here which specialises in lobster and every night the owner ferries people over from Gaios for dinner. Car and moped hire are available in Gaios although it should be noted that the island only has one reasonable road which joins Gaios and Lakka. Elsewhere you will have to follow rutted tracks which are not really suitable for two wheels. Boat hire is also available. Greek Islands Club, for example, have a fleet of wooden and fibreglass boats powered by Seagulls or Evinrudes in Gaios and Longos.

Tour Operators:
GAIOS: Beach Villas (S); Corfu à la Carte (S); C.V. Travel (S); Enterprise (H); Greek Islands Club (S); Olympic – Main Brochure (S); Pan (R,S); Sun Club (S); Sunmed (R,S).
LONGOS: C.V. Travel (S); Greek Islands Club (S); Loggos Tourist Co. (S); Olympic – Main Brochure (S).
LAKKA: Corfu à la Carte (S); Greek Islands Club (S); Olympic – Main Brochure (S); Pan (S); Sunmed (P,R,S).

LEFKAS (LEFKADA)

Lefkas is separated from the mainland only by a canal and its character is more akin to that of the mainland, being a bit scruffy and lacking in romance. The island's interior is mostly mountainous and barren although the eastern coast is dotted with orange and olive groves. At present the tourist industry is low-key but is being developed.

Connections: By bus – three times a day from Athens (6 hours) and Patras (4½ hours); also regularly from Igoumenitsa. By boat – one or two boats a week, in season, from Nidri and Vassiliki to Ithaca and Kefalonia.

Centres: The capital, also called LEFKAS, is situated on the northern tip of the island facing the mainland to which it is connected by a chain-ferry and a long causeway. The town was badly affected by an earthquake in 1948 and many of the houses were rebuilt using timber frames and corrugated iron. Extraordinarily, scaffolding was used to reconstruct the bell towers of two churches making them look more like oil rigs than places of worship. There is no beach in Lefkas town and no real reason for staying here although there are a number of hotels including the 'B' class Lefkas (0645 23916/8) and the less expensive Hotel Byzantion (0645 22629). Tavernas provide what evening entertainment there is.

NIDRI, on the east coast, is a small, characterless resort but is beautifully situated facing the wooded islets of Mandouri, Sparti, Skorpios and Meganissi. There are rooms to rent in Nidri, a reasonable beach and wooded coves near-by.

VLIHO, 2 miles further on, is a pleasant village which is set in a deep, almost enclosed, bay. There are rooms to rent here. A little to the west is the rocky DESSIMI BEACH with an organised campsite. POROS, the next village, also has a beach and a campsite (0645 95298). Eventually the road reaches VASSILIKI, a quiet, little resort at the foot of wooded slopes with a pretty harbour. This is a pleasant place to stay with a hotel, the 'D' class Paradise (0645 31256), rooms, restaurants and beaches.

AGIOS NIKITIS, on the west coast, also has rooms to rent.

Beaches: Beaches are mostly shingle or rocky. AGIOS NIKITIS*, on the west coast, has a sandy beach and north of here are miles of deserted white pebbles which can be enjoyed without clothes. VLIHO has a small, secluded, sandy beach which may be suitable for nudism (reached from the top of the hill outside the village). VASSILIKI is sheltered in a deep bay but, unfortunately, the narrow, pebble beach is rather badly affected by litter.

Things To Do: Few things to see except for boat trips to the caves, the cliffs at Cape Lefkados and the islets.

Getting Around: Seven buses a day to Nidri; three a day to Vassiliki and Vliho; three buses a day to Agios Nikitis. Car, moped and bicycle hire in Lefkas town. Bus and boat excursions in high season. Caiques to the islets of Mandouri, Sparti, Skorpios and Meganissi, although you can't go ashore on Skorpios which is owned by the Onassis family.

Tour Operators:
LEFKAS TOWN: Manos (H).
NIDRI: Falcon (R,S).

ITHACA (ITHAKI)

Ithaca appears as two small islands of equal size connected by a narrow isthmus. It consists of scrubby and rocky hills with woods and some cultivation in the more sheltered areas. The villages are pretty but there are few tourist facilities. The ancient palace of Odysseus was supposed to have been located here and there are other Homeric associations which is probably the reason why most people come here.

Connections: By boat – daily from Patras via Kefalonia (5 hours); caiques in season from Fiscardo on Kefalonia to Stavros on Ithaca.

Centres: VATHI, the capital and main port, is set in a deep bay. The whitewashed Venetian-style houses surrounding the harbour have been faithfully reconstructed after the 1953 earthquake destroyed many of them. There are some rooms to rent as well as a number of hotels including the Mentor (0674 32433/32293) and the Odysseus (0674 32381) – both 'B' class. Tavernas provide what evening entertainment there is.

STAVROS is a fair sized village with a couple of restaurants and rooms to rent. 15 minutes' walk away is Polis Bay with a small beach where people camp.

FRIKES is a little village nestling in a protected bay. There are several houses with rooms to rent, two quiet waterfront tavernas and a village shop.

KIONI, two miles further south, has similar facilities although it is somewhat larger.

Beaches: Mainly rocky or pebbly coves. In VATHI small caiques ferry people across the bay to sunbathe on small and rather uninspiring concrete strips. There is a small beach at POLIS BAY near Stavros. Between FRIKES and KIONI are innumerable coves and pebble beaches; all of them empty and suitable for nudism.

Things To Do: See the Grotto of the Nymphs and the Fountain of Arethusa (both mentioned in 'The Odyssey') and the ancient city of Alkaklomenai.

Getting Around: In high season boats between Vathi and Kioni leave twice daily in each direction. Buses leave Vathi's waterfront for Kioni (via Stavros and Frikes) at 07.00, 08.00, 09.00 and 14.30 and return at 10.00 and 15.30. Bicycles and mopeds for hire although there are few roads. Motorboats for hire in Vathi.

Tour Operators:
VATHI: Aegina Club (P); Greek Sun (H); Manos (H); Thomson – 'Summer Sun' Brochure (H).
FRIKES: Greek Islands Club (S).
KIONI: Greek Islands Club (R,S).

KEFALONIA (ARGOSTOLI)

Kefalonia, approximately 16 miles by 31 miles at its widest points, is the largest of the Ionian islands. The interior is very mountainous and, although some parts are relatively lush, it cannot compare in terms of natural beauty with either Corfu or Zakynthos. The small fishing village of Fiscardo was the only place to survive the 1953 earthquake undamaged; virtually every other town and village on the island was levelled. The mountainous terrain and poor public transport make travelling around difficult. While catering quite well for tourists the island is still relatively unvisited although an increasing number of tour operators are adding Kefalonia to their list of destinations.

Connections: By air – daily with Athens and three times a week with Zakynthos. By sea – ferry at least once a day from Patras on the mainland (3½ hours); three ferries daily in season between Poros (on the east coast of Kefalonia) and Killini on the mainland; caiques in season between Fiscardo and Ithaca. By bus – three times a day from Athens.

Centres: ARGOSTOLI, the island's capital, is new and modern and not very attractive although there are some comfortable modern hotels here including the 'C' class Kefalonia Star (0671 23180/3). There are a good selection of tavernas and bars as well as four discos. The discos are all situated at LASSI, about 1½ miles away on the outskirts of town, and also here is the 'C' class Lassi Hotel (0671 23415/6). The nearest beaches are within 20 minutes' walking distance but most people take the bus to the sandy beaches at Makri Yialos and Plati Yialos.

From Argostoli boats leave eight times a day for the pretty village of LIXOURI which is situated across the bay on a wide peninsula. There are two or three hotels here including the 'C' class Summery (0671 91771). The village only has a small pebble beach but elsewhere on the peninsula are miles of beautiful unspoilt coastline.

SKALA is a small, sleepy fishing village on the south-east coast. Its little houses, many of which are built of wood, cluster around the main street and here you will find three good tavernas, a number of cafe-bars, a few village shops and the 'C' class Hotel Skala (0674 23247). Skala has a long, clean sandy beach.

Densely wooded Mount Ainos stands sentinel over the small east coast resort of POROS. There are rooms to rent here as well as the 'B' class Hercules Pension (0674 21235). Nightlife centres around a number of tavernas and there are also two or three music bars. Poros has a long, pebble beach.

SAMI is the dismal main ferry port and is of no other interest except that there is an organised campsite here, Caravomilos Beach Camping (0674 22480), complete with snack bar, restaurant, disco, self-service shop and waterskiing and windsurfing facilities.

FISCARDO, situated in a sheltered bay on the north-east tip of Kefalonia 25 miles from Argostoli, is a small village of pretty whitewashed houses some of which are Venetian in style. Here is the 'B' class Panormos pension (0674 51340), a few tavernas and cafes and a colourful harbour with fishing boats and visiting yachts. There are two pebble beaches just outside the village and these are picturesquely situated in coves surrounded by cypress and olive trees. Car hire is recommended.

ASSOS, on the north-west coast, is a picturesque fishing village with just one taverna and the 'C' class Gerania pension. Close by, standing high above the village on a small peninsula, is the magnificent Castle Assos which dates from 1595. The village has a small pebble beach. Car hire recommended.

Beaches: All along the coastline between Argostoli and Poros are a succession of beaches and coves, the quieter of which can be used for nudism.

LASSI* (1½ miles from Argostoli). It is a ten minutes' walk (through a field of thistles!) to this three-hundred-yard-long sandy beach which is usually quiet enough to be used for nudism.

PALIOSTIFADO BEACH** is reached from in front of the Hotel Méditerranée. Walk to the left as you face the sea and climb over the small pile of rocks which divides the beach. The next part of the beach is topless and, after about 200 yards, you will come to some more rocks. Climb over these onto the naturist beach.

MAKRI YIALOS, about 2 miles from Argostoli, is situated on a beautiful, long, sandy bay. It can, however, get fairly busy here and there are also a number of villas and apartments which overlook the beach. Windsurfing and waterskiing are available and there is a good taverna. A little further on is PLATI YIALOS. This is another fine, sandy beach. Unfortunately, the bay is totally dominated by the 200 bedroom White Rocks Hotel and it gets busy here. Sun umbrellas and sunloungers are available as well as waterskiing and windsurfing.

In the middle of the south coast is AFRATA, a long beach of fine sand near to the village of Blaxata. It should be possible to enjoy nudity here.

The long, sandy beach at SKALA is fringed with pines. It is usually quiet and may be suitable for nudism.

POROS*. Although the beach at Poros is shingle it is not uncomfortable to lie on. It runs for about 2 miles and is secluded enough at its northern end to be used for nudism.

1 mile north of FISCARDO and reached by footpaths is an area of flat rocks by the sea which is sometimes used for nude sunning. Walk around the harbour towards the lighthouse before climbing the path which leads up and over the headland to the rocks. There are pebble beaches just outside the village. However, these are small and, when busy, are probably unsuitable for nudism.

MYRTO* is a superb beach of fine sand just south of Assos. It is spectacularly situated in a bay encircled by cliffs and is usually deserted. You can walk here from Assos and there are also caique excursions (these are dependent on demand – ask in Assos).

AGIOS GEORGIOUS*, to the south of Lixouri, is a long stretch of golden sand most easily reached by caique. All around this western peninsula are miles of beautiful coastline which remain untouched by tourism.

Things To Do: Two interesting caves. Drongarati Cave is near to the village of Haliotata (about 2½ miles from Sami and reached by walking inland along the Argostoli road). It is open from 07.00 to 19.00 daily and has orange and yellow stalactites and stalagmites. The other cave, Melissani, is the more interesting of the two and is near the village of Vlahana. It is half an hour's walk to here from Sami or, alternatively, you can take the Fiscardo bus at 13.30 and ask to get off at Melissani. Open 07.00 to 19.00. It has a salt water lake in its centre which can be explored in a rowing boat.

There are two museums in Argostoli. The Archaeological Museum is open weekdays 09.00-13.00 and 16.00-18.00, Sundays 10.30-14.30, closed on Tuesdays and the Historical and Cultural Museum is open every day except Sunday, in the morning and after siesta.

Mount Ainos is the highest mountain rising to 5,000 feet and there is a road leading to a T.V. relay at the top. The view is magnificent not only taking in all Kefalonia but also Ithaca, Zakynthos and Patras.

Getting Around: Buses are surprisingly few and some, to more distant parts, don't return until the next day. Buses from Sami to Argostoli daily at 07.30, 08.15, 14.30 and 17.30 returning at 07.45, 12.00, 13.00 and 15.00. Bus to Fiscardo at 13.30 (but doesn't return until the next morning). Kefalonia is hilly and the roads are not very good although the stout-hearted can hire bicycles in Argostoli. Car and scooter hire is also available here and mopeds can be hired in Lixouri. A few excursions are available in high season.

Tour Operators:
ARGOSTOLI: Aegina Club (H); Freedom (H); Grecian (H); Greek Sun (H); Sunmed (H,R,S); Thomson – 'Small and Friendly' Brochure (H,T); Thomson – 'Villas and Apartments' Brochure (S).
LASSI: Greek Islands Club (S); Greek Sun (H); Olympic – Main Brochure (H).
PALIOSTIFADO BEACH: Aegina Club (Hotel Méditerranée); Amathus (Hotel Méditerranée); Grecian (Hotel Méditerranée and Lassi Apartments); Thomson – 'Summer Sun' Brochure (Hotel Méditerranée); Thomson – 'Villas and Apartments' Brochure (Lorentzatou Apartments).
POROS: Freedom (H,P,S); Greek Sun (H); Sunmed (H,P,R,S).
FISCARDO: Greek Islands Club (S); Greek Sun (R).
ASSOS: Greek Sun (P).

ZAKYNTHOS (ZANTE)

Zakynthos, approximately 11 miles by 22 miles at its widest points is, like Corfu, a very green and scenically interesting island with cultivated plains and sandy bays contrasting with rugged mountains and precipitous cliffs. A strong Italian influence, particularly noticeable in many of the buildings, bears witness to the island's 350 years of Venetian occupation. Although the main town and port, also called Zakynthos, is attractive, the island's villages tend to be dull and lacking in interest. After Corfu, Zakynthos is the busiest and most developed of the Ionian islands and is particularly popular with the British who have all but swamped the main resorts.

Not recommended for those looking for authentic Greek atmosphere, sophisticated nightlife or a high standard of food.

Connections: By air – direct flights from the U.K.; daily with Athens and four times a week with Kefalonia (but only up to 22nd June). By sea – three ferries a day (one, out of season) between Zakynthos and Kyllini (mainland) and on to Kefalonia; on Sundays in season there is a direct ferry between Zakynthos and Kefalonia (until 16th August). Buses twice a day from Athens and Patras.

Centres: The island's capital and main port of ZAKYNTHOS was virtually rebuilt following its destruction by an earthquake in 1953. By usual Greek standards it is a masterpiece of town planning and reconstruction. Much has been done to retain the original Venetian influence and there are squares, bell-towers and colonnaded walk-ways.

Your first sight of the town will probably be from the busy boulevard which follows the long sweep of bay on which the town stands. The drive-on ferry virtually backs onto this busy road to discharge its load of cars and lorries causing periodic traffic chaos. Further along are the offices of the tourist police (0695 22550) and close by is the elegant and spacious main square,

Platia Solomou, which contains the imposing Neo-Byzantine Museum. Cutting across this square, a road (Vassileos Georgiou B) leads to another pretty square, Agiou Marko Platia. This square seems to serve as the town's centre and there are some pleasant pavement cafes (the one opposite the Ionian Bank serves very good pizzas) and a restaurant which charges high prices for unremarkable food. In fact, the most disappointing thing about Zakynthos is the unoriginality and, in many cases, poor quality of the food served up in restaurants and tavernas. Pizzas, pasta and other fast foods are much in evidence but you will be hard pressed to find a restaurant serving decent Greek dishes. One of the better ones is the Kallino Restaurant on Vassileos Georgiou B (on the right before you enter Agiou Marko Platia). Nightlife in town is also virtually non-existent and the liveliest venue is the Zakynthi Pub which is situated behind the Kallino Restaurant. This is quite a stylish place with good music and cocktails.

The other main tourist centres are at Laganas, Argassi and Alikes. LAGANAS is about 4 miles from Zakynthos town and to call it a village would be a misnomer. It consists of some hotels, tourist shops and tavernas spaced spasmodically along a tarmacadamed road which ends at the beach. The fine sandy beach extends for about three miles around the bay. The first part of the beach is covered with sun loungers and sun umbrellas and is generally very busy. Further along, past the Zante Beach Hotel, it becomes emptier until a rocky headland prevents further progress. A track leads inland around this obstacle to another sandy beach above which stands the Turtle Bay Hotel. Near-by is the tiny 'resort' of KALAMAKI, 4½ miles from Zakynthos town. There are a few rooms and apartments here but little else. Not recommended in view of the isolated location and distance from the sea (about fifteen minutes' walk).

Nightlife in Laganas centres around the tavernas although there is a cocktail bar (on the left of the main road travelling towards town) and the Zante Beach Hotel has a disco. A usually good and inexpensive place to eat is the Tassos Taverna which serves simple food (souvlaki, fish, veal, etc.) cooked over a charcoal grill. The waiters are the owner's sons and they periodically entertain the diners with some very good Greek dancing.

ARGASSI, 2½ miles from town, also owes its existence to tourism, being a collection of bars, souvenir shops and holiday accommodation straggling both sides of the main road. In fact, it is difficult to see why a resort grew up here in the first place. There is hardly anything which could reasonably be described as a beach other than a narrow strip of sand strewn with pebbles outside the Chryssi Akti Hotel (in Greek Chryssi Akti means golden beach and at home such a description would court instant prosecution under the Trade Descriptions Act). The Mimosa Beach Bungalows have a grassed area bordering the sea which people use for sunbathing in the absence of a beach.

Nightlife centres around a few bars and there are also a couple of discos situated about a half a mile or so outside Argassi towards Zakynthos town. These are the Manhattan and the Station (in front of the island's power station). Two bars worthy of mention are the Magic Mushroom and Dennis's Bar. Both serve reasonably priced cocktails and good English breakfasts which represent excellent value for money. Eating out is generally uninspiring although just a stroll up the hill out of Argassi is Porto Davia, with a narrow strip of wet sand and a taverna which serves good food (by Zakynthos standards anyway). It can, however, get very busy. Although there are no nudist beaches close to Argassi this resort does have the advantages of a good choice of accommodation, some nightlife and plenty of transport to hire – cars, mopeds and bicycles. You could consider hiring transport and using Argassi as a base to visit the nudist beaches further down the coast.

ALIKES, situated 10 miles or so north of Zakynthos town, is a small, quiet resort on a long sandy bay. There are no easily attainable nudist beaches and the resort is also somewhat isolated.

Beaches: Although Zakynthos has some superb sandy beaches many of them have, unfortunately, been affected by oil spillages. This pollution manifests itself in the form of tiny black pellets buried in the sand and it is not always possible to avoid getting oil on your feet. This is not a serious problem but you are advised to take some suitable cleaning solvent with you.

At LAGANAS* the beach becomes quieter the further along you go and, at this far end, it is backed by low, scrubby dunes. Nudism should be possible here although there are better places on the island.

The best choice of beaches and some of the nicest, are to be found off the metalled road which runs south from Argassi. The first of these is PORTO ZORO (4 miles or so from Argassi). The beach is approached by a steep track (drivable) off the main road and is well signposted. It is a pleasant, sandy bay with rocks at the water's edge at one end. A taverna stands on the beach and, although nudity is not unknown here (at the top end near to the rocks) the beach is relatively small and its popularity with conservative British holidaymakers inhibits nudism.

Just over a mile after the turn-off to Porto Zoro, a track on the right leaves the main road signposted DAFNI BEACH**. This track is passable by car or on two wheels but caution should be exercised as it is bumpy and steep in places. It is about 3 miles (10 minutes' careful driving) to the sea. There is a scruffy taverna and some low pines at the back of the beach. The proprietors of the taverna used to operate a mini-bus service to transport young backpackers arriving in Zakynthos town from the harbour to Dafni where they camped under the trees. However, Zakynthos is a breeding ground for the threatened Loggerhead Turtles and this beach in particular is a favourite laying ground. The turtles come ashore at night and lay their eggs in the soft sand. However, dozens of young people camping virtually on the beach, as well as the antics of a moronic minority who used torches to search for laying turtles, soon caused those interested in conservation to quite rightly take an interest. At the time of writing the taverna appears to have closed down and tranquillity reigns once again on Turtle Beach. The beach is long and sandy but, unfortunately, there is evidence of both oil on the beach as well as litter at the back of it. Although isolated and quiet it is, in the opinion of the writer, not as nice as Gerakas and is much less easily accessible.

Continuing along the main road for another 4 miles or so you will see a road on the left which is signposted 'Restaurant Ionian Beach. Rent Rooms'. The road leads to a taverna which overlooks the sea and there are rooms to rent and a campsite close by. A path leads down to the sea and to the right a long, flat, sandy beach stretches into the distance. The beach is usually deserted and is suitable for nudism. There is no natural shade here.

The next turn left off the main road is signposted AGIOS NIKOLAOS (Saint Nicolas Beach)**. This is a fine sandy bay with a beach bar which serves drinks and simple food (yogurt, spaghetti, toast). Pedeloes can be hired here as well as a windsurfer. To the right of the main beach is a low headland and an easy scramble over the rocks reveals another nice bay of fine sand. The bay is sheltered and has a gently sloping bottom making it suitable for young children. Unfortunately, the back of the beach is affected by litter and the far end is covered with dried seaweed. Nevertheless, this is in many ways an ideal place where it should always be possible to enjoy nudity although you may be the only naked person there. There is no natural shade on either of these beaches. The Vassiliko Beach Hotel (0695 24114/51325) is in an unobtrusive position well back from the beach. It has comfortable rooms with showers and balconies. The fact that it is only partly completed, coupled with its isolated position, ensures that it is not used by tour operators. You should have no difficulty in getting a room at a keen price here. Close by are the Botonis Houses with rooms to rent by the sea. Agios Nikolaos is a good choice for those who want accommodation close to a naturist beach although, in the absence of transport, evening entertainment is non-existent.

Still further along the main road is PORTO ROMA. This is a narrow, sandy beach overlooked by a rather run-down looking taverna at one end. The beach becomes stonier the further along you go and here stones in the water make entering the sea difficult. The great attraction of Porto Roma is, however, that it is protected on windy days and can often be enjoyed when other beaches are unusable. It is usually fairly busy and, while it cannot be claimed to be a naturist beach, the writer has enjoyed nude sunning here when other places have been too windy (necessity being the mother of invention) and, as so often happens, has sometimes been joined by those lying near-by. It is most suitable about 200 yards along before the beach starts getting too stony and where you can distance yourself a little way away from the nearest clothed person.

Soon after the turn-off to Porto Roma the tarmacadam disappears from the main road and a short distance further on the road ends completely at

GARAKAS BEACH**. A flat grassy area is used for parking and a short distance away is a taverna with a sign which offers free camping. A track leads down onto the long beach of fine sand which is backed by cliffs. Nudism can be enjoyed at either end and you will often be in the company of other naked bathers enjoying this superb location. The sandy bottom shelves gently making swimming safe for children but there is no natural shade. At the time of writing there is a very temporary-looking bamboo shack on the beach which calls itself a 'coffee bar' and pedeloes and a windsurfer can be hired here. One of the best nudist beaches on the island.

Although there are other beaches none are reported as being suitable for nudism. Of these, TSILVI is the best. It is a long, narrow beach of fine sand situated halfway between Zakynthos town and Alikes near to the little village of Planos. It is in a fairly isolated location although there is some holiday accommodation part way along. When not too busy, you may be able to strip off.

Things To Do: Visit the Neo-Byzantine Museum in Platia Solomou (open daily 09.00-13.00 and 15.00-18.00, closed Tuesdays). There is a good collection of icons here. In the small museum in Agiou Marko Platia you can thumb through an interesting album containing photographs of the town before and immediately after the earthquake. Visit the Venetian kastro which stands on a cliff above the town. The battlements are intact, in spite of the earthquake, and there are some good views from up here. Caique trips from Zakynthos town and Alikes to see the Kianoun Cave (popularly called the Blue Cave) on the northern tip of the island.

Getting Around: Buses to Porto Roma leave Zakynthos town at 08.00 and 13.00 daily and return immediately. The trip takes thirty minutes and costs 40 drs. If you want to make your own way to the Blue Cave (rather than going on an organised excursion), buses leave town for the village of Korithi at 05.00 and 13.00 on Wednesdays and Saturdays only (100 drs.). In Korithi you can hire a boat to the cave. All buses leave from the bus station which is situated on Filitia Street (walking south down the promenade towards the massive Church of St. Dennis, turn right before the Fina petrol pump).

Roads are generally good and there are many cars, mopeds and bicycles for hire. Although there is no shortage of petrol pumps, you should avoid running low on Sundays because most of the pumps are closed. Although a rosta of 'duty' pumps operates it is unintelligible – even to the locals!

Tour Operators:
LAGANAS: Aspro (H,R,S); Enterprise (H); Flair (H); Freedom (H,P); Grecian (H,P,R,S); Manos (H); Olympic – Main Brochure (H,S); Pan (P); Sunmed (H,P,R,S); Sunvil (H,P); Thomson – 'Summer Sun' Brochure (H); Thomson – 'Small and Friendly' Brochure (R); Thomson – 'Villas and Apartments' Brochure (S).
ARGASSI: Avra (H,S); Sunmed (H,P,R,S).

KYTHERA

Only suitable for those with a pioneering spirit. Not particularly attractive and few tourist amenities. The coastline is rocky and inaccessible.

Connections: The island is difficult to reach and is totally unconnected with the other Ionian islands which are far to the north-west. By air – up to two flights a day from Athens. By sea – Pireus to Ag. Pelagias by ferryboat on Thursdays and by hydrofoil daily except Mondays; ferry three times a week from Neapolis (mainland); there is also a sea connection with Porto Heli on the mainland.

Centres: KAPSALI is the island's main port and is beautifully situated on a sweeping bay 900 feet below KYTHERA (or Chora) the island's picturesque capital. There is no bus service and Kythera is reached by a steep 25 minute walk. There are rooms to rent at both Kapsali and Kythera. AG. PELAGIAS, a hydrofoil port in the north of the island, is somewhat untidy and straggles along a beach. There is a hotel here and tavernas.

Beaches: KAPSALI has a half rocky, half sandy beach near to the harbour. Other beaches are less easily accessible. The island's main road joins Kythera and Potamos and from here you can hitch to the nudist beach at AG. ELEFTHERION** on the west coast or head north for the sandy beach at AGIA PELAGIAS. Further north still is the reputedly fine beach at PLATIA AMMOS.

Things To Do: Little to see of real interest.

Getting Around: Difficult. There are occasional buses to some villages (including one to Potamos – one hour journey) and a few taxis.

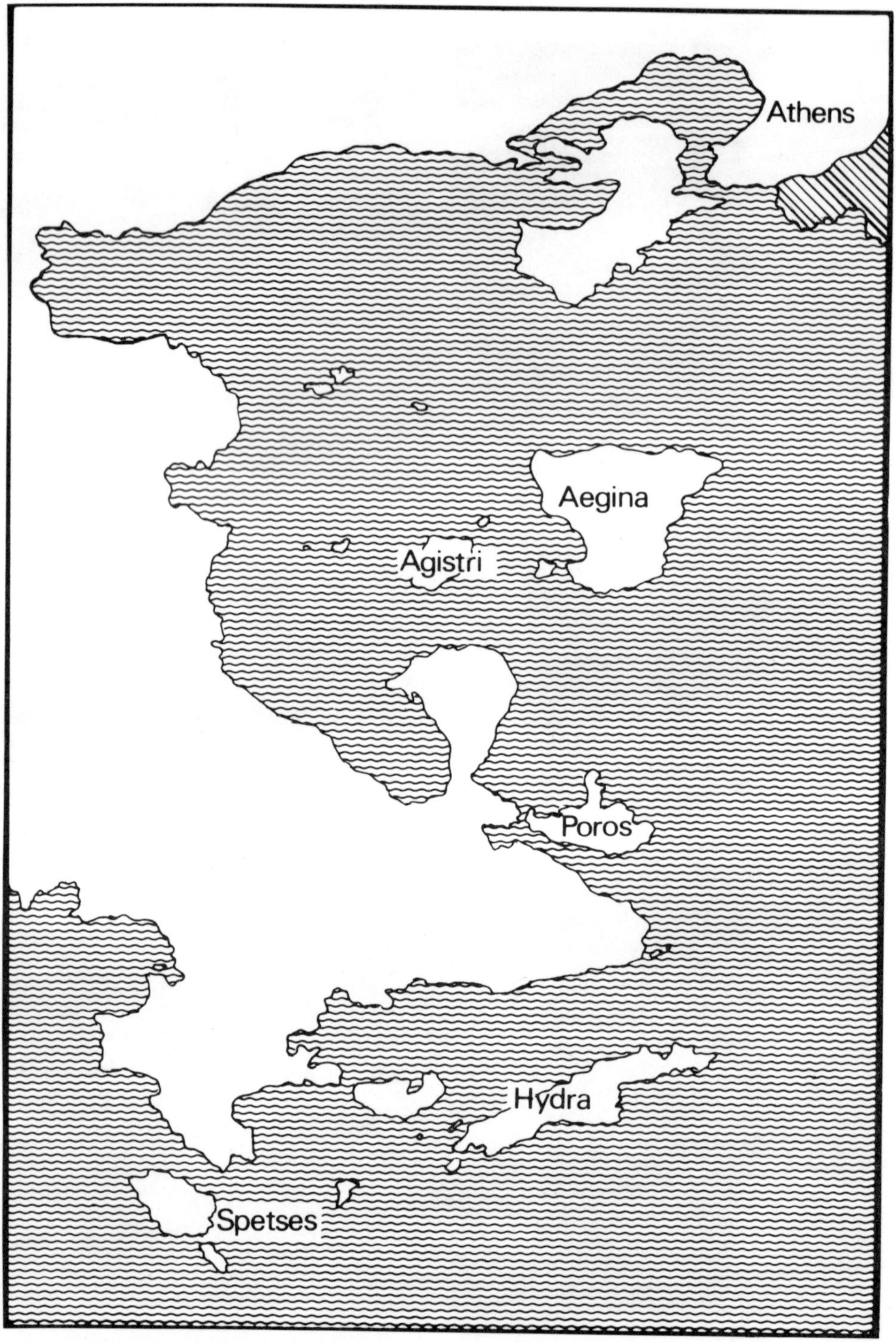
Athens
Aegina
Agistri
Poros
Hydra
Spetses

THE SARONIC ISLANDS

Their proximity to Athens makes them ideal for the island wanderer with limited time. Connected by high speed hydrofoils and ferryboats almost hourly with Athens and with each other, they are the most accessible of all the Greek islands. This accessibility has made them extremely popular. In addition to the many foreign visitors, Greek families like to spend their weekends here and, in season, the Saronics can become unpleasantly overcrowded. If possible, you should try to see the islands during the week and avoid arriving at week-end. Another consequence of this popularity is that they are among the most expensive places in Greece.

AEGINA

Aegina (pronounced Eggina), approximately 8 miles by 7 miles at its widest points, is within commuting distance of Athens. The island is consequently well developed with as many Greek as foreign tourists. The island lacks pretty scenery and genuine Greek atmosphere.

Connections: Fourteen times a day with Piraeus (35 minutes by hydrofoil). Frequent connection with Poros, Hydra and Spetses.

Centres: The island's capital is also called AEGINA and is the main port and commercial centre of the island. In Aegina town there is plenty of accommodation in both hotels and rooms. There is a small sandy beach. South of the town the coast is pleasantly quiet and fertile but with few beaches.

From Aegina town a boat leaves three times a day for the quiet little island of Agistri (30 minute trip) which has many pine trees and some beaches. Another islet, Moni, has beaches, woods and wild goats and the Greek National Tourist Organisation operate a camping site here. Open from the end of June until September. During this period the island can be reached by a boat which leaves three times a day from Aegina town.

Buses run regularly across the island to the main resort of AGHIA MARINA (30 minute trip). On the way the bus stops at the ruined Temple of Aphaia (fourth century B.C.). You can leave the bus here for a short guided tour before catching the next bus to Aghia Marina (temple gates locked between 13.30 and 15.30). It is worth stopping if only for the spectacular views. From the temple it is only a mile down to Aghia Marina (walkable) where you will find hotels, numerous private houses offering rooms as well as discos, bars and all the other trappings of a booming tourist resort. Aghia Marina is a classic example of what was once a typically Greek village which has been transformed, some would say ruined, by tourism.

Beaches: The best and only really sandy beach on the island is at AGHIA MARINA and it gets very busy here in season. There are no reports of any beaches being used for nudism.

Things To Do: Visit the ruined Temple of Aphaia (see above). Take a boat from either Aegina town or Aghia Marina to the pretty wooded islet of Moni which has beaches. Visit Perdika in the south, a fishing village with a small beach, which is still relatively untouched by tourism.

Getting Around: Renting a bicycle is a popular way to travel. Car and scooter hire also available. Buses leave Aegina town for Aghia Marina (via the Temple of Aphaia) and Perdika from the bus station on the waterfront (to the left of the ferry landing stage).

Tour Operators:
Aegina Club (H,R,S); Cook, Thomas – 'Hotels, Coaches and Cruising' Brochure (H); Cook, Thomas – 'Villas, Apartments and Tavernas' Brochure (S,T); Cosmos – 'Summer Sun' Brochure (H,P); Ellerman (H,P); Freedom (H); Grecian (H,S); Intasun – 'Plain and Simple' Brochure (H); Manos (H,R,S,T); Olympic – Main Brochure (H,S); O.S.L. (S);
Sunvil (H,S); Tanntours (H); Thomson – 'Summer Sun' Brochure (H); Thomson – 'Small and Friendly' Brochure (H,R,T); Thomson – 'Villas and Apartments' Brochure (S).

AGISTRI

The small island of Agistri, 30 minutes by boat from Aegina, has only recently opened up to tourism. The island is mountainous and is covered with pine and olive trees. There are three small villages, no proper roads and few vehicles.

Connections: Ferry from Piraeus (2 hours). Boats three times a day in season from Aegina town.

Centres: SCALA and MILOS consist of a few tavernas, a handful of buildings and little else. They are separated by a thirty minute walk and these two places have most of the island's holiday accommodation. Nightlife is unsophisticated.

Beaches: SCALA has a nice beach of fine sand and shallow water which is ideal for children. MILOS also has a sandy beach but it is littered with driftwood and flotsam brought ashore by the prevailing wind. There are waterskiing and windsurfing facilities on both of these beaches.

A twenty minute walk from Scala along a rough coastal track is CHALIKIADA BEACH***. The Hotel Alkyoni perches on top of the cliff above the pretty bay and from here it is a not too difficult scramble down to the lovely beach of white pebbles. There are no facilities.

Things To Do: Visit Aegina. Day trips to Athens are also possible.

Getting Around: There is one fourteen seater bus on the island which operates without a schedule or a fixed route! The only transport which can be hired is bicycles and there are no taxis.

Tour Operators:
SCALA: Sunmed (H,R); Tanntours (H – Hotel Alkyoni, S – studios close by).

POROS

The island is about 6 miles by 5 miles at its widest points and is separated from the mainland by a narrow channel. It is a peaceful island and is popular with Athenians and British 'package' tourists. Poros is really two islands separated by a canal and joined by a narrow bridge. Kalavria is much the larger island and consists mainly of pine forests. There are roads on Kalavria and an unpredictable bus service. The best way to explore it is to hire your own transport. Most of the inhabitants and all of the facilities are crammed into the smaller island, Sferia.

Connections: Nine boats and two hydrofoils a day from Piraeus; frequent connections with Spetses, Hydra and Aegina.

Centres: POROS town, picturesquely situated on a hillock, is the only centre. There are rooms to rent here as well as a number of hotels. The town has quite a few good tavernas and restaurants and there are a number of discos. A short walk away across the canal bridge is the coastal road which has been tarmacadamed for a couple of miles in either direction and along here are some newer hotels and self-catering accommodation.

Beaches: Nearly all the beaches around the island consist of shingle or larger stones and are not particularly good. Anywhere resembling a decent beach tends to get busy and none are reported as being used for nudism. However, it is possible that the quieter coves may be suitable.

From Poros town water taxis provide a shuttle service to the small beach of rocks and pebbles at NEORION (about a mile from town). The beach is pleasantly shaded by trees and waterskiing and windsurfing are available although, unfortunately, the water in this bay can be less than crystal clear. Closer to Poros town, on the west coast of Sferia island, is the beach known as AGAPIS (Limenaki tis Agapis). It is beautifully situated among the pine trees and can be reached from Poros town by water taxi. This is a quieter beach without a taverna and it may be possible to go nude here when it is not too busy. At the eastern end of the canal is KANALI BEACH (you may be asked to pay here) and further around the bay is busy ASKELI BEACH with a beach bar and watersports school. These beaches are both shingly. A mile or so further on is the quieter, stony, MONASTERY BEACH with three tavernas.

Things To Do: One of the few sights is the eighteenth century monastery of Zoodochos Pigi. The trip can be made by bus from the harbour or, more interestingly, by boat (ask one of the old men around the harbour). The cost of the round trip should be small and will take about 30 minutes each way. Further north are the few blocks which are all that remain of the Temple of Poseidon. Excursions to the near-by mainland are also available.

Getting Around: Frequent buses. Bicycle hire in Poros. Water taxis (known locally as 'benzinas') to the beaches.

Tour Operators:
Aegina Club (H,S); Airlink (S); Amathus (S); Freedom (H); Grecian (H,R,S); Gryphon (H,R,S); Intasun – 'Plain and Simple' Brochure (H); Kosmar (H,R,S); Laskarina (S); Manos (H,S); Meridian (P,R,S,T); Olympic – Main Brochure (H,R,S); Sunmed (H,R,S); Sunvil (H); Tanntours (H,R,S,T); Thomson – 'Summer Sun' Brochure (H); Thomson – 'Small and Friendly' Brochure (P); Ventura (H,S); Zeus (S).

HYDRA

Hydra (pronounced Eedra), approximately 13 miles by 3 miles at its widest points, is picturesque, fashionable and expensive.

Connections: Three boats and five hydrofoils a day from Piraeus. Daily connections with Aegina, Poros and Spetses.

Centres: Only HYDRA town. The waterfront is colourful and lively and the tavernas and restaurants here are the centre of life in the evenings. There are a number of lively discos. Cement bathing area beside the town. There are no roads on the island and few things to see apart from the town itself.

Beaches: It is reported that Hydra's police are not as enlightened as some and that naturists have had to pay stiff fines in the past. There is a rocky island just off Kamina which used to be popular with nudists but caique owners have now been prohibited from taking visitors there. In any case there are practically no beaches and, although Hydra has undoubted attractions, it is not a good choice if an all-over tan is high on your list of priorities.

Things To Do: Few things to see apart from the town itself. Easy to get to both the mainland and neighbouring islands.

Getting Around: There are no roads on the island – rough tracks only.

Tour Operators:
Aegina Club (H,R); C.V. Travel (S).

SPETSES

The island is about 4 miles by 3 miles at its widest points. The interior is uninhabited and is covered with pine forests. Spetses is popular with Athenians and British 'package' tourists. Cars are only allowed with a permit.

Connections: At least twice a day with Piraeus, Hydra and Poros; less often with Aegina.

Centres: DAPIAS is the only resort and is the port and island capital. The town has extended along the coast and development has been rather haphazard. Palio Limani at the edge of town is smarter. The streets in the old part of the town are paved with pebble mosaics commemorating the island's history. In season it is difficult to find accommodation. Check with the Mania Express (main travel agents on the harbour), Takis's travel agents (eastward towards the old harbour) and with the tourist police (200 yards up the narrow street behind the Saronikos Hotel). The town is a maze of bars, tavernas and tourist shops and in the evening the town is lively and this is not an early to bed place. There is a small, crowded town beach (pebble).

Beaches: Every day at 10.30 the 'Nautilus' leaves the harbour for the 45 minute trip to AGIOS ANARGHERI, stopping at other beaches on the way. The cost is about £1.00 return and the boat back leaves at 16.00. Anargheri is the longest and most popular beach consisting of pebbles and sand. There are rocks at one end between which you may be able to enjoy the beach in relative privacy. There is a taverna on the beach. The adjoining bay is PARASKEVI*** – mixed nudist and non-nudist. Hire a moped and explore the island's perimeter road (which is mostly dirt track). There are lovely views and you will find a succession of small coves set amongst pine trees with beaches of coarse sand or shingle and crystal clear water.

Things To Do: Few things to see. There are excursions to Epidaurus on Saturdays and Sundays and a one day tour comprising Epidaurus, Mycenae and Nafplion on Wednesdays. The 'Daphne II' operates one day cruises to Leonidon (on the south-east Peloponnese coast), to Hydra and to lovely Monemyasia (south-east Peloponnese). The same boat also departs at 21.00 on Saturdays for a bonfire and barbecue at Anargheri beach, returning at midnight.

Getting Around: Daily bus around the coast. Rent a bicycle through the tourist office. Probably the best way of seeing the island and getting to those secluded coves is to hire a moped or motorcycle. There is one taxi on the island. Caiques travel around the island to the main beaches.

Tour Operators:
DAPIAS: Aegina Club (H,P,R,S); Airlink (H,R,S); Club 18-30 (H,T); Cosmos – 'Summer Sun' Brochure (H); Falcon (H,R,S); Freedom (H,P); Laskarina (P,R,S); Manos (H,R,S,T); Meridian (H,R,S); Olympic – Main Brochure (H); Sunmed (H,P,R,S); Sunvil (H,P); Tanntours (H,R); Thomson – 'Summer Sun' Brochure (H); Thomson – 'Small and Friendly' Brochure (H); Thomson – 'Villas and Apartments' Brochure (S); Zeus (H,R,S).

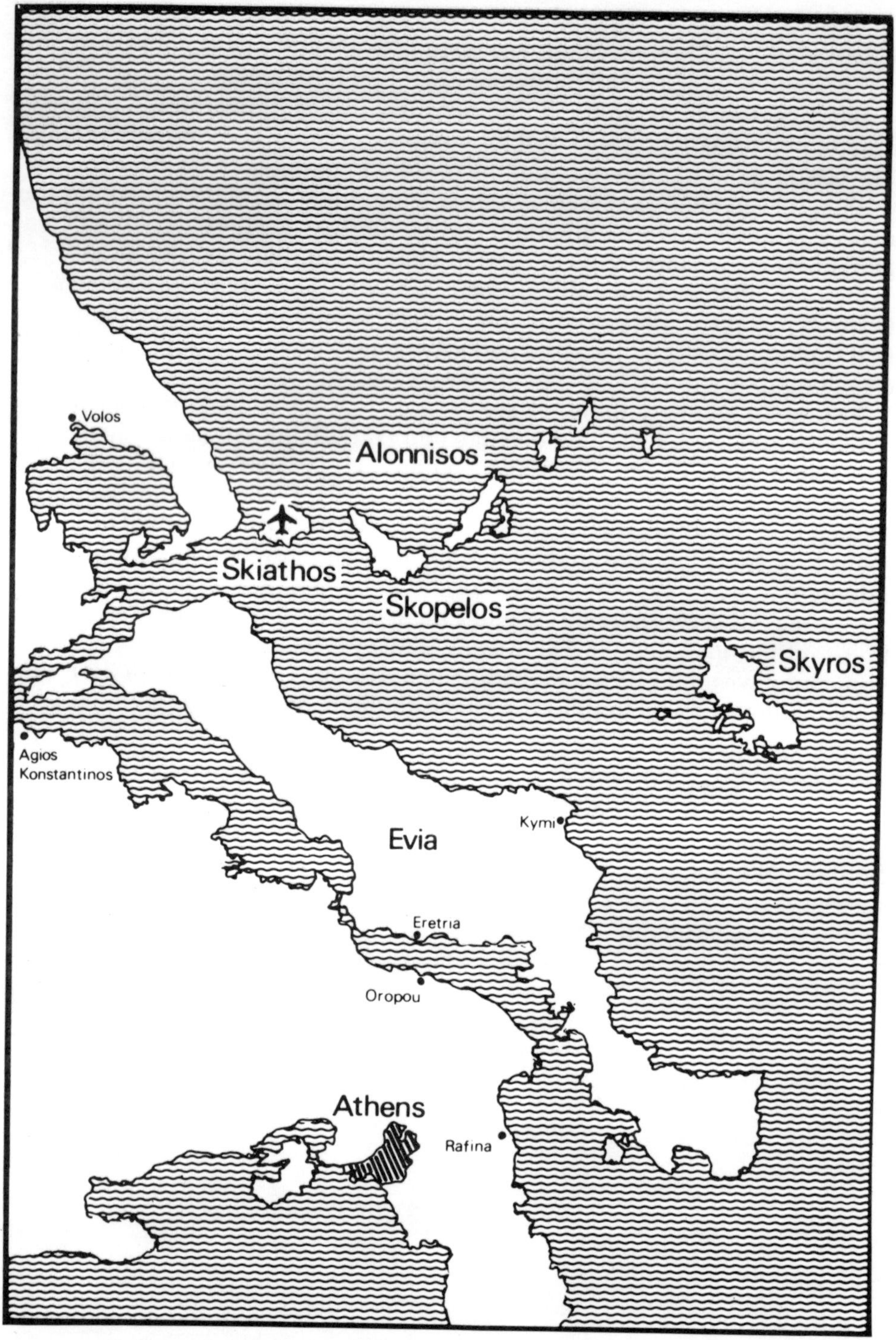
Volos
Alonnisos
Skiathos
Skopelos
Skyros
Agios
Konstantinos
Kymi
Evia
Eretria
Oropou
Athens
Rafina

THE SPORADES

The Sporades (meaning the sprinkled islands) are green and wooded with rolling hills and some superb sandy beaches. Their comparative inaccessibility ensures that they are not overrun. Skiathos, with an airport, is the busiest and, unless you fly there first, the trip to the other islands involves either a bus or train ride to Volos, or a bus trip to Agios Konstantinos, both followed by a ferry trip to the island. Skyros is the most difficult to get to. There are ferry connections only with Kymi on Evia and Volos. The crossing from Volos is a long one and the other route involves a bus trip from Athens to Oropou, a ferry to Eretria on Evia (every hour), a further bus ride to Kymi and a ferryboat from there to Skyros.

Although, strictly speaking, Evia is not one of the Sporades it is included here for the sake of convenience.

EVIA

Evia, approximately 110 miles long and 31 miles wide, is so close to the mainland that it is easy to regard Evia as being part of it. However, although it is joined to the mainland by a bridge at Halkis, it is the second largest island in Greece (after Crete). The scenery is varied, being greener towards the north, and much of the island is covered with large areas of farmland. The east coast is rocky and mainly inaccessible while the west coast is more gentle. Evia is little visited by foreigners and is mostly quiet and unspoiled.

Connections: By sea from Rafina – three times a day to Karistos, a small fishing port in the extreme south of the island (2 hours), three times a day to Marmari (1¼ hours) and eight times a day to Nea Stira (50 minutes) – both on the west coast; from Oropou to Eretria every hour from 06.00 to 23.00 (25 minutes); twelve times a day between Arkitsa and Edipsos – in the north of the island – (50 minutes); from Glifa to Agiokambos (also in the north) every two hours between 06.00 and 20.00 (30 minutes); once a week with Volos (8 hours). By bus – from Athens (260 Liossion Street) every half an hour from 06.00 to 21.00 (1½ hour journey); from Athens (Mavromateon and Alexandras Avenues) to Rafina at least hourly from 07.00 to 23.30 (1 hour journey); buses to Oropou leave from the same place. By train – nineteen each day from Athens (Larissis station) to Halkis. The trip takes 1½ hours.

Centres: HALKIS is the island's capital and also its largest town. It is heavily industrialised and is not an appealing place to stay.

KARISTOS, close to the southern tip of the island, is a small fishing port with a Venetian fortress. It is quiet and unspoiled with a good, long, sandy beach. There are a number of hotels here, rooms to rent and a youth hostel as well as some nightlife.

KYMI, on the east coast, and its port of Paralia Kymi 2½ miles away, are connected to one another by bus. Kymi is quite a nice town set high above the sea and surrounded by forests but the port is unremarkable. There is a passable beach here which gets very crowded. Accommodation is mainly in hotels.

PEFKI, also on the east coast, has a very long, sandy beach, numerous tavernas and some rooms to rent but it tends to get crowded in summer with Greek tourists.

LOUTRA EDIPSOU, on the north-west coast, is a health spa – it attracts the infirm from all over Greece who come here looking for relief. The town is somewhat reminiscent of a Riviera resort and has no less than 104 hotels. Visitors are mainly older and hotel accommodation tends to be expensive. There are numerous narrow beaches in the long bay which curves to the north-west of the town and you can often find one to enjoy without anyone else disturbing you.

Beaches: Not a good choice if an all-over tan is high on your list of priorities. Its closeness to the mainland ensures that Evia is popular with Greek tourists and many of the better beaches are busy. The size of the island makes it difficult to get to the more remote and quieter beaches. The only beach reported as being used for nudism is CHILIADOU**. This is reached from Halkis by driving to the east coast village of Lamari via Steni Dirfios and on to Chiliadou. The very long beach is used by naturists at its northern end and there is a large cavern here which provides shade when not already occupied.

Things To Do: Nothing of spectacular interest. See the old Turkish quarter in Halkis. Here are the remains of a Turkish fortress, an aqueduct, the Byzantine Museum on El. Venizelou (which is housed in the old Turkish mosque) and the church of Agia Paraskevi which was converted into a Gothic cathedral in the fourteenth century by the Crusaders.

On the main road, 2½ miles south of the town of Krieza and then a half a mile or so west along a farm track, is the ancient city of Dystos which stands on a marshy lake. The walls of the acropolis are well preserved and there are also remains of fifth century B.C. houses.

Modern Eretria is built on an ancient site and here are the ruins of an agora and a temple dedicated to Apollo Daphnephoros. There is a small museum in town which exhibits local discoveries and which is open in the mornings. Near here a theatre has been excavated and beyond this are the ruins of a gymnasium.

Getting Around: Good bus service from Halkis to most parts of the island.

Tour Operators:

Intasun – Main Brochure (H); Intasun – 'Plain and Simple' Brochure (H); Sunmed (H).

SKIATHOS

Skiathos, about 7 miles by 6 miles at its widest points, is a verdant island of gently rolling hills covered in pine woods, orchards and olive trees. Its magnificent beaches of fine white sand are amongst the best in Greece. These attributes have resulted in a considerable amount of building development in recent years, most of which has taken place along the island's single surfaced road which runs for 7½ miles from Skiathos town to Koukounaries. The island is very popular, particularly with the British (a good many of the villas are English owned) and gets crowded in season.

Connections: Direct flights from Gatwick (tour operators offering direct flights include Olympic Holidays and Freedom Holidays). Up to six flights a day from Athens. Alkyon Travel, 98 Akadimias Street, Athens (362 2093) sell combined bus and boat tickets to Skiathos. Buses leave at 08.30 every morning (except Friday when they leave at noon) to meet the boat at Agios Konstantinos. The journey to Skiathos takes about 5½ hours. Daily connections by boat with Agios Konstantinos (3¼ hours); two or three times a day with Volos (3 hours), there is also a Flying Dolphin hydrofoil (in season) between Volos and Skiathos which is quicker but more expensive; once a week with Kymi (5½ hours); several times a day with Skopelos (1½-2¼ hours) and on to Alonnisos.

Centres: The only town is SKIATHOS town and most of the island's 4,000 or so inhabitants live here. Its predominantly white and somewhat

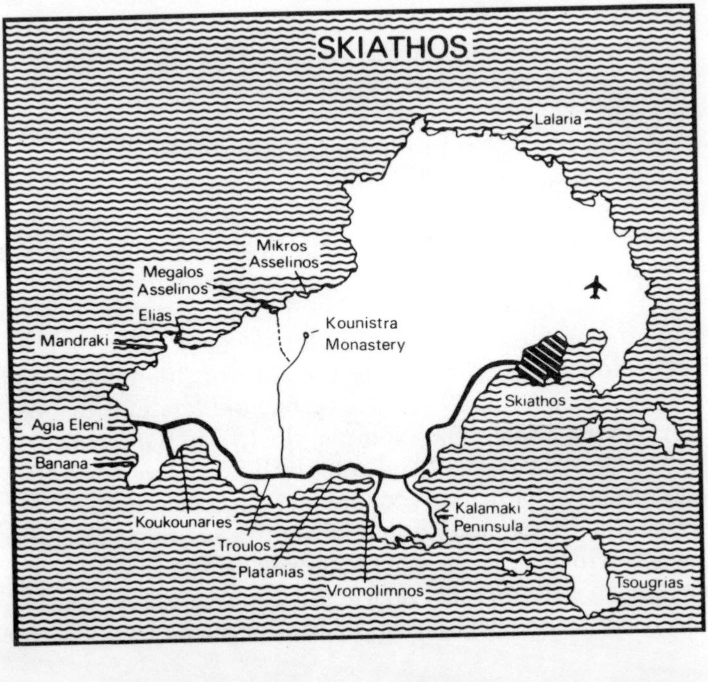

characterless buildings cover two hills which rise on either side of the pleasant harbour. The harbour is also the town's focal point (it is situated around the corner from where the ferries dock). It has thankfully been made pedestrian and this is a good place to sit under the sun-awnings of one of the cafes and watch the world go by. If you continue along the harbour front and up the steps past the tavernas you will come to a more peaceful part of town where Greek family life appears to carry on untouched by the tourist invasion just a short walk away.

There are plenty of places to eat in Skiathos town and the quality is good by Greek island standards. Recommended are two tavernas which are reached by climbing the steps from the harbour (to the right as you face the sea). At the top of the steps are a number of tavernas. The second one along is 'O Stamatis' where you will get a good, reasonably priced meal (the lobster is especially good). Further along on the left is the Taverna Anemos where some of the tables have a great view of the harbour. Try the hors d'oeuvres and the excellent fish.

There are a number of discos in Skiathos including the Bonaparte (on the main street), the Captain Nemo and the Scuna Club (both of these are a little way out of town).

If you don't fancy crowded discos try one of the small bars such as the Kaliri Bar. You can find the Kaliri by walking down the rather bitty main street (Papadiamanti Street) towards the harbour. Turn right after passing the National Bank of Greece (the turning just before you come to the Olympic Airways office on the left). Follow this street to the 'T' junction and turn left, the Kaliri bar is on the right. If you enjoy cocktails you'll like the Kaliri and the French owner, Patrick, plays some great music for you to groove to on the small dance floor.

Accommodation is plentiful in hotels and rooms in town and there are a number of modern hotels along the south coast. However, Skiathos can get so crowded in season that there are no rooms left in the town, although you will usually be able to find somewhere along the road to Koukounaries. The Skiathos Owners' Association operate an information service on the availability of rented accommodation. Their kiosk is situated on the right of the quay (as you face the sea) where the ferries dock.

If you stay in town you will have to travel a considerable distance to the naturist beaches – by boat to Tsougrias, by bus to Platanias, by bus or caique (in season) to Banana Beach. For example, the trip to Banana (the best beach but also the furthest away) takes 30 minutes by bus followed by a 10-15 minute walk. As an alternative, you could consider staying near to the Koukounaries end of the bus route in the area known as Mandraki (not to be confused with Mandraki Beach which is some distance away on the north coast). To walk from here to Banana will probably take about 20-30 minutes. The path is steep in places and it can be heavy going in the heat of the day – not recommended with young children. There are a couple of tavernas at Mandraki but little else in the way of evening entertainment. The best solution is to hire transport, although this is expensive. Failing this, it might be best to stay in town. At least you are at the beginning of the bus route (the bus gets crowded further along) and you also have the alternative of a pleasant trip by boat to Banana. In addition there are the advantages of plentiful accommodation, a good choice of places to eat and nightlife.

Beaches: There are reputed to be over sixty beaches but only those on the south and north-west coasts are easily accessible. Many of the south coast beaches have been developed commercially and this, coupled with the ease of access from the main road, has inhibited the spread of nudism. Naturist beaches are to be found on the island of Tsougrias, at Platanias, Banana Beach, Agia Eleni, Mandraki, Elias and Asselinos. None of these beaches are easily accessible from town.

Boats to TSOUGRIAS** leave the town harbour between about 10.00-11.00 each day for the 20 minute trip across to the island. Return trips are usually at 14.00, 16.00 and 17.00 and the cost of the round trip is 250 drs. per person. The beach where the boats land is not nudist. At one end you will notice some trees on higher ground at the back of the beach and behind these is the path which runs straight ahead (don't follow the one which leads up the hill – it's a dead-end although there's a good view). The path leads through thick brush and it's a 15 minute walk to the nudist beach. You should cover your legs to prevent scratching and the walk is not recommended if you have young children. The beach is a long spit of fine sand. Some shade is provided by bushes at one end. This is a nice, sandy beach but getting there involves a lot of effort and there are better alternatives.

If you follow the main Skiathos-Koukounaries road you will pass some lovely beaches including beautiful Vromolimnos but none are naturist. There are secluded sandy coves on the Kalamaki Peninsula which are suitable for nudism but they are difficult to get to.

PLATANIAS BEACH* can be reached by bus (18 minutes from town – ask to get off at Agia Paraskevi). Near to the bus stop you will see a signpost on the left of the main road stating 'To The Beach. Water Ski. Wind Surfing. Motor Boat For Rent. Cruises.' The path near to this signpost leads directly onto the beach. Platanias is a long, sandy beach which probably never gets crowded, although it is popular with British villa parties and it can get busier at week-ends when it is used by Greek families. It should be possible to go nude at one or other end of the beach. There is a snack bar on the beach and a good taverna near-by on the main road at Paraskevi.

MANDRAKI BEACH* is a 20-25 minute walk off the main road. If you are travelling by bus ask to get off at Mandraki (which is the stop but two before the road ends at Koukounaries). A signpost on the left of the road which states 'Beach – Mandraki – Refreshments' points towards the track to the beach

Skiathos Beaches

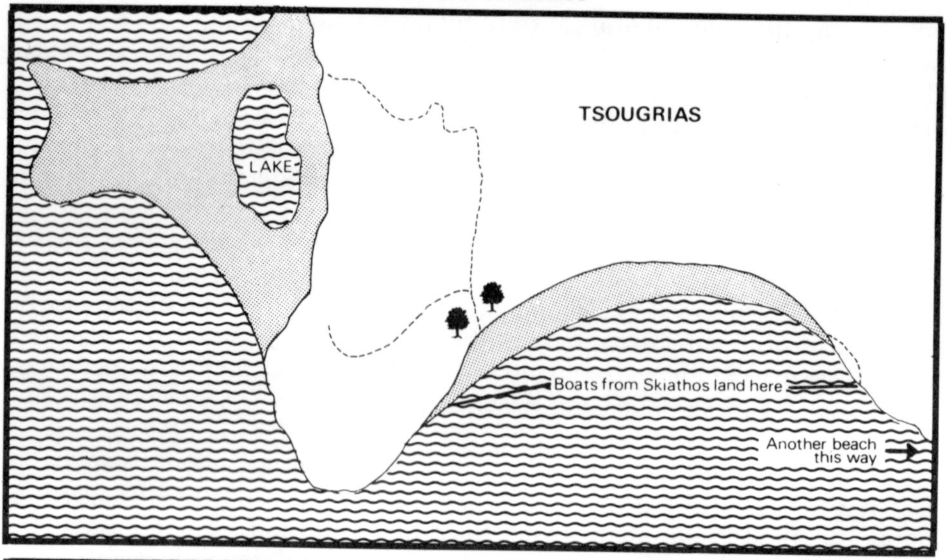

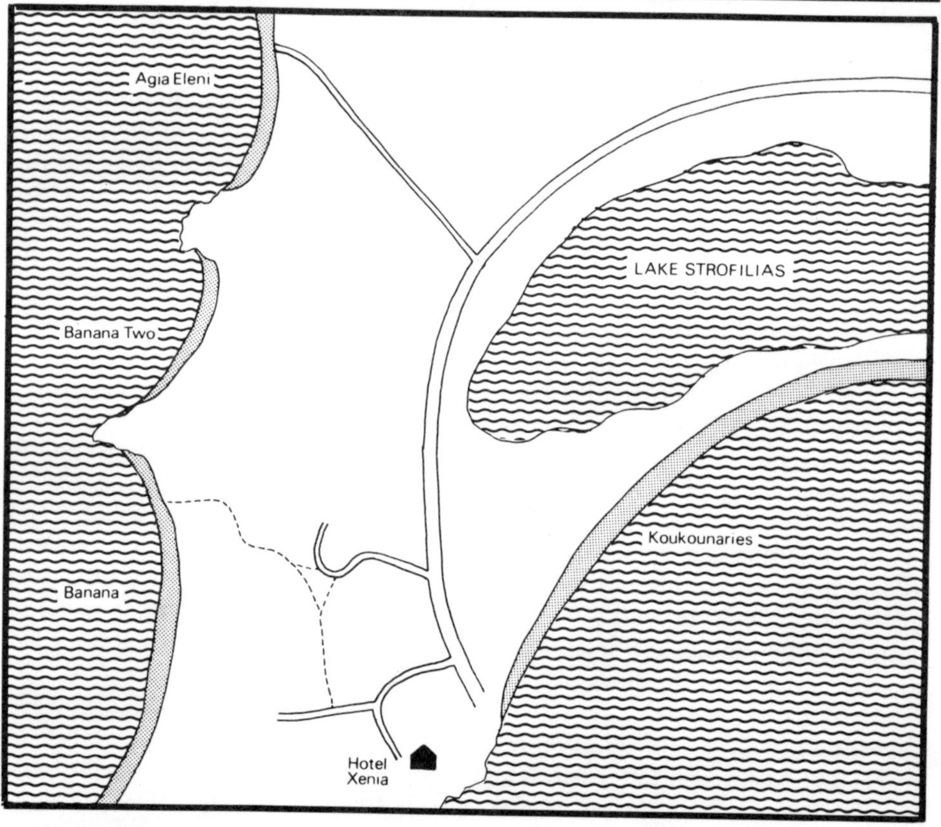

which runs alongside a taverna. After a short distance the track ends and you continue along a sandy path (no access for motor vehicles) which winds its way through the pine woods. After about 100 yards, the path divides. Straight ahead leads to Elias Beach while the left fork emerges at the long and sandy Mandraki Beach. There is plenty of room for both nudists and non-nudists here but, unfortunately, the beach is dirty with seaweed and junk which has been washed ashore by the prevailing winds. This wind can also wash jelly fish inshore and when the writer was there the north coast was badly affected by these unpleasant creatures although the south coast beaches were free (all the north coast beaches can be affected by strong winds). The beach bar has been abandoned and there are now no facilities and there is no natural shade.

ELIAS BEACH* is a 20 minute walk and is well signposted from the divide in the path mentioned above. It is a lovely, sandy beach which stretches for well over three-quarters of a mile. It can, like Mandraki, be windy here and the beach is similarly littered with flotsam and jetsam. Nevertheless, there is plenty of soft, clean sand on which to lie and sheltered sunbathing is provided by the dunes. There is no natural shade although recent reports suggest that a taverna may have opened. Behind the rocks at the northern end of Elias is a further sandy beach which is similar, although somewhat smaller, than the main beach.

It is possible to take a short cut from Elias to Mandraki Beach. Re-enter the wood via the dunes and after about 100 yards turn right onto a small track. The track widens and after a short distance it divides. The left-hand path returns to the main road while the right fork descends to Mandraki Beach.

AGIA ELENI* is a 10 minute walk from the main Skiathos-Koukounaries road (the bus stop is called Agia Eleni). Close by, a surfaced road branches off on the right (up a fairly steep hill) signposted Agia Eleni. Agia Eleni is a lovely, sandy beach with a taverna and water-sports. Naturists can sometimes be found at the far end of the beach (to the left facing the sea) or behind the rocks at this end of the beach. There is no natural shade here but there are sun umbrellas all along the beach.

The best used naturist beach on the island is BANANA BEACH*** (its Greek name is Krassa, although everyone now calls it Banana). It can be reached on foot from either the Agia Eleni bus stop on the main road (10-15 minutes' walking time) or from the Koukounaries beach bus stop which is the last one on the route (also 10-15 minutes' walking time). If you have your own transport you can drive part of the way by following the main Koukounaries road. Pass the turn-off to Agia Eleni on the right and look out for a dirt track also on the right (there are usually a number of cars parked at the bottom). The track climbs steeply and is very uneven and you should think twice about attempting it on anything other than four wheels. Part of the way up the hill you will come to a parking area near to some metal gates. Park here and follow the path down to the beach. Banana is a fantastic beach of beautiful white sand

and must rank as one of the best nudist beaches to be found anywhere in the Mediterranean. It is well used and the majority of people are nude. Windsurfing, waterskiing, pedeloes and sun umbrellas are available from a wooden beach hut where you can also get sandwiches, doughnuts and cold drinks (no need to get dressed). The proprietor makes sure that the beach is kept clean and litter bins are provided and emptied at the end of each day. If you get too hot, the pines at the back of the beach provide pleasant shade and you can cool off here without having to get dressed. Banana can get crowded in season and if it becomes too busy for your liking try 'Banana Two'. This is another long, sandy beach and is situated around the rocks to the right of the main beach. It is also used for nudism and there is plenty of room for the few people who decide to go there (no facilities).

MEGALOS ASSELINOS** Asselinos is signposted off the main road near Troulos. After about a mile and a half the road forks. The left-hand fork leads to Megalos (Big) Asselinos along a mile or so stretch of poorly surfaced road. This is a large, sandy beach with a big new taverna and an official campsite. There is no natural shade although a bamboo construction opposite the taverna can be used by those seeking respite. Attempts are being made to keep the beach clear of the rubbish which is brought ashore by the prevailing northerly wind. For this reason and because of the superior facilities (there are even two hot showers on the beach!) many will prefer this beach to Mandraki. Although some of the excursion boats stop here on their tour of the island, Megalos Asselinos can best be reached by the daily coach operated by Lakis Tours. This leaves Skiathos town at 11.30 and returns at 17.00. Most nudists are to be found at the eastern end of the beach.

MIKROS ASSELINOS** Instead of turning left (see above) to Megalos Asselinos take the right fork to the Kounistra Monastery. From here continue along a small track for about 1½ miles (drivable on two wheels only). There are some lovely views before the path descends steeply to the sandy beach. The beach is quiet and remote and the few who find it usually don't bother with clothes. There are no facilities although drinks and small lunches (delicious fresh salads) are available at the Kounistra Monastery which is, in any case, worthy of a visit.

There are many other fine, sandy beaches including VROMOLIMNOS and KOUKOUNARIES. Many holiday brochures describe Koukounaries as the best beach in Greece but fail to mention that the long crescent of fine sand gets jam-packed in season. The beach at LALARIA*, on the northern coast and only accessible by boat, consists of extraordinarily smooth, white pebbles. It is spectacularly situated with a natural archway formed by the rocks at one end.

Things To Do: Caique trips around the island and to the beaches. Near to Lalaria are two caves which can only be explored from the sea, Skotini Spilia (the 'Dark Grotto') and Glazia Spilia (the 'Blue Grotto'). Near-by are the ruins of the medieval walled city of Kastro. Lalaria Beach, Kastro and the caves can be reached by excursion boat from town. The Monastery of Evangelismos (open 08.00-12.00 and 17.00-19.00) can be reached by mule trip and has an exceptionally beautiful stone church. Excursions to Skopelos and Alonnisos.

Getting Around: Frequent bus service between Skiathos town and Koukounaries. The trip takes about 30 minutes and costs 45 drs. (25 drs. to Paraskevi). Buses get crowded in season. Boats to Koukounaries and Banana leave the town harbour at about 11.00 every morning returning at about 16.30. Cost – 75 drs. each way. Car, moped and bicycle hire in town.

Tour Operators:
SKIATHOS TOWN: Aegina Club (P); Allsun (S); Avra (R); Freedom (P,R); Grecian (H,P,S); Greek Sun (H,R); Ilios (H,S); Laskarina (H,P,S); Skiathos Travel (H,P,R,S); Sunvil (H,P,R,S); Tanntours (H,S); Timsway – 'Original Holidays in Greece' Brochure (H,S).
AGIA PARASKEVI: Laskarina (S); Meon (S); Skiathos Travel (S).
AGIA ELENI: Ilios (S).
KOUKOUNARIES: Aegina Club (H); Allsun (H); Amathus (H); Club Mark Warner – Club Koukounaries (H); Freedom (H); Grecian (H,S); Laskarina (S); Manos (H); Olympic – Main Brochure (H); Skiathos Travel (H); Sunvil (H,S); Timsway – General Brochure (H).

SKOPELOS

Skopelos, about 11 miles by 10 miles at its widest points, is another beautiful pine-covered island. It is fertile and grows an abundance of fruit and nuts – pears, plums, walnuts and almonds. In spite of its pretty scenery and magnificent beaches it is not well developed and has yet to be discovered by mass tourism.

Connections: Five times a week (excepted days are Thursdays and Saturdays) with Kymi (3½ hours); two or three times a day with Volos (4½ hours) also Flying Dolphin hydrofoils in season (quicker but more expensive). Daily with Agios Konstantinos (5½ hours); several times a day with Skiathos (1½-2¼ hours); every day with Alonnisos in season (½ hour) and nearly every day out of season. On most days with Skyros (via Kymi).

Centres: SKOPELOS, the main port and capital of the island, is one of the most picturesque towns in the Sporades. Its whitewashed buildings are set on a hillside around an almost circular bay and its streets climb steeply to the ruins of a Venetian fortress. There is ample accommodation in hotels, pensions and rooms in private houses. Along the waterfront are a number of restaurants and tavernas. Jimmy's (O TZIMH) comes highly recommended (at the end of the harbour near to where the ferryboats dock). Nightlife, however, is low-key and this is not a good place for a lively time.

There are rooms to rent and a few basic hotels along the west coast and on the south coast there is unofficial camping on Velanio beach.

GLOSSA, in the north of the island, is the other main town. It is situated high above the sea and, as well as being a pretty place, there are magnificent views from here. There is, however, nowhere to stay and hardly anywhere to eat. Glossa is connected to its port of LOUTRAKI (2 miles away) by bus and most of the ferryboats also stop here on their way to and from Skopelos town. There are some rooms to rent, as well as a couple of hotels, tavernas and a small pebble beach.

Beaches: The long, sandy beach at Skopelos town is not nudist and, in any case, it is dirty. An official notice in town states that Velanio is the official nudist beach on the island and that nudity is forbidden elsewhere. Other beaches are, however, used – apparently without hindrance. The island's only bus service operates between Skopelos town and Loutraki and passes several beautiful beaches on the way. The first of these, STAFYLOS, is long and sandy but it is also very busy. There is a lovely cliff-top taverna here which is shaded by pine trees. If you walk the length of the beach and climb over the headland at its eastern end you will come to the official nudist beach at VELANIO***, an excellent beach of coarse sand and fine shingle backed by crumbling cliffs. There are no facilities here. The next village along the bus route is AGNONTAS with a small, crowded beach. From here you can catch one of the caiques which run every half an hour to LIMONARI*, a long crescent of fine sand surrounded by towering green hills. Trees at the back of the beach provide shade and there is also a taverna here. The beach is generally uncrowded and could be suitable for nudism when not too busy. After Agnontas the bus turns northwards to PANORMOS**, a long beach consisting mainly of small pebbles. Part of the beach can be viewed from the main road but elsewhere the beach is sometimes used by the occasional naturist. There is a taverna here and a few boats for hire. A little further on is beautiful MILIA**. This secluded beach, which extends for over a mile, consists of sand and some pebbles and is backed by scrub and pine woods. It is partly nudist and is accessible from the main road by means of a dirt track. The bus driver will put you down at the start of the track if you ask.

Things To Do. There are 09.00 departures most days in season for a boat tour of the island. This takes 4½ hours and includes a stopover at one of the beaches and lunch at Loutraki or Glossa. Day trips to Alonissos – depart Skopelos 10.00 (1 hour journey), return at 16.00.

Getting Around: Buses from Skopelos leave for Stafylos at 10.00, 10.30, 11.30 and 16.00; for Agnontas at 10.30, 11.30 and 16.00 and for Glossa and Loutraki at 07.15 and 11.30. In addition there are coach excursions to Agnontas, Panormos and Milia. These usually leave Skopelos town at about 10.30 and 11.00 and return at 16.00 and 17.00. At present a single road crosses the island although a new road is being constructed to join Skopelos town and Agnontas. Car and moped hire in Skopelos.

Tour Operators:
SKOPELOS TOWN: Aegina Club (H,P,S); Freedom (H,P,S); Grecian (H,S); Greek Sun (H,R); Ilios (H,S); Laskarina (H,P,S); Olympic – Main Brochure (H,R); Sunvil (H,P,S); Tanntours (H,P); Timsway – 'Original Holidays in Greece' Brochure (H,P,S).
STAFYLOS: Laskarina (S).

ALONNISOS
Sun-dappled forest tracks, the deep blue Aegean glinting through the pines, sounds of sea and singing birds; otherwise peace, tranquillity and solitude. These are the attractions of Alonnisoss, an island about 13 miles long by 3 miles wide. A major contributor to this peacefulness is the absence of traffic. A single made-up road joins Patitiri (the capital) with Votsi close by. Other places on the island are reached by tracks of variable quality. This is not the place for nightlife, sandy beaches or people who don't enjoy walking and many will find the island too quiet for a stay of more than, say, a week.

Connections: Once a week with Agios Konstantinos (6 hours); five times a week with Kymi on Evia (2¾ hours); virtually daily with Volos (5 hours); daily in season with Skopelos – nearly every day out of season (½ hour); daily with Skiathos – direct (1½ hours) or via Skopelos (about 2¼ hours).

Centres: There are only two villages of any note on the island, Patitiri and Votsi. PATITIRI is the island's capital and port and has been mostly built since the 1956 earthquake destroyed the one-time capital of Chora (now usually referred to as Old Alonnisos). Although not unattractive, Patitiri is an unremarkable place. A few tavernas bordering the white pebble beach, a couple of grocery shops (grandly calling themselves supermarkets), an agent of the National Bank of Greece (opposite the landing stage), hotels and private homes offering rooms to rent. You can explore the town thoroughly in half an hour. Hotels include the Alkyon (on the harbour front) and the three star Galaxy (situated in a commanding position overlooking the harbour). Telephone 0424 65251.

VOTSI, the other town and a short distance away from Patitiri, is an unattractive jumble and is not recommended for a stay.

A number of tour operators go to CLUB MARPOUNTA, a Club Méditerranée-style village. Marpounta, reached by means of a fairly rough track from Patitiri, is beautifully situated on a rocky promontory. The restaurant, bar, disco, tennis courts, swimming pool and other facilities are at sea level. The studio-type accommodation is attractively laid out in Greek village style and is situated at the top of a steep pine-covered hill (this makes Club Marpounta an unsuitable choice for the infirm). The studios, although small, are adequate consisting of a bedroom with a separate shower and toilet. A number overlook the sea and have spectacular views from their little

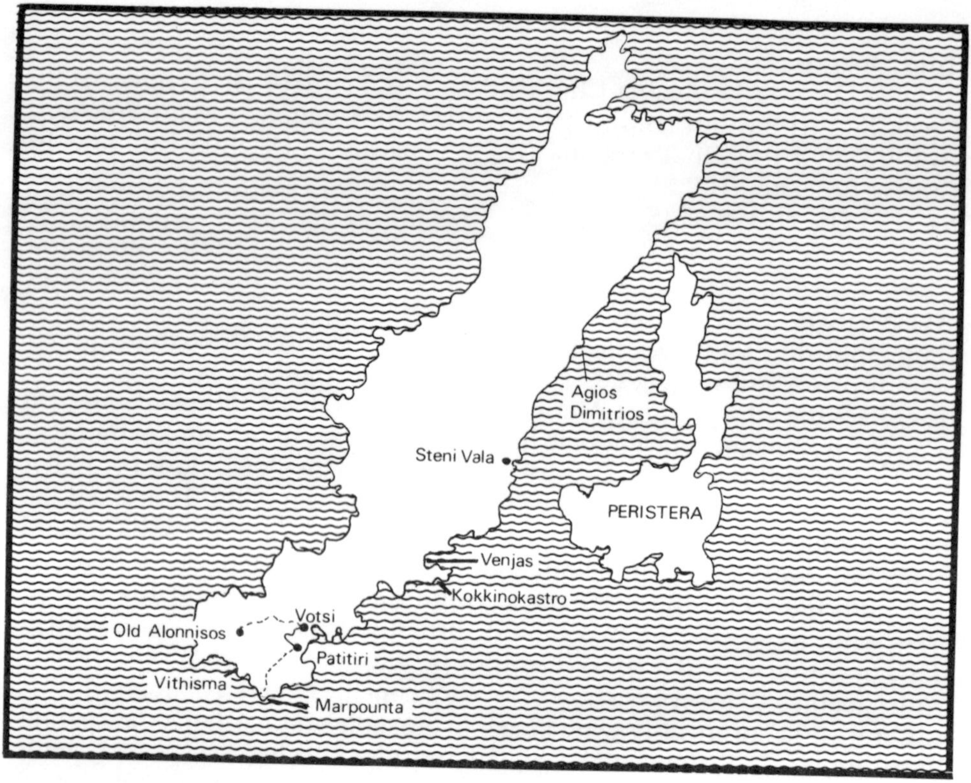
Agios
Dimitrios
Steni Vala
PERISTERA
Venjas
Kokkinokastro
Votsi
Old Alonnisos
Patitiri
Vithisma
Marpounta

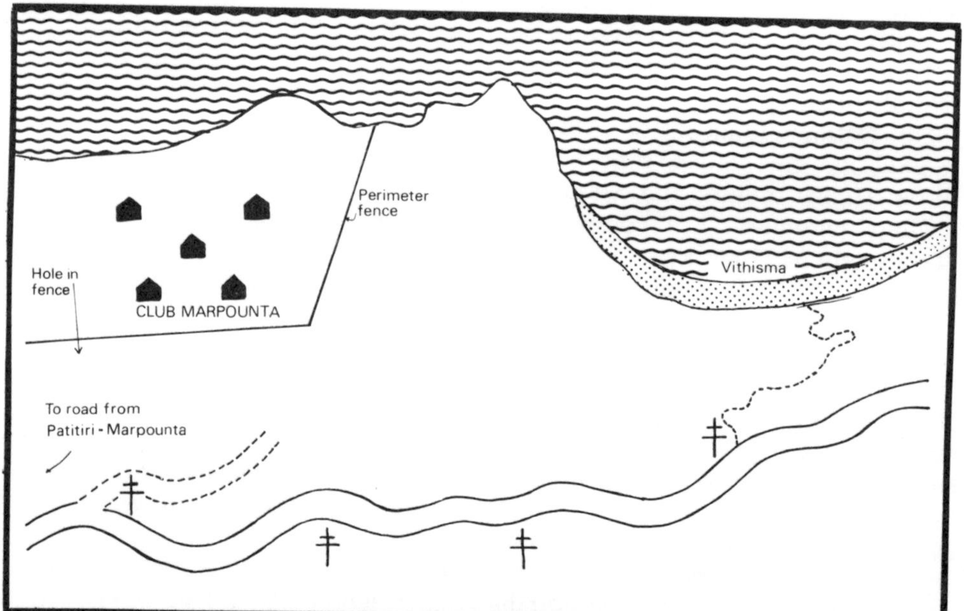
Perimeter
fence
Hole in
fence
CLUB MARPOUNTA
Vithisma
To road from
Patitiri - Marpounta

terraces. Some may feel that Marpounta is too isolated although the club mini-bus runs into Patitiri at certain times of day (for which there is a small charge) or you can walk into town (30 minutes). There are two beaches – one has been improved by the addition of imported sand, the other consists of pebbles. There is a small boat with an outboard motor for hire (about 1500 drs. a day) as well as pedeloes and a windsurfer. Half-board minimum is obligatory. Drinks and extras at the club are expensive and you will probably find it difficult to get a meal outside the set times. The writer found the food mediocre and, although the club has much to recommend it, was left with the impression that Club Marpounta may have seen better days. You might consider staying at Club Marpounta as part of a package two-centre holiday.

If you're looking for nightlife, forget it! There's a disco at Marpounta which doesn't get going properly until June and The Rocks disco on the Marpounta road is so isolated that it's surprising that anyone goes there at all!

Beaches: There are numerous coves and beaches on the island. Most of the beaches consist of pebbles and shingle – sand is a scarce commodity on Alonnisos! The coastal scenery is interesting and it is worthwhile taking a boat as far as Agios Dimitrios and back to see it. Cliffs and contorted rock formations contrast with tranquil beaches framed by pine and olive trees. Getting to the beaches is a problem. There is no car hire although you could risk breaking your neck on a scooter (always assuming that you can find a map which bears any relationship to what's actually on the ground!). The best way is by caique from Patitiri. The boats leave between about 10.00-11.00 each day and run as far as Agios Dimitrios visiting other beaches on the way. The best beach along this stretch of coastline and possibly the best beach on the whole island is KOKKINOKASTRO***. It is beautifully situated and consists mainly of pebbles with some gritty sand. Some shade is offered by crevices in the rocks and by the pine trees on the steep slope at the back of the beach. It is a long beach and is well used by naturists. There are no facilities so at least take something to drink. The cost by caique is about 150 drs. return.

AGIOS DIMITRIOS** is a vast beach of sloping pebbles and is used by naturists. It is beautifully situated on a promontory with magnificent views down the straight which separates Alonnisos from the near-by island of Peristera. There is no taverna and no natural shade.

Between Patitiri and Agios Dimitrios are other isolated beaches which are suitable for nudism. Don't worry if, when you arrive, someone has beaten you to it and prefers to retain clothing. Find your own piece of beach and strip-off – nobody is likely to mind. Try the beaches to the north of Steni Vala and the beautiful pebbly beach at VENJAS* (just around the headland from Kokkinokastro). Ask the boat-man to drop you off at any of these beaches and he will pick you up later in the day (probably between 16.00-17.00) but remember at least to take something to drink.

For those staying at Club Marpounta, the best beach is near-by

VITHISMA**. It can be reached from Patitiri by taking the Marpounta 'road'. After travelling a little way you will come to a boundary wall on the left on which is the name 'Naiada'. Just before this you will notice a track leading off on the right. Follow this track until you see, across the fields on your left, buildings amongst the trees. This is part of Club Marpounta. A small track on the left runs down the hill into the fields at the back of the club and near to this is a telegraph pole (actually it's a pole supporting an electricity supply line). This pole is your point of reference (if you are staying at the club you can get here by climbing through the hole in the perimeter fence at the back of the club and walking across the fields). Continue along the main track passing two more telegraph poles on the right. The next pole is on the left and near-by is a large rock. The path to the beach runs down behind this rock. The path is steep and, in places, difficult but the beach is worthy of the effort. It consists of pebbles with some fine, dark sand in parts. There is a little shade in the morning and later on in the afternoon from overhanging trees. Vithisma must have been more accessible at one time for there is a small abandoned beach bar here which carries '7-Up' advertising signs (Vithisma was promptly renamed the '7-Up beach' by our party) but now there is nothing except natural beauty, peace and tranquillity. If you continue along the track which you followed to Vithisma you will come to another pebble beach with (surprisingly enough in this remote place) a taverna.

The beaches at Club Marpounta are not nudist. However, it is possible to enjoy nude sunning and swimming on the rocky promontory which runs between the main beach and the pebble beach. The best part can be reached from the top of the steps which lead down to the pebble beach. Instead of walking back towards the club buildings along the path, follow the line of the low cliffs. Below is a rocky inlet with some flat rocks which are suitable for sunbathing. Although you can be seen by anyone standing on top of the embankment the writer was able to sunbathe without experiencing any problem – so get there early and stake your claim!

Things To Do: Visit Old Alonnisos, a village of considerable character situated on a hilltop. Most of the inhabitants abandoned the village when the earthquake destroyed many of the houses. However, a large amount of renovation is taking place and life is once again returning to the village. The walk to Old Alonnisos, either by means of the path which is hedged with raspberry bushes or by the unsurfaced road which is lined with pear trees, takes about ¾ hour. The easiest way, however, is to catch the small coach which is operated by one of the travel agents on the harbour front in Patitiri. It carries the day trippers from Skiathos and Skopelos up to the old town and departs at about 11.00 and 14.15 each day and at other times to suit the ferries (check the times beforehand). The cost is 100 drs. return.

Many guide books refer to the Kokkinokastro peninsula as the site of an ancient city, the remains of which are still supposed to survive. To spare you the effort – the writer was unable to find any trace but was told that there are some remains beneath the sea.

Getting Around: There is no public transport. Caiques to the beaches in season. No car hire but scooter/motor bike hire in Patitiri.

Tour Operators:
PATITIRI: Aegina Club (S); Freedom (P,S); Grecian (H,P); Laskarina (R,S); Sunvil (P,S); Tanntours (P); Timsway – 'Original Holidays in Greece' Brochure (P,S).
CLUB MARPOUNTA: Aegina Club, Freedom, Sunvil.

SKYROS

Skyros, about 9 miles by 15 miles at its widest points, is barren and mountainous in the south but in the north the scenery is more typical of a Sporadic island. Old customs and traditions are still much in evidence with many of the men wearing traditional baggy blue breeches and straw hats and the women in their long skirts and yellow scarves. It is less visited than the other islands in this group but is attracting a growing number of (mainly young) island hoppers.

Connections: Daily with Kymi on Evia; four times a week with Volos (11 hours).

Centres: Buses join the port, Linaria, with the island's capital, SKYROS. It is beautifully situated on a hillside with magnificent coastal views and an impressive fort. It is reminiscent of a Cycladic town with its hilly narrow streets and sugar cube houses. Accommodation is limited consisting of a hotel at Magazia, the 'B' class Xenia (tel. 91209) and rooms in Skyros town. In high season it can be difficult to get accommodation at all. A long path leads from town down to MAGAZIA with its nice, sandy beach. Along the way are tavernas and a lively disco.

Beaches: The beach of dark sand below Skyros town is one of the longest in the Sporades extending through the villages of Magazia and Molos and onwards around the point. It is a 15 minutes' walk down stone steps from the town centre to the beach or, alternatively, there is an hourly bus service. You can catch the bus from either the main square or from in front of the Post Office. That part of the beach which is closest to town gets crowded in season. Turn right and walk for 15 minutes in a southerly direction to a quieter part of the beach (beyond the rocks) where nudism appears to be well tolerated. Other beaches on the island are relatively inaccessible and quiet and it should be possible to enjoy nude sunning without too much difficulty. KALAMITSA* can be reached by taking the bus to Linaria followed by a 45 minute walk along the dirt road which runs south of the port. There are some magnificent views and your effort will be further rewarded by the lovely crescent of clean sand and a shaded taverna. In season, Skyros Travel (in town) organise bus and boat excursions to Kalamitsa as well as to PEFKOS*, north of Linaria, where there is a good sandy beach and a taverna. A longer trip goes to ATSITSA*, a sandy beach fringed with pine trees, which is reported as being suitable for nudism. There is a taverna here.

Things To Do: Few things to see. Caique trips to Tris Boukes to visit the grave of Rupert Brooke (if you think that it's worth the effort).

Getting Around: Bus from Linaria to Skyros and then to Magazia. Hire a taxi to get to the remoter beaches or rent a moped or a motor-boat.

Tour Operators:
MOLOS: Sunvil (P,S).

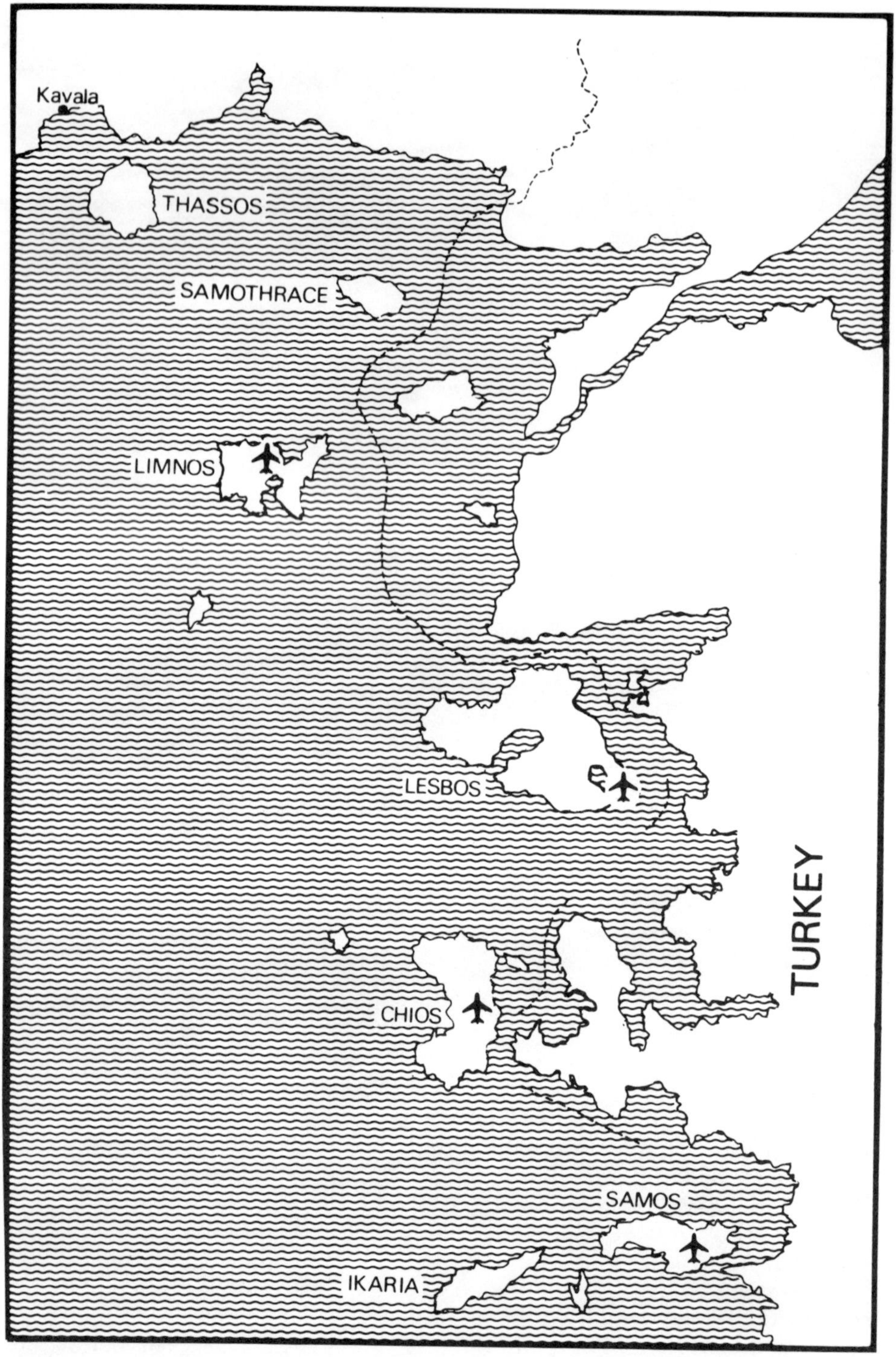

Kavala
THASSOS
SAMOTHRACE
LIMNOS
LESBOS
CHIOS
SAMOS
IKARIA
TURKEY

THE NORTH-EASTERN AEGEAN ISLANDS

This grouping is for geographical convenience rather than for cultural or historical reasons. The North-Eastern Aegean Islands are Chios, Ikaria, Lesbos, Limnos, Samos and Thassos. Ikaria is the closest to Athens although even this is a 12 hour boat trip. There are regular ferry connections between the islands.

THASSOS

Thassos, about 15 miles by 16 miles at its widest points, is one of the greener islands with high, pine-covered mountains, fine, long sandy beaches and attractive hill villages.

Connections: Ferryboat from Keramoti (mainland) to Limenas thirty times a day; from Kavala to Limenas four times a day; from Kavala to Prinos eight times a day; from Kavala to Limenaria once a day. Daily flights from Athens to Kavala and buses from Athens to Kavala.

Centres: LIMENAS (also known as Thassos) is the island's capital. With the exception of the pretty fishing harbour, the town has little to recommend it. There are discos and tavernas and if you are looking for lively nightlife this is the place to stay for elsewhere on the island evenings are quiet. There are numerous relatively inexpensive hotels and rooms to rent. The tourist police are to be found by the quayside (tel. 22122) and have a list of rooms to rent although, as with many other islands, householders offering rooms meet arriving ferryboats.

LIMENARIA also has some hotels and rooms but it is an uninteresting place to stay.

Camping sauvage takes place everywhere in spite of notices stating that camping outside official areas is forbidden. The official camping sites are Rachoni Camping, Skala Rachoni (open mid-May to mid-September), Ioannidis Camping also at Rachoni (tel. 71377/71477) and Skala Panayias Camping and Golden Beach Camping (both on the east coast).

Beaches: 5 miles south of Limenas is the pretty village of Panagia. From here it is 2 miles down to the coast and the seemingly endless golden sand beach of CHRISI AMMOUDIA* with an official campsite. Continuing along the main road, the next village is Potamia (6½ miles from Limenas). The beach, SKALA POTAMIA, is about 2 miles away and you can rent a room at the water's edge here. There are unconfirmed reports that this beach is used for nudism. The sandy beach at ALIKI (20 miles from Limenas) is set on a wooded peninsula and is considered to be one of the best on the island. People camp here and there is a single taverna although this tends to be a bit expensive. Westwards, along the 12 miles of road between Aliki and Potos, are four strips of sand which could be used for nudism. They are little used because it is a scramble down to them from the road. The beach below the

Monastery or Archagelos (about 6 miles west of Aliki) is dramatically situated in a narrow, steep-sided valley. The pebble beach in Limenaria is not particularly inspiring but there are good beaches at PEFKARI** (about 2 miles east) and POTOS (a mile further on). Pefkari is a lovely, sand beach bordered by pine trees and a lot of people camp here. It can be reached by caique from Limenaria. It is a popular place but, in spite of this, the beach is apparently used by naturists. On the north-west coast there are reports of nudist beaches at KALI** and PRINOS**. Beaches to avoid are Glyfada and Makriamos, both near to Limenas. Makriamos in particular is frequented by well-off tourists who are prepared to pay an entrance fee and eat at the expensive restaurant.

Things To Do: Various archaelogical sites in Limenas as well as an Archaeological Museum.

Getting Around: Buses make a full circuit of the island a few times a day. Car and bicycle hire in Limenas. Excursions by boat and bus.

Tour Operators:
Aegina Club (H); Manos (H).

SAMOTHRACE

Samothrace, approximately 13 miles by 9 miles at its widest points is, after Santorini, the most dramatic of all the Greek Islands. It rises abruptly from the sea and climbs steeply to Mount Fengari which, at 5,250 feet, is the highest point in the Aegean Sea.

Connections: By boat – twice daily in season from Alexandroupolis on the mainland (2½ hours) which has up to three flights a day from Athens; twice a week with Kavala; once a week with Kymi.

Centres: Boats dock at the little port of KAMARIOTISSA where there are some rooms, a few tavernas and a small, pebbly beach where unofficial camping takes place. The only village of any size is CHORA, situated high in the hills with the ruins of a Byzantine fort standing sentinel above the town. There are some rooms here and three or so restaurants. Other villages are tiny and not easily accessible. There is only one hotel on the whole island (situated close to the archaeological site), the expensive, 'B' class Xenia (tel. 41230). Camping sauvage is possible almost anywhere.

Beaches: Beaches are scarce on Samothrace. Remote AMMOS* is the only sandy beach on the island. It is a 3 mile walk south-east of the village of Lakoma. An easier way of getting there is by caique (see Getting Around).

Things To Do: The main reason for visiting Samothrace is to visit the Sanctuary of the Great Gods at Palaeopolis (but probably only if you are an archaeology buff).

Getting Around: Buses run fairly regularly in season to the site of the sanctuary and to Chora. Occasional caique trips in season from Kamariotissa to the beach at Ammos.

LIMNOS

Limnos, about 25 miles by 19 miles at its widest points, is a peaceful, relatively unvisited island. The landscape is mostly flat and uninteresting and water is short in summer.

Connections: By air – once or twice a day with Athens, daily with Thessaloniki, four times a week with Lesbos; ferryboats twice a week from Kavala and Thessaloniki, twice a week with Lesbos, Chios, Samos, Ikaria, Patmos, Leros, Kalymnos, Kos and Rhodes; ferryboat three times a week from Kymi on Evia.

Centres: MYRINA, the island's capital, isn't a particularly pretty town although it is spacious and leafy and its old houses give it a touch of charm. The town is divided into two parts by its acropolis and castle and there is an animated fishing harbour. Most of the island's accommodation is in Myrina in basic hotels and rooms although here also is the luxury class Akti Myrina Bungalows with their own private beach.

Beaches: MYRINA has a peaceful strip of sandy beach. Isolated beaches and places to camp are easy to find along the barren hilly coastline which runs south of Myrina. PLATIS, 1½ miles from Myrina, has a good beach which may be suitable for nudism. THANOUS*, 2½ miles further south, is more spacious with a taverna and rolling breakers.

Things To Do: There are few things to see except for some isolated archaeological sites.

Getting Around: Buses go to most villages although the service is rather infrequent. Car hire in Myrina.

Tour Operators:
MYRINA: Allsun (S); Amathus (H); Greek Sun (H,S); Olympic – Main Brochure (H).

LESBOS (MYTILINI)

Lesbos, approximately 32 miles wide and 32 miles long, is the third largest island in Greece. The scenery varies between flat, featureless plains, the pretty south-east and exposed barren hillsides in the west. Some of the villages have little to recommend them and, in certain areas, olive oil refining factories give the impression of industrialisation. Other villages are charming with a distinct Turkish influence.

Connections: By air – five flights a day from Athens every day except Thursday (four); daily with Thessaloniki; four times a week with Limnos. By sea – nine times a week with Piraeus; four times a week with Chios; twice a week with Limnos, Samos, Patmos, Leros, Kalymnos, Kos and Rhodes. In summer daily connections with Turkey.

Centres: MYTILINI, the island's capital, is a large town of crumbling mansions and a shortage of accommodation. The four main hotels are usually full in season. Rooms are also difficult to find although you could try the tourist police who are to be found at the end of the harbour. Just north of the harbour is a wooded hill which is used by campers with a small beach, Tsamakia, close by. Mytilini is not particularly tourist orientated and there isn't a great deal to do.

METHIMNA (also known as MOLYVOS), a very attractive village beneath an impressive Byzantine and Genoese castle, is the main resort. It overlooks the fishing harbour and the long, not too attractive, stony beach. More beaches are to be found on the other side of the cape, about an hour's walk from town but, as there are no facilities, you should go prepared. In Methimna is the 'B' class Delfina (tel. 71315). There are many rooms to rent but the town gets full in season. The bus stops outside the tourist office and you should enquire there. Methimna has a lively, youthful atmosphere and is the most attractive resort on the island.

PLOMARI is a large village resort with famous ouzo distilleries. There is only one hotel, the 'C' class Oceanis (tel. 32498), which is usually full. The beach is half a mile from the town centre. Not many tourists stay here.

AGIASSOS – If you want to experience true rural Greece stay inland at this picturesque, old village set in a landscape of wooded mountains. There are rooms to rent here.

Beaches: Easily accessible beaches are not easy to find and are rarely sandy.

METHIMNA (MOLYVOS)** has a crowded pebble beach just in front of the town. A more attractive pebble beach, which is used by naturists, can be reached by walking through the grounds of the Hotel Delfina. Turn left onto the beach and walk to the quieter nudist area. PETRA*, 4½ miles south, has a delightful waterfront, a few rooms to rent and a wide, pebble beach which stretches for over a mile. The village of EFTALOU**, about 3½ miles north of Methimna (Molyvos), can be reached either by walking (about 1½ hours along a hilly, dirt track) or by means of an inexpensive taxi ride. Walk past the main beach and the taverna to the end of the road where you will see a house with what looks like an air-raid shelter attached. This is, in fact, a hot spring and may be full of nude and obese Greek businessmen – not a pretty sight! Continue walking until you come to a succession of pebbly bays and coves where there is hardly a clothed person in sight. From Methimna (Molyvos) the road runs south-easterly to Mantamandos and, from here to the village of Therma, it hugs the coastline and passes a number of narrow little beaches. In the south there are sandy beaches at KRATIGOS (with many trees), AG. ERMOGENIS and at PERAMA. These beaches are relatively quiet. SKALA ERESSOS, on the west coast, is probably the best beach on the island with a long stretch of sand which could be suitable for nudism. There are rooms to rent here as well as unofficial camping. The bus fare from Mytilini is about 300 drs. or you could try hitching.

Things To Do: See the petrified forest near Sigri. It is one of the most impressive in Europe with hundreds of fossilised trees up to 1 million years old.

Getting Around: Buses from Mytilini run to Methimna (Molyvos) at around 09.00, 11.00 and 13.30; to Mantamandos at 13.30 (returns at 18.00); to Sigri (petrified forest) only on Wednesdays and Saturdays and to Plomari at 07.15, 11.00, 12.30, 15.00 and 18.30. Car and moped hire in Methimna (Molyvos) and Mytilini although it should be noted that many of the island's roads are unsurfaced. Bus tours from Mytilini.

Tour Operators:
METHIMNA (MOLYVOS): Aegina Club (H,P); Freedom (H); Sunmed (H,P,R,S); Sunvil (H).
SKALA ERESSOS: Sunmed (P,R,S).

CHIOS (HIOS)

Chios, about 32 miles by 18 miles at its widest points, is a well-populated island situated four or five miles from the Turkish coast. The scenery is surprising in its variety ranging from the barren lunar landscape of the north-east to fertile agricultural plains and areas of dense forest elsewhere. The fertile south produces citrus fruits, figs, wine and mastic. In the past much of the island's prosperity was due to the mastic trees which grow only on Chios and which produce a sort of natural chewing gum. Mastic gum, sweets and a liqueur made from mastic are still important products.

Connections: Up to four flights a day from Athens. By boat – five times a week with Lesbos and Piraeus; twice a week with Limnos, Samos, Ikaria, Patmos, Leros, Kos and Rhodes; once a week with Thessaloniki and Kavala; daily with Turkey.

Centres: CHIOS is a mainly modern town and most of the accommodation is here in hotels and rooms. Nightlife is low-key and Chios is not the place for a lively time.

Beaches: There are some (stony) beaches near to Chios town but the best is at KARFAS, a long sandy strip of beach with little shade, about 3½ miles south. KOMMI, in the far south, has a beach of brown sand but the best beach in this part of the island is at the small fishing village of EMBORIO***. The beach consists of black sand and pebbles and the last cove to your right (facing the sea), past three short rock climbs, is nudist. Cutting across the island via the villages of Pirgi and Mesta, the western coast is reached at PASS LIMANI, not a memorable place but with secluded beaches in either direction. Also to be found on the western coast are pretty LITHIO beach and, near to the village of Volissos, the sand and pebble beach at ST. MARKELLA. A little way south of Volissos is a village of just four houses, Limnia, with a long, empty stretch of sand, SKALA VALIS*. On the north-east coast is beautiful, empty NAGOS*, a beach of multi-coloured stones.

Things To Do: Buses go twice a day to Neo Moni monastery where you can see superb mosaics in the church. Women should wear skirts. Opening times – morning until noon and from 17.00 to 20.00. A track leads from here to a fascinating ruined village, Anevatos, the scene of Turkish brutalities during their occupation of the island. Also worth a visit is the southern village of Pirgi which dates from the thirteenth century. This excellently preserved medieval village with its tiny arched streets is a fascinating place to explore. Two other medieval villages, Olymbai and Mesta, are on the road from Pirgi to Pass Limani.

Getting Around: Buses to most villages. Car and moped hire in Chios. Sightseeing tours from Chios.

Tour Operators:
Aegina Club (H); Manos (H); Thomson – 'Summer Sun' Brochure (H).

SAMOS

Samos, about 27 miles by 12 miles at its widest points, is one of the most beautiful of all the Greek islands with miles of sandy beaches, awe inspiring cliffs, mountains and pretty hill villages. It is verdant and much of the island is planted with vines. Most holiday development has taken place around Pythagorion. Elsewhere the island is undeveloped. Nightlife is practically non-existent and Samos will suit those looking for a quiet, relaxing holiday surrounded by beautiful scenery.

Connections: Twice daily flights from Athens. By boat – almost daily with Piraeus and Ikaria; twice a week with Limnos, Lesbos, Chios, Patmos, Leros, Kos, Kalymnos, Rhodes, Syros and Mykonos; once a week with Kavala and Thessaloniki.

Centres: The ferryboat schedules refer to Vathi although the port is, in fact, in Samos town and Vathi is the old town situated up on the hill. The boats from Piraeus stop at Karlovassi first but there are few places to stay here and the bus service is bad so you would be well advised to stay on to Samos town.

SAMOS town is not a particularly attractive place but is a good base for exploring the island. There are a number of hotels here and some rooms. A Youth Hostel is situated near the waterfront on Sofouli and Smyrnas Streets.

The majority of tourists stay at PYTHAGORION with its attractive and colourful harbour. Accommodation consists of hotels and rooms and there is a shortage of both in season. The best beach is Portokali and is about half a mile from town.

An alternative to Pythagorion is the attractive fishing village of KOKKARI. The village is backed by wooded mountains and there are several beaches to choose from. There are a number of hotels including the Kokkari Beach (tel.

28538/28563) and the Venus (tel. 28530/28560), both 'C' class and the 'D' class Lito (tel. 28507).

Beaches: The nearest decent beach to Samos town (Vathi) is at GAGOU, a very small piece of sand situated on the coast road about a half a mile north-east of Samos town harbour. It gets very crowded here in summer and is best avoided. There is a two or three hourly bus service from Vathi which serves the island's northern coast as far as Karlovassi. There are beaches with tavernas at Kokkari (about 5 miles west of Vathi), Avlakia (two miles further on) and Karlovassi (about 18 miles west of Vathi) as well as various little rocky bays and sandy strips which are usually empty because to get to them requires a lengthy scramble down from the main road. KOKKARI has a long beach of smooth pebbles with houses at the back which make it unsuitable for nudism. However, a short walk away are the beaches of TSAMADOU** and LEMONAKIA** which offer fine sand and natural beauty and where nudity is not unknown. Tsamadou, just over a mile west of Kokkari, has a cafe and a fresh-water tap on the beach which make it a good choice for those who want to camp – although it can get busy. At KARLOVASSI you can travel by bus to a good beach at the foot of wooded mountains about a half a mile west of the port. There is a reasonable taverna here and even a disco. Alight at the far end of the beach (where the road finishes) from where you can walk along forest paths to smaller, more secluded, coves.

Travelling in the opposite direction from Vathi are two fine sandy beaches set in deep sheltered bays, POSSIDONION (about 8 miles from Vathi) and PSILI AMMOS (about 5½ miles from Vathi). Both are situated on the south coast facing Turkey and there are beautiful views across the Straits of Mykale. You can get to both of these beaches by bus from Vathi (see Getting Around) or by excursion boat from Pythagorion. PYTHAGORION has a small beach to the east of the town and a much larger one to the west. Both of these beaches are used for camping although the one to the west is better and less crowded.

The south-western coast of the island is the best area for nudism. ORMOS MARATHOKAMPOS* is a peaceful fishing village with a huge, sandy beach, rooms and a taverna. A mile or so west is the spacious beach at VOTSALAKIA* and, after another mile, the even better beach at CHRISSI AMMOUDIA*. There is a fresh-water stream here which makes this a good place to camp. There are tavernas and some accommodation in PSILI AMMOS (not to be confused with the one on the south-east coast) as well as a good beach which may be suitable for nudism.

Things To Do: A mile north of Pythagorion is the impressive and mostly intact Eupalinos Tunnel. The tunnel was cut through the mountains to ensure a water supply and escape route in times of siege. 5 miles to the west of Pythagorion are the remains of the Temple of Hera. However, little survives intact of what used to be the second largest temple in Greece.

Boat and bus excursions around the island and boat trips to Patmos and Turkey.

Getting Around: Buses from Vathi to Possidonion and Psili Ammos at 09.30 and 12.45. About five buses a day run from Vathi to Pythagorion between 07.00 and 17.00. Buses to Kokkari at 13.00 and 18.00. Buses between Vathi, Kokkari and Karlovassi run from 07.00 to 19.00. The best way of getting around the remote western end of the island is on two wheels. Car and moped hire in Vathi and Pythagorion. Bicycles can be rented just off the main square in town and taxis are available at reasonable prices.

Tour Operators:
KOKKARI: Aegina Club (P,S); Greek Sun (H,P).
ORMOS MARATHOKAMPOS: Greek Sun (H).

IKARIA

Ikaria, about 22 miles long by 6 miles wide, is a quiet, unspoiled island which is known for its thermal baths. The hot springs at Therma are considered the most radio-active in Europe. There are ten springs on the island and the plentiful supply of fresh water keeps the island green. Ikaria is also known for its wind and the Ikarian Sea is one of the roughest in Greece.

Connections: Four times a week with Samos and Piraeus; twice a week with Limnos, Lesbos, Chios, Patmos, Leros, Kalymnos, Kos and Rhodes; once a week with Thessaloniki, Mykonos and Syros.

Centres: AGIOS KIRYKOS is the capital and port. THERMA, ten minutes away by road, is where most of the island's hotels are situated. There are rooms and tavernas at RACHIS. ARMENISTIS, on the northern coast, is quite a large village where, in spite of the fact that rooms are plentiful and cheap, most people seem to sleep on the beach.

Beaches: There are reports that camping and nudity are both frowned upon by the locals. In spite of this people camp at RACHIS, a beautiful place, with a forest of tall pines sweeping down from the mountains to the sandy shore. The majority of young visitors make for ARMENISTIS, also on the northern coast, where the sand is fine and white and the water crystal-clear. Boats leave town every morning (from the harbour below the Hotel Akti) bound for the isolated Faro peninsula on the eastern tip of the island. The boat takes you to the little village of FANARI with a long, sandy beach and this is probably the best place to acquire an all-over tan.

Things To Do: Few things to see.

Getting Around: An old bus runs between Agios Kirykos and Armenistis although you should note that it is unwise to rely on a bus back if it is important that you travel on a particular day.

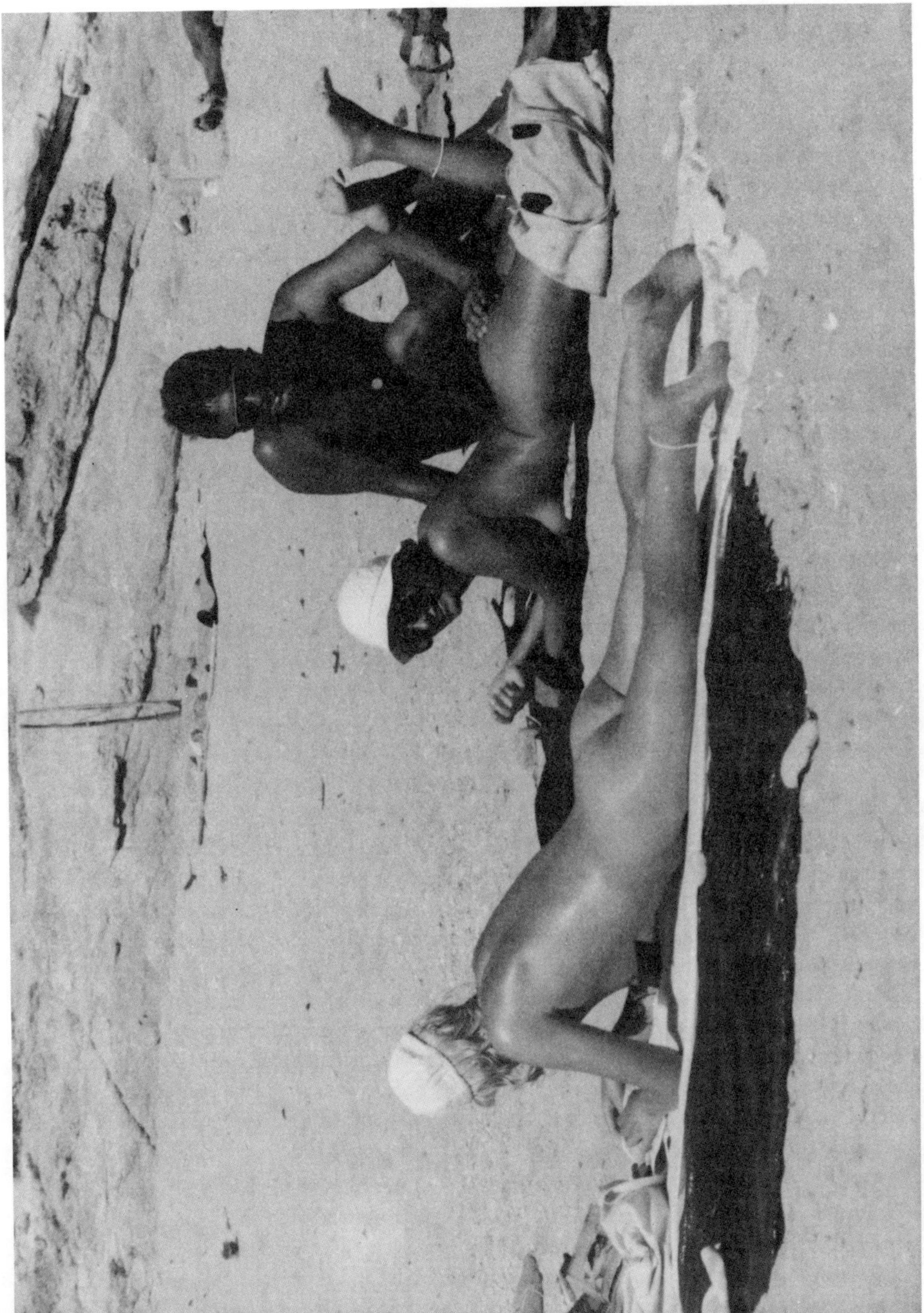

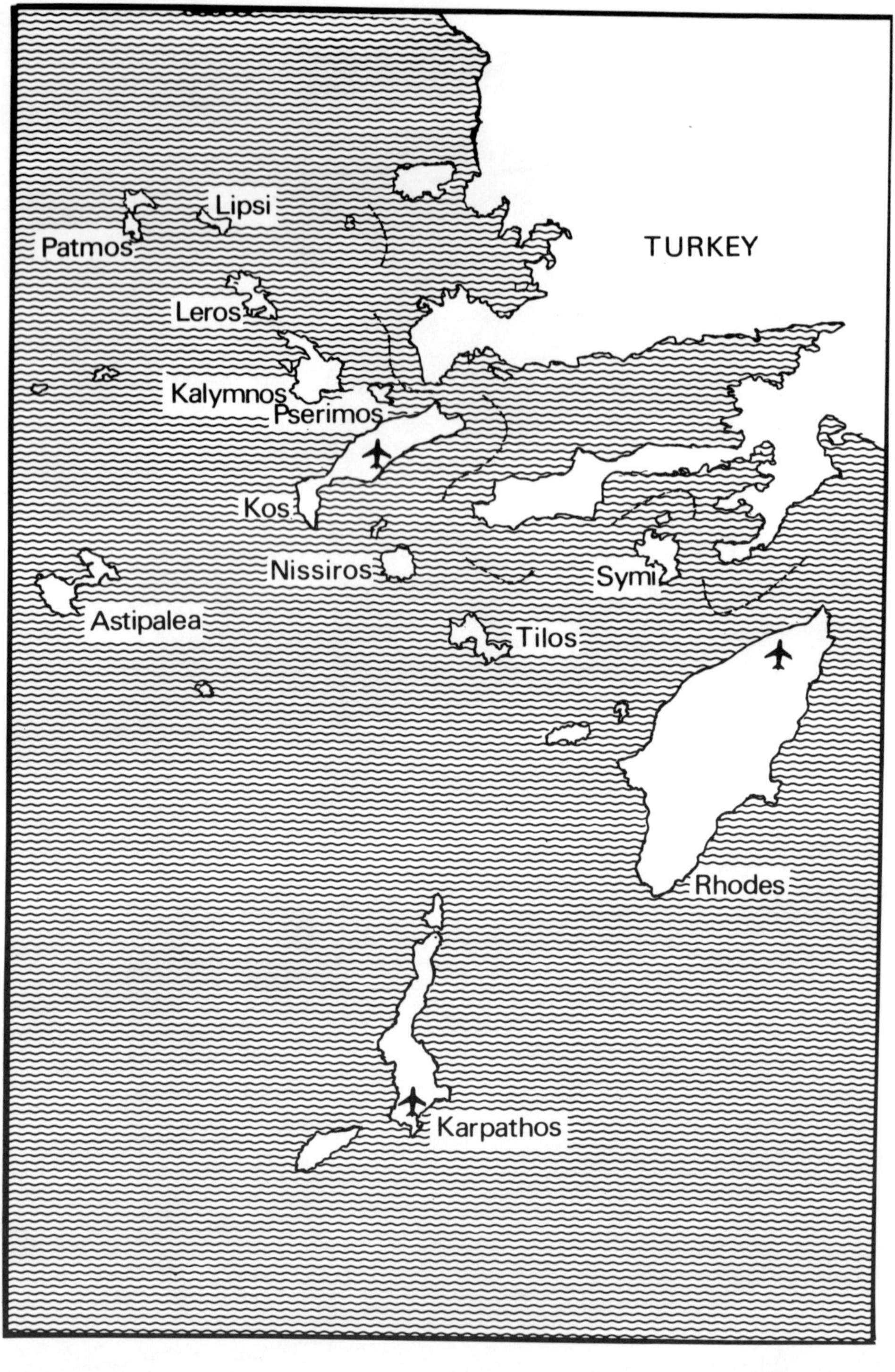
Lipsi
Patmos
TURKEY
Leros
Kalymnos
Pserimos
Kos
Nissiros
Symi
Astipalea
Tilos
Rhodes
Karpathos

THE DODECANESE

The Dodecanese consist of a chain of islands situated close to the Turkish coast. In the thirteenth century they belonged to the Knights of St. John who made Rhodes their headquarters. Three centuries later they fell to the Turks and in 1912 the Italians took possession. After the Second World War they were ceded to Greece. Rhodes and Kos are the major holiday centres and are popular with German and Scandinavian holidaymakers. Their climate makes them particularly suitable for out of season holidays. Direct flights are available from the U.K. to Rhodes and Kos. Most of the Dodecanese are connected by ferry with one another.

PATMOS

Patmos, approximately 8 miles long and 4 miles wide, is a beautiful island of barren hills contrasting with attractive farmland. It also has a magnificent coastline of bays and capes. There are few tourist amenities and rooms can be in short supply in season. It will suit those who are looking for a peaceful time, picturesque villages and attractive scenery.

Connections: Six times a week with Piraeus (10 hours), Leros (1 hour), Kalymnos (3 hours), Kos (5 hours) and Rhodes (15 hours); twice a week with Ikaria, Samos, Tinos, Syros, Symi, Chios, Lesbos and Limnos; once a week with Naxos, Kavala and Thessaloniki.

Centres: CHORA, a beautiful village of cobbled streets and white sugar-cube houses, is the island's capital. Below is the pleasant, modern port of SKALA and most of the accommodation is here. In high season Skala's few hotels are nearly always full but the ferryboats are met by townsfolk and finding a room is usually a simple matter. It is a half-hour climb from Skala to Chora or you can catch one of the nine buses a day. Most visitors stay in the port ensuring that Chora remains peaceful and relatively unaffected by tourism. The town is a maze of small streets and hidden amongst them are no less than twenty-two churches and monasteries. Here also, at the top of the hill, is the monumental Monastery of St. John the Theologian and many visitors come to Patmos primarily to see the priceless treasures contained within its fortified walls. There are a few pensions and rooms in Chora but you will have to search them out. What eating places there are tend to be better and cheaper than in Skala.

There is a good campsite at MELOY (tel. 31287) with its own cafe. It is situated two minutes away from the beach. GRIKOS in the south has some rooms to rent, a luxury hotel and a couple of tavernas.

Nightlife is low-key. There are some music bars and two or three small discos which have been discreetly located out of earshot.

Beaches: The town beach is crowded and small and the nearest good beach is at MELOY, a twenty minute walk north along the waterfront and over a small hill.

The magnificent crescent of sand at PSILIAMOS*** is not only probably the best beach on Patmos but is also renowned locally as *the* nudist beach on the island. There is a taverna here and the owner cleans the beach regularly. Some shade is provided by the trees which grow on the beach and sunloungers and umbrellas are also available. Psiliamos is about a two hours' walk from Skala although it is easier to take the boat which leaves Skala in the morning and returns in the evening (see Getting Around).

GRIKOS** has a comparatively empty beach and naturists are to be found on the south side of the pebble spur at the southern end of Grikou Bay. You can walk here easily from Chora or there is a bus service (see Getting Around).

SAPSILA*, situated between Skala and Grikos, has very few visitors and is suitable for nude sunning.

To the north of Skala is the small village of Kambos with pensions and a modest beach situated below the town. From the northern end of this beach a well-defined track leads to more isolated beaches where nudism should go undisturbed, although the beaches are sometimes visited by Greek families. The first of these, VARGA*, is not very attractive but further on is LIGGINOU* which actually consists of two shingle beaches separated by a headland. There are trees here which provide some shade. Further on still is the lovely beach of LIVADI YERANOU*. Boats go here occasionally from Skala. There are no facilities on these beaches and you should at least take something to drink.

The extremities of the multi-coloured pebble beach at LAMBI** are occasionally used for nudism. This beach can be reached by boat from Chora or you can walk there in about half an hour from Kambos (see Getting Around for times of buses to Kambos).

Things To Do: Visit the eleventh century Monastery of St. John the Theologian at Chora. The monastery is open 08.00 to 12.00 and 15.00 to 18.00 except for Wednesdays and Thursdays when it is open 08.00 to 12.00. Inside its huge fortifications are arcaded courtyards and beautiful frescoes. In a glass case in the centre of the library is the Codex Porphyrius, St. Mark's gospel written in the fifth century. There are many other treasures and this is one monastery which is probably worth seeing but, as usual in Greece, both men and women should cover-up well. Below Chora and above Skala is the Holy Cave where St. John lived and wrote the Apocalypse. It has a seventeenth century chapel inside and is open to visitors at the same time as the monastery.

Getting Around: The island's single bus runs from Skala to Chora and back nine times a day between 07.40 and 22.30, to Grikos at 09.15, 13.30, 16.30, 19.30 and 22.30 and to Kambos at 08.15, 10.30, 18.30 and 21.30. The current bus and boat schedule is posted outside the police station, where the buses stop. Excursion boats leave Skala at 10.00 returning at 16.00. The round trip to Kambos costs 100 drs.; 300 drs. to Lambi or Psiliamos. There are caique trips to near-by islets and to the Turkish coast. Motorbikes can be rented on the waterfront in Skala and bicycles are also available.

Tour Operators:
SKALA: Aegina Club (H,P); Freedom (H); Greek Sun (H); Timsway – 'Original Holidays in Greece' Brochure (H); Twelve Islands (H,R,S).
GRIKOS: Aegina Club (H); Greek Sun (S); Timsway – 'Original Holidays in Greece' Brochure (S); Twelve Islands (S).

LIPSI

Lipsi is a rocky island with one village and about 550 inhabitants. There is an excursion boat from Patmos six days a week costing 400 drs. return. Most people return the same day but the island is well worth an overnight stay. Basic rooms are not difficult to find and are cheap. Camping takes place on the fine town beach but it gets crowded here in the afternoons when the local children are let out of school. However, the island has very good almost deserted beaches where nude sunning should go undisturbed (follow the tracks from town). The best beach is at KATZADIA*, a half-hour walk out of town to the south on the road which runs parallel to the waterfront behind the Pension Flisvos.

LEROS

Leros, approximately 5 miles wide and 8 miles long, has a number of bays on opposite sides of the island which cut so deeply inland that they almost meet in the middle. It is rocky, although the low lying parts are quite green and fertile. There is little to see and few tourists and many would probably find it dull, certainly for a long stay.

Connections: By air – up to two flights a day from Athens; on Mondays, Wednesdays and Fridays with Kos and on Mondays, Wednesdays, Fridays and Saturdays with Rhodes. By sea – four times a week with Piraeus; six times a week with Kalymnos, Kos and Rhodes; up to six times a week with Patmos; once a week with Kavala and Thessaloniki; three times a week with Samos; twice a week with Ikaria, Chios, Lesbos and Limnos; once a week with Mykonos and Tinos. A small boat leaves Xerocampos (on the south coast) at 07.30 daily for Myrties on Kalymnos. The return trip is at 13.00.

Centres: PLATANOS is the island's capital. It stands astride a coll protected both by the sea and by the Franco-Byzantine fortress set high above the town on a spectacular hillside. The town has gradually extended in both directions to join up with the colourful port of AGIA MARINA on the northern edge of the coll and the fishing village of PANTHELI to the south. The modern Hotel Anemi (0247 22152) is here and rooms in private houses should be easy to find. Nightlife in this trio of villages is surprisingly lively (including a cinema and two discos).

Further around the bay to the north is ALINDA, the old commercial port of Leros, with pleasant beachside tavernas and the 'B' class Alinda Pension (0247 23266). LAKKI, on the west coast, is an ugly port with little to recommend it although it has the island's only official campsite which is pleasantly situated in an olive grove (0247 23372).

Beaches: There are many deep inlets surrounded by deserted coves which are ideal for naturism. Beaches consist mainly of long, narrow strips of sand and shingle. There are two beaches at PANTHELI. One is rather pebbly. The other, around the bay to the south, is better, consisting of sand and shingle. There is also a taverna here. North of Agia Marina is the more developed resort of ALINDA with a long beach of sand and shingle. The beach is lined with villas and is popular with holidaying Greeks. However, if you walk to the north (left as you face the sea) for about twenty minutes you will come to a quieter part which is well established as an unofficial naturist beach. Alternatively, you can get a taxi here. In spite of its having a taverna, BLEFOUTI BAY*, on the northern coast, has the island's most isolated beach. It is situated five minutes' walk to the east of Partheni, a tiny village which is overshadowed by an army base and airstrip. Other good beaches can be found at Gourna, Lepitha, Vromolithos and Xerocampos.

Things To Do: Nothing to see of real interest.

Getting Around: Bus service six times a day between Platanos, Lakki and Xerocampos. The same bus runs between Platanos and Partheni via Alinda three times a day. Taxis are reasonably priced. Moped and bicycle hire in Lakki.

Tour Operators:
ALINDA: Aegina Club (P); Greek Sun (H); Twelve Islands (R).

KALYMNOS

Kalymnos, approximately 8 miles by 10 miles at its widest points, is an hour and a half by boat from Kos. Excursion boats run frequently but, other than this, tourism is low-key. The impressive coastline is wild and mountainous and inland the barren mountains are intersected by a number of valleys. The main one runs from Pothia, on the west coast, to Kantouni on the east coast. It is verdant and most of the island's population live here. Kalymnos is famous for its sponge fishing. The sponge fleet leaves shortly after Easter each year amid much celebration for four months of diving in Greek and Italian waters.

Connections: Daily by boat with Piraeus (12 hours), Leros (1½ hours), Patmos (3 hours), Kos (1½ hours) and Rhodes (7-11 hours). Once a week with Astipalea, Amorgos, Santorini, Folegandros and Mykonos. Once a week with Symi, Karpathos and Crete. Once a week with Samos, Ikaria, Chios, Lesbos and Kavala.

Centres: POTHIA (also known as Kalymnos) is the island's capital and port. Viewed from the hills it looks attractive with blue and white painted houses but a closer inspection shows it to be a rather sprawled-out place. It is also busy and noisy. Most holidaymakers stay at Myrties or Massouri, both of which are situated on bays facing the near-by islet of Telendos. MYRTIES (pronounced Meertee-ez) is about five miles across the island from Pothia. Here is the 'C' class Delfini (tel. 28914). MASSOURI is a little north of Myrties and has a sandy beach and the 'D' class Marilena (tel. 47289). Other accommodation is mostly in villas and apartments although there are also a few cheap rooms. There are no food shops in either of these two places although bread, fruit and pies are sold by mobile shops which announce their arrival through loudspeakers. Further south, about 2½ miles from Pothia, is the mini-resort of KANTOUNI with a good sandy beach.

Beaches: Notices prohibit nudity on all the main beaches and, because a large number of locals regularly visit them, topless bathing is also something of a rarity. The only beach reported as being used by naturists is on the small mountainous island of TELENDOS***. This can be reached by means of a regular caique service from Myrties. The nudist beach is to the right of the landing jetty, four bays along and about seventeen minutes' walk. It is in a small, quiet and beautiful bay.

In the north of the island around ARGINONTAS* and EMPORIOS* the beaches are much emptier and should be suitable for nudism. In the south, KANTOUNI* stands at the end of a huge, sandy beach which extends for 2-3 miles.

Things To Do: Visit Chorio, the old capital of Kalymnos, a mile or so from Pothia. It's a pretty village of white houses and, above the town, are the remains of an impressive fort and medieval settlement with surrounding walls. Also Vathi, east of Pothia, a fishing port spectacularly situated at the end of a Norwegian-like fjord and surrounded by orchards of tangerines and lemons.

There are good walks for suitably shod hikers. The terrain is mountainous affording panoramic views although there are no trees and little shade.

Getting Around: Buses run twice a day between Pothia and Vathi. There is also a regular but infrequent bus service from Pothia to Kantouni, Myrties and Massouri. On Mondays, Wednesdays and Saturdays the bus continues northwards to Arginontas. Taxis also run regularly between Pothia and Kantouni, Myrties and Massouri. Moped hire in Pothia. The valley roads are metalled with generally good surfaces.

Tour Operators:
MYRTIES: Aegina Club (H); Greek Sun (H); Small World (T); Timsway – General Brochure (H); Timsway – 'Original Holidays in Greece' Brochure (H,S); Twelve Islands (S). TELENDOS: Small World (T).

KOS

Kos, approximately 24 miles long and 6 miles across at its widest points, is mainly flat and given over to agriculture, although there is a single, barren, mountainous ridge in the south-east. The main town is lively and interesting and elsewhere on the island are relaxed seaside villages and magnificent beaches. Its climate makes it a good choice for late holidays. The average daily temperature in October is over 70 with an average of 8 hours' sunshine.

Connections: By air – direct flights from a number of U.K. airports; up to four flights a day from Athens; once a day with Rhodes; to Leros on Mondays, Wednesdays and Fridays. By sea – to Rhodes every day except for Monday (4½-9½ hours); to Piraeus every day except for Monday and Saturday (at least 12 hours); daily to Kalymnos (1½ hours) and Leros (3½ hours); on Mondays and Tuesdays to Patmos (5 hours); once a week to Astipalea, Amorgos, Karpathos, Crete, Santorini, Samos, Ikaria, Chios, Lesbos and Kavala.

Centres: KOS town is not very inspiring architecturally. Much of it has been rebuilt on anti-seismic principles following the 1933 earthquake but, in compensation, there are colourful gardens with bougainvilleas, palms and other trees. There is much to see in Kos town. The mosque, the Ancient Agora, the ruins of the Temple of Aphrodite, the huge plane tree under which Hippocrates supposedly taught, the castle of the Knights of St. John and the Casa Romana (surrounded by extensive ruined Roman Baths). There is a wide promenade and a good place for dinner at night is in one of the restaurants along the lively harbour. North of the harbour is a long, sandy beach with water-sports. Nightlife is good, ranging from tavernas to discotheques and nightclubs. There is plenty of accommodation (although there might be a shortage in the height of the season) in hotels and rooms. The tourist police (tel. 28572) are to be found slightly to the right along the harbour as you leave the boat and skirt the Venetian fortress to enter town. They have a list of hotels with rates and also details of private rooms to rent.

KARDAMENA, once a fishing village, is now a busy resort. It is situated on the south coast and has a sandy beach which stretches for miles. Nightlife is based on the tavernas but there is also a disco or two. In Kardamena is the 'D' class Paralia (tel. 51205) and rooms are also available.

MASTIHARI and TIGAKI are quieter villages with good beaches and rooms to rent.

Beaches: Kos has lots of sandy beaches near to the main places to stay and quieter ones elsewhere. Even in the height of the tourist season you can easily find long stretches of secluded beach.

KARDAMENA**, on the south coast, has a lovely, wide sandy beach which is at least six miles long. A ten minutes' walk along the beach to the west of the village brings you to the start of the long stretch which is used by naturists. A track leads along the back of the beach here and if you hire a bicycle and cycle for 10-15 minutes from Kardamena you can have the beach all to yourself for as far as the eye can see. There are trees between the track and the beach which provide shade in the heat of the day. There are no facilities outside the village so at least take something to drink.

Also on the south coast is the long stretch of sand known as 'BUBBLE BEACH'***. This is situated off the main road to Kefalos about one mile before the Club Mediterranean complex. It has the advantage of being sheltered from the strong winds which can be a problem (especially on the north coast) and is well used by naturists.

About eight miles west of Kos town is TIGAKI**, a narrow beach backed by dunes. Tigaki can be reached by bicycle from Kos town (half an hour) or by bus (see Getting Around) and consequently it can get crowded in summer. However, there are reports that it is used for nudism when not too busy. There are several tavernas on the beach which is also used for camping. Further along this coast, about eighteen miles from Kos town, is Mastihari (see Centres) and from here there is a frequent boat service to the islet of PSERIMOS (less than a mile away) where, to greet you as you come ashore, is a notice stating that nudity is forbidden. There are three tavernas on the superb sandy beach and definitely no nudity. There are, however, two other good, sandy beaches on the island. These can only be reached by walking for half an hour and consequently are unlikely to be much used.

Things To Do: Besides the places already mentioned, visit the museum on the main square. Open 09.00 to 13.00 and 16.00 to 18.00, closed on Sunday. The prize exhibit is the statue of Hippocrates. The castle of the Knights of St. John in town is well preserved and is open from 09.00 to 13.00 and 16.00 to 18.00. Located up on a hill about two miles east of the town is the Asklepeion. This was one of the most sacred shrines to the healing god Asklepios who was worshipped by a secret order of priests whose philosophy was that baths in beautiful surroundings did much for spiritual well-being and bodily health (sounds like a good idea!). You can walk there if you're feeling fit, rent a bicycle or get a taxi.

Getting Around: Buses to Kardamena leave Kos town at 09.30, 12.30 and 17.00 (return trips at 07.45, 10.30 and 16.00). Buses to Tigaki at 10.00 and 16.00. Daily bus to Mastihari at 12.30 (returning to Kos at 19.45). Cars, jeeps, mopeds and bicycles for hire in Kos town. Daily tourist boat to Kalymnos. In addition there are numerous excursions, including round the island bus tours. Greek evenings and boat trips to near-by islands and Turkey.

Tour Operators:
KARDAMENA: Grecian (H,P,R,S); Horizon (H); Intasun – 'Plain and Simple' Brochure (H,P,R,S,T); Lancaster (H); Manos (H,S); Meon (P,S); Olympic – Main Brochure (H,R,S); Olympic – 'A touch of Greece' Brochure (R,S); Sigma (H); Sunmed (H,P,R,S); Thomson – 'Summer Sun' Brochure (H); Thomson – 'Villas and Apartments' Brochure (S); Timsway – General Brochure (H,P,S); Timsway – 'Original Holidays in Greece' Brochure (H,P,R,S); Twelve Islands (H,S).

TIGAKI: Intasun – Main Brochure (H); Intasun – 'Plain and Simple' Brochure (H); Thomson – 'Small and Friendly' Brochure (H).
PSERIMOS: Small World (P); Timsway – 'Original Holidays in Greece' Brochure (P); Twelve Islands (P).

ASTIPALEA

Astipalea is more like a Cycladic island both in terms of its barrenness and its architecture. There is one cultivated valley at Livadia and this is where the island's agriculture is concentrated. Tourism is low-key.

Connections: By boat – twice a week with Piraeus (10 hours), Amorgos (3 hours), Symi and Rhodes (10½ hours); once a week with Kos and Kalymnos.

Centres: The capital, ASTIPALEA, is a quiet fishing village overlooked by a Venetian castle and a row of nine derelict windmills. Its streets of whitewashed houses with decorated wooden balconies lead down steeply to the harbour where there is a long beach of grey sand. There are rooms to rent and just three 'D' class hotels – the Aegeon (0242 61236), the Astynea (0242 61209) and the Paradissos (0242 61224).

Half an hour's walk from Astipalea is LIVADIA with a good beach and shady restaurant by the waterfront. There are rooms to rent here.

Beaches: LIVADIA gets crowded in summer but just south-west of the main strand is SENAKI*** where the cognoscenti enjoy nude bathing in almost complete solitude.

Things To Do: Little, except to sunbathe and generally relax.

Getting Around: Bus service to Analipsi and to Vathi, a sleepy fishing village in the north.

Tour Operators:
ASTIPALEA TOWN: Twelve Islands (H).

NISSIROS

Paradoxically Nissiros, with its volcano, is a fertile, green island. The main tourist activity happens every day at about 11.00 when excursion boats, packed with holidaymakers intent on seeing the volcano, arrive from Kos. Otherwise Nissiros has little to offer visitors. The main town, Mandraki, is pleasant enough but there are no good, easily accessible beaches and public transport is infrequent. A number of older Greek visitors are attracted here by the large thermal baths at Loutra which are supplied by naturally-heated subterranean mineral water. Much of the island's income has come from quarrying and off-shore, towards Kos, can be seen the vast pumice quarries on the island of Yiali.

Connections: Three ferries a week between Rhodes, Symi, Tilos and Nissiros and on to Kos and Kalymnos. Once a week with Leros, Patmos, Lipsi, Samos, Astipalea, Amorgos, Paros and Piraeus. Daily tourist boat, in season, to Kos at 14.00

Centres: MANDRAKI is the main port and town and most visitors stay here. It is a short walk from the port to the centre with its tightly-packed houses and narrow streets. Although it extends for some way, Mandraki is really quite small and, curiously, the main part is built around a central area which remains green and undeveloped. Even in high season Mandraki is not over-busy. There are two hotels by the port, the Three Brothers and the Romantzo (0242 31340) and in August the Romantzo was offering double rooms, which according to the published tariff should have cost 1400 drs., for 800 drs. In the evenings there is nothing to do except eat and drink and most people who stay in these two hotels prefer to eat in the village. Even so, there are only enough people to make two of the tavernas really busy (one is on the waterfront as you enter the main part of the town and the other, the 'Nissiros', is on a side street to the left of the main 'drag'). Mandraki gives the impression of having geared itself up for a tourist boom which, with the notable exception of day excursions from Kos, never quite materialised. Traveller's cheques can be changed at the post office in Mandraki.

PALI. It takes about an hour to walk from Mandraki to this little fishing village or you can catch one of the five buses a week (see Getting Around). There are several cafes, a shop and one or two places offering rooms but very little else. The beach is disappointing but it is an easy 15 minute walk back up the hill to the White Beach (see Beaches).

Beaches: In MANDRAKI the beach, such as it is, is a 10 minute walk beyond the harbour on the road to Loutra. It consists of a small strip of dirty sand which is so unattractive that it is difficult to see why anyone should want to use it at all.

WHITE BEACH*** This is the best of the accessible beaches and can be reached from Mandraki by walking for 45 minutes along the main road. At Loutra the road begins to climb, passing the thermal baths and the thoughtlessly situated refuse tip. Within sight of the top of the hill (before the road begins its descent to Pali) are some pumice quarry workings (now abandoned) and from here it is possible to look down onto the beach. At the time of writing a hotel or apartment block is in course of construction. A track leads down to the new building and, part way along, a footpath continues the descent to the beach. The beach consists of coarse, light-coloured granules which look almost like crystals of sea salt and which, from a distance, give the beach its white appearance. On one side of the bay the remains of a rickety metal jetty (used to load pumice from the quarry into waiting ships) are gradually disintegrating into the sea. The bottom shelves steeply and, although there are some rocks below the waterline, is mainly sandy. There are, at present, no facilities and there is no natural shade. Although the beach is well used by nudists, the building of the new hotel or apartment block could not only ruin the best beach on the island but could also prevent its use for naturism. White Beach can be reached by bus (see Getting Around).

The scrubby beach at PALI consists of a long, narrow strip of dark sand which is dirty with seaweed. A road runs alongside the beach and, although the beach is hardly used, its proximity to the village and the road makes it unsuitable for nudism.

There are other beaches on the island but none are easily accessible.

Things To Do: The chief attraction is the volcano. Day-trippers from Kos arrive at about 11.00 every day and are met at the quayside by two or three buses (if you are staying on Nissiros you should get there before the tourist boats arrive or you may have to stand the whole way). The road twists and winds its way up the mountainside before descending to a flat plain where the crater is situated. It is possible to walk down the steep-sided crater and as you approach the acrid smell of sulphur drifts up to meet you. The bottom is flat and in places there are cavities from which drafts of hot air issue like the opening of oven doors. Elsewhere, steam drifts from tiny blow-holes around which form bright yellow crystals of pure sulphur. After exploring the crater you can have a drink in the small cafe near-by before your bus returns to Mandraki (arriving at about 13.00)

The spectacularly situated villages of Emborio and Nikia are worth a visit but are difficult to get to.

Getting Around: Daily buses at about 11.00 to the volcano. The 'Green Bus' runs at 09.45 on Monday, Tuesday, Wednesday, Friday and Sunday to Loutra, the White Beach and Pali. The fare to the White Beach and Pali is 35 drs., one way. The bus returns at about 14.30 (but check with the conductor). The 'Blue Bus' runs every Friday to the volcano, Nikia and Emborio departing at 17.00 All these buses leave from the harbour in Mandraki.

There is at least one taxi on the island but it's never there when you want it!

Tour Operators:
MANDRAKI; Twelve Islands (H).
PALI: Small World (R).

TILOS

In spite of the fact that there are far fewer trees than on Nissiros, its nearest neighbour, sleepy Tilos has a charm and beauty of its own with rocky hillsides, some lovely views and two picturesquely-situated villages. Although there is some agriculture, local produce is scarce and most food has to be shipped-in (including bread which comes from Symi or Rhodes). The few tavernas really only operate in high season and nightlife is non-existent. Tilos is a sanctuary from the commercialisation which mass tourism has brought to so many of the islands in recent years and a stay here will appeal to those looking for simplicity, complete relaxation and genuine Greek atmosphere.

Connections: Three ferries a week between Rhodes, Symi and Tilos and on to Nissiros, Kos and Kalymnos. Once a week with Leros, Patmos, Lipsi, Samos, Astipalea, Amorgos, Paros and Piraeus.
Centres: There are just two places to stay on Tilos, Livadia the tiny port and Megalo Chorio which is not much bigger. There is a taverna on the quayside in Livadia and if you want rooms either here or in Megalo Chorio this is the place to ask (they can also help in getting transport to Megalo Chorio). LIVADIA, surrounded by high rocky hillsides, is picturesquely situated at one end of a long, sweeping bay. There are about three tavernas and some rooms to rent including six bungalows, built from communal funds, at the back of the beach. There is one hotel, the Hotel Livadia (tel. 53266), which offers double rooms for about 750 drs. Unofficial camping takes place in the fields at the back of the beach.

The island's only made-up road runs for 4½ miles and joins Livadia with Megalo Chorio. MEGALO CHORIO is a small village of whitewashed houses. It nestles at the foot of a rocky escarpment on top of which stand the ruins of a Venetian castle. Accommodation is limited but Sevasti Ikonomou (tel. 53237) offers nice double rooms (with shared facilities) for about 700 drs. a night. Her modern house is one of the first on the left as the road climbs to enter the village. There are just two places to eat. At the 'Tilos' the owner's wife prepares good, simple food in her tiny kitchen and a meal for two here (including pre-dinner ouzos and a bottle of Retsina) should cost about 700 drs. Megalo Chorio is a charming place and those who relish the sights and sounds of Greek village life will find a stay here particularly rewarding. Not recommended for those who dislike walking.

Warning: it can be difficult to cash traveller's cheques on Tilos. The island's post office (situated in Livadia) does not do so even though it displays a sign which suggests that it might. In case of difficulty try the 'supermarket' in the square (opposite the post office).

Beaches: LIVADIA** has a long beach of white pebbles which extends around the wide bay. At intervals trees overhang the beach and provide pleasant shade when the sun is at its hottest. The beach is backed by a road and nudists can usually be found at the end furthest away from the village (after the concreted section of the road finishes). Here the beach is narrower and consists of small pebbles which are not uncomfortable to lie on. The pebbles can make access to the sea difficult and the bottom shelves quite steeply but this is, nevertheless, a very pleasant and quiet beach with a lovely view around the bay to the village.

Before reaching Megalo Chorio, you will see a track on the left of the road which is signposted 'Nausica'. NAUSICA** is a long, wide beach which consists of sand at the water's edge and a mixture of sand and pebbles further back. There are trees at the back of the beach and people often pitch tents here. Nausica can be used for naturism for the whole of its length (it is often empty and a dozen visitors would constitute a busy day). A ridge of pebbles at the water's edge can make access to the sea a little difficult and the bottom shelves quite steeply. It is a pleasant 40 minute walk from Megalo Chorio to Nausica. Take the first unsurfaced road on the right leading out of the village (at the bottom of the hill). You will pass what looks as if it used to be a small monastery (a detachment of the Greek army is now billeted here) and, a little further on, you will see the small, oil-fired power station which supplies the island's electricity. At the bottom there is a T-junction. Turn left and follow the track through a verdant valley. Vegetables, lemons, oranges and pomegranates grow in profusion thanks to the water which is brought to the surface by wind-operated pumps (assisted these days by electricity as well). On the right, just before reaching the sea, is the Tropicana Taverna. There are, in fact, two tavernas near to this beach. The other is called the 'Nausica'. It too is set back and is signposted both from the track and off the beach itself (about halfway along). Both of these tavernas offer simple rooms to let at 600 drs. for a double. Nausica is the best of the easily accessible beaches.

The pebbly beach at PLAKA** is used by both nudists and campers. It can be reached from Megalo Chorio by following the same unsurfaced road which leads to Nausica. However at the T-junction, instead of turning left, turn right and walk for about 40 minutes until the sea comes into view. Look out for a white house on the right. Virtually opposite here a track branches off to the left. The main track (bearing right) leads to the tiny fishing hamlet of Agios Andonis. Take the left fork and walk for 40 minutes before reaching the beach at Plaka. This walk is not recommended during the hottest part of the day and should only be attempted if you are used to walking distances.

Although there are other beaches on the island, none are easily accessible.

It is worthy of comment that the inhabitants of Tilos seem to take beach nudity in their stride. That part of the beach which is used for nudism at Livadia is bordered by an unsurfaced road along which vehicles and pedestrians pass fairly frequently. Similarly, at Nausica nude campers often pitch their tents under the trees at the top end of the beach where local people sometimes come to swim. In both these places local people seem completely relaxed about nudity although they rarely strip-off themselves.

Things To Do: The remains of the Venetian castle at Megalo Chorio are reached by means of a steep track. Follow the road through the small village square, passing the 'supermarket' on the left. The road loses its surface before it loops around to the left (ignore the track which leads straight ahead). After a short distance take the first path on the right. It appears to lead to a house but actually continues on into the fields before ascending to the summit. On the way up you will notice the remains of 12,000-year-old Pelasgian walls – relics of the earliest known Greeks. The entrance to the castle is substantially intact as is a small church (note the faded murals on the back wall) and the views (especially when the sun is setting) are magnificent.

See the abandoned village of Mikro Chorio (situated to the right of the main road before it descends to Livadia). Once a thriving village of 1,200 souls it fell victim to the island's depopulation as the younger generation left to seek their fortunes in such places as the U.S.A. and Australia. It was finally abandoned after the Second World War. Its only inhabitants now are sheep but many of the houses are amazingly intact and the church is still maintained.

Getting Around: There is no public transport, no taxis and no car or scooter hire. There are not more than twenty vehicles on the whole island and most of these are pick-up trucks. It is easy to get a lift when the ferry docks in Livadia (just ask one of the waiting drivers – although you may have to share your journey with crates of vegetables or other imported produce). In Megalo Chorio one or two people supplement their incomes by providing transport. The man who lives in the next house on the left up the hill from Sevasti Ikonomou (see Centres) speaks reasonably good English and is very obliging although, naturally, he will expect payment for this service. Otherwise, you will have to rely on your own two feet. Although transport is sparse, passing vehicles will often stop (without being asked) and pick up walkers and, usually, payment will not be expected.

Tour Operators:
LIVADIA: Twelve Islands (S)

SYMI

Symi is small, rocky and, except for the daily influx of day-trippers from Rhodes, off the beaten tourist track. Most people would probably find Symi too quiet for a stay of more than a few days.

Connections: Boat at 08.30 every morning from Rhodes; twice a week with Kos.

Centres: The island's capital consists of the port, Yialos, and Chorio, the village on the hillside above. Collectively these two are known as SYMI. The town itself is picturesquely situated with neo-classical mansions and steep streets leading down to a colourful quayside. Symi is short of water and it is for this reason that, mercifully, no large hotels have been built here. However, as a consequence, the islanders have to rely heavily on the daily influx of trippers from Rhodes to make their living and prices tend to be somewhat inflated here. There are a few rooms to rent and a number of small hotels including the Haskas (0241 71340), the Glafkos Hotel (0241 71358) and the six room, 'B' class Niraeus (0241 71386). Nightlife is low-key although there is one small disco and a good selection of restaurants on the harbour front with other less expensive ones just behind.

Beaches: Although beaches are rarely sandy and are often poor Symi's coastline is notched with many deep, narrow bays which offer seclusion and superb swimming. NOS BEACH, ten minutes on foot from Yialos (north along the waterfront and past the shipyard) is very small, pebbly and shaded by the early afternoon. From Nos it is a 45 minute walk west to EMBORIO, not a great beach, but worth the walk for the views along the way. The beach at PEDHI is a fifty minute walk to the east. There is a taverna here but the pebbly beach is minuscule. From Pedhi a goat track to the right of the bay leads over the headland before descending (after walking for about half an hour) to a tiny but deserted bay with a church and olive trees known as AGIOS NIKOLAOS**. Other secluded coves can be discovered either with a small boat or on foot.

Things To Do: The huge monastery of St. Michael Panormitis is a popular excursion destination. It is set in a beautiful bay with a small sandy beach and within the monastery complex are a small museum, two expensive restaurants, shops and guest rooms to let (very enterprising monks, these!). The best way to get there is by excursion boat from town.

Getting Around: There are hardly any roads on Symi and therefore no cars or bikes for hire. There are two taxis which compete with each other up and down the only real road – a two mile stretch around the cliff between Yialos and Chorio. Caiques or smaller boats can be hired to take you to one of the numerous coves around the island.

Tour Operators:
SYMI TOWN: Aegina Club (R,S); Beach Villas (S); Lancaster (H); Laskarina (H,S); Manos (H); Meon (S); Olympic – Main Brochure (H); O.S.L. (S); Small World (H,R); Sunvil (H,S); Timsway – 'Original Holidays in Greece' Brochure (H,S); Twelve Islands (H,S).
PEDHI: Aegina Club (P); Lancaster (S); Timsway – 'Original Holidays in Greece' Brochure (H).

RHODES (RODOS)

Rhodes, approximately 40 miles long and 23 miles across at its widest points, has more hours of sunshine than most places in Greece with average daily temperatures never falling below 70 Fahrenheit from the beginning of June to the end of October. The western side of the island is green with wooded mountains, the eastern side is less verdant. Rhodes is well developed touristically with, in places, conglomerations of hotels reminiscent of Spain but there are also quiet villages and far flung beaches where natural beauty and peacefulness can still be found.

Connections: By air – direct flights from most U.K. airports; up to seven flights a day from Athens; up to three flights a day from Karpathos; daily flights from Iraklion (Crete), Kos and Mykonos; two flights a day from Sitia (Crete) on Tuesdays, Thursdays and Saturdays and one on Sunday; flights from Leros on Tuesdays, Thursdays and Saturdays; flights from Paros on Tuesdays, Thursdays, Saturdays and Sundays; flights from Santorini on Tuesdays, Thursdays and Saturdays. By boat – daily with Piraeus (15-24 hours), Kos (4½-9½ hours), Kalymnos (7-11 hours), Leros (11 hours), Patmos

(15 hours) and Symi (2 hours) also daily hydrofoil to Kos; twice a week with Astipalea (10½ hours), Karpathos (7 hours), Crete (13 hours), Amorgos and Santorini; once a week to Folegandros, Milos, Naxos, Paros, Mykonos, Syros, Samos, Ikaria, Chios, Lesbos, Kavala and Thessaloniki.

Centres: Where to stay in Rhodes presents something of a problem. The main beach in Rhodes town is probably the most crowded in Greece and from here to Trianta, 5 miles away, the story is a similar one with crowded (and sometimes not very good) beaches backed by high-rise hotels. The best beaches are along the east coast and the closest, Tsambika, is about eighteen miles from town. You could consider staying at Lindos (thirty-five miles from Rhodes town), Faliraki (about eight miles from town) or somewhere in between such as Afandou or Arhangelos.

RHODES town is divided into the old and new towns. The new town consists of hotels, tourist shops, restaurants and discos. The harbour front is interesting but the rest is rather uninspiring. The old town is one of the most perfectly preserved medieval walled cities to be found anywhere in the world. The town walls average forty feet in thickness and the old town is entered through gates, the most magnificent of which is the Gate of Emery d'Amboise, near the Palace of the Grand Masters and built in 1512. Inside there is a maze of cobble-stone streets full of the usual souvenir shops as well as classy fur and jewellery shops and boutiques, cafes and restaurants. Here also are attractive squares, fountains, the Mosque of Suleiman and the magnificent Street of the Knights (Ippoton Street). The street begins at Museum Square (Plateia Mousion) and leads up the hill past the Inns of the Tongues (each group of knights lived in different inns named after the eight nationalities which comprised the Order) to Citadel Square and the impressive Palace of the Grand Masters. The original palace, built on the site of a sanctuary dedicated to Helios, was completed by the Knights in the fourteenth century. After the Turkish invasion it was used as a prison but was largely ruined by a huge gunpowder explosion in 1856 (presumably this was accidental). During the Italian occupation, Mussolini ordered its reconstruction and many of the lovely mosaics and sculptures were transported here from Kos by the Italians. There is plenty of nightlife especially in the new town with discos, bars and restaurants. Accommodation is plentiful and varied but for easy access to the beaches you should stay elsewhere.

FALIRAKI, about eight miles from Rhodes town, is an unremarkable little place which owes its very existence to the package holiday. A hotchpotch of gift shops, hotels, tavernas and discos. The main beach is very long and sandy with hundreds of beach umbrellas and loungers. However, Faliraki does have a nudist beach and there is plenty of accommodation. Many U.K. tour operators offer holidays here. In addition, there is a regular bus service to Rhodes town and Faliraki is also on the Rhodes-Lindos bus route. It is a good base from which to visit the nudist beaches at Tsambika (about eleven miles

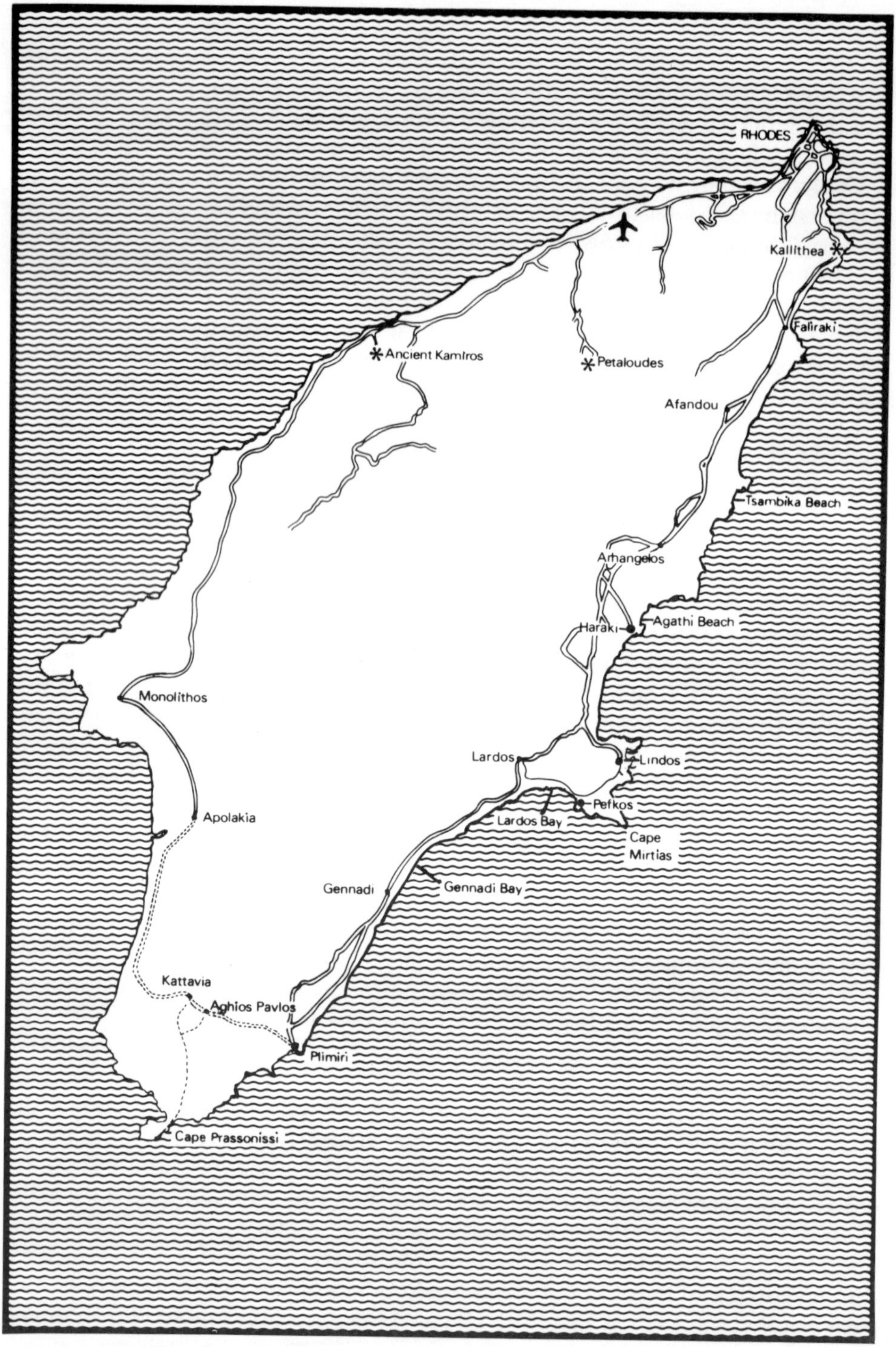
RHODES
Kallithea
Faliraki
Ancient Kamiros
Petaloudes
Afandou
Tsambika Beach
Arhangelos
Haraki
Agathi Beach
Monolithos
Lardos
Lindos
Pefkos
Lardos Bay
Cape Mirtias
Apolakia
Gennadi
Gennadi Bay
Kattavia
Aghios Pavlos
Plimiri
Cape Prassonissi

away) and Agathi (about nineteen miles).

Other places worthy of consideration because of their closeness to these beaches include Afandou and Arhangelos. AFANDOU is situated about twelve miles from Rhodes town, six miles from Tsambika and fourteen miles from the beach at Agathi. There is an eighteen hole golf course here as well as tennis courts but little else. A number of tour operators offer self-catering accommodation and here also is the 'B' class Hotel Xenia (tel. 51121). ARHANGELOS, off the main Rhodes to Lindos road, is the largest village on Rhodes and a stay here would probably appeal to those wanting to experience something of Greek village life. Arhangelos is twenty-one miles from Rhodes town, four miles from Tsambika and six miles from Agathi. Here is the 'E' class Arhangelos, 184, 7th Martiou, (tel. 0244 21230).

LINDOS, thirty-five miles along the east coast from Rhodes town, is a picturesque village of whitewashed houses and narrow cobbled streets. Above, on a hilltop, stands the acropolis and below is Lindos bay with its beautiful sandy beach. The magnificent setting of the town makes it a must for a visit and Lindos is often very crowded. There are rooms to rent but they are often full in summer.

Beaches: Travelling along the east coast from Rhodes town the first nudist beach is to be found at FALIRAKI***. The main street in Faliraki ends at the beach which stretches for several miles in a north-easterly direction. This beach, although long, is generally busy and is not used by nudists. Turn right and walk along the beach away from the main strand and around a headland to another much smaller beach. Continue, passing George's Taverna and a restaurant, before rounding a second headland to the nudist beach. The walk takes about twenty to twenty-five minutes. Alternatively, instead of turning left for Faliraki off the main Rhodes-Lindos road, continue along this road for a short distance until you come to a cross-roads. Ignore the road on the right (which leads to the village of Kalithies) but turn left down a small tarmac road which leads past the Hotel Evie to the beach. This road ends at George's Taverna from where you can walk to the nudist beach. The beach is sandy, although rocky at the water's edge, and a bit dirty (tin cans, bottles, etc.) but in August was well used every day by about forty to fifty nudists. There is no taverna here although, at the time of writing, a Greek naturist sells cold drinks (until he runs out) from a tent at the back of the beach. The nearest place for refreshments otherwise is the restaurant, back around the headland, on the George's Taverna beach. There is also a shower here on the outside wall of the restaurant.

TSAMBIKA* is a beautiful bay with a long, wide, sandy beach. The impressive Mount Tsampicas, with its monastery perched on top, dominates one side of the bay. Also at this end is the busy taverna, the inevitable (on Rhodes at least) sun umbrellas and loungers, water-sports and paragliding. As you move away from this crowded end of the beach you will begin to see the nudists. This is a very long beach and there should never be any shortage of room. Tsambika Beach is signposted off the main Rhodes-Lindos road after passing through Kolimbia.

The magnificent sandy beach known as AGATHI*, near the village of HARAKI, is rather more difficult to find. Follow the main Rhodes to Lindos road passing the signs for the village of Arhangelos which is to the left. After climbing a steep hill the road drops down again and at the bottom, before crossing the river bridge, is a road to the left which leads to Haraki. Follow this road for a mile or so looking out for a track which leads off on the left. The track can be identified by an old free-standing advertising sign. It has yellow lettering on a black background and states 'Typaldos Lines Bungalow Hotel Beaches'. Follow the track passing the abandoned, partly completed bungalows until you see the beach below. A magnificent stretch of fine sand which is hardly used. There are no facilities here so you would be wise to at least take something to drink.

At LINDOS, nudists congregate on the rocks which border the sea below the acropolis and there is occasional nudism in St. Paul's Bay (on the far side of the acropolis). There are also reports of nudism at the northern end of the main beach at Lindos. It may be possible out of season but otherwise you would have to be very brave to strip-off on what is usually an extremely busy beach.

PEFKOS** can be reached from Lindos by following the cobbled track

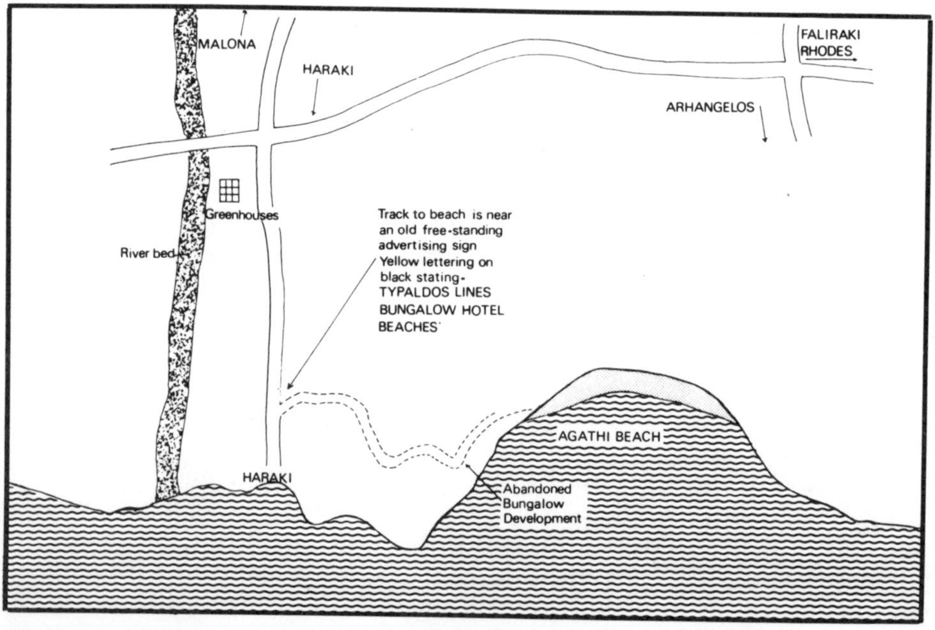

which starts at the back of the village. The road soon becomes metalled and, after about 3 miles, the sleepy hamlet set amongst fig orchards and vineyards comes into view. The mile long beach of fine sand, backed by dunes and cliffs, slopes gently into the sea, making it very safe for children. There is a snack bar and taverna here and, although there is no natural shade, there are sun loungers and sun umbrellas on the central (clothed) part of the beach. The far end of the beach is where those intent on getting an all-over tan congregate. Windsurfers can be hired in season.

Leaving Pefkos, turn right by the two tavernas and follow the track for 2 miles to CAPE MIRTIAS* where you can usually enjoy a small, sandy beach all to yourself.

From Pefkos the road rejoins the surfaced road near Lardos. Continue travelling south along the main road which rejoins the coast at the western end of LARDOS BEACH*. Look out for a sign on the left of the road pointing the way to the Lardos Beach Cafe. The beach beyond the cafe is usually empty and is suitable for nude sunning.

Between Lardos Bay and Cape Prassonissi there are deserted stretches of beach offering fine swimming and almost total solitude. In some places the beaches consist of grit rather than sand but this is at least as comfortable as sand to lie on and, if you use sun oil, the beach won't stick to you like sand does.

After Lardos Bay continue for 3 miles or so until you come to a dirt road on the left signposted KIOTARI*. This track leads to the old road which runs along the coast parallel to the main road which you have just left. Turn left at the bottom and, to the right of the road at a distance of about 150 yards, you will see long, deserted beaches consisting of shingle at the water's edge with sand further back. Alternatively, if you turn right at the bottom and drive for three quarters of a mile you will pass more deserted beaches. Warning – the going along this old road can be rough in places, especially if you are on two wheels. A little further along the main road is GENNADI*, again with miles of deserted beach which is suitable for nudism away from the tavernas. Still further along is PLIMIRI* (signposted off the main road) with a mile of deserted beach and a taverna which offers some very basic beds. From here the road cuts inland to AGHIOS PAVLOS. Continue for a quarter of a mile before bearing left over a bridge. 4-5 miles further on park your car at the dunes from where it is just a 200 yard walk to miles of deserted, sandy beach. From Aghios Pavlos continue to KATTAVIA (there are one or two rooms to be had here if you ask around) from where an unmade road runs south for about 6 miles to the isthmus at CAPE PRASSONISSI* (turn left past the derelict windmills). Do not attempt to drive onto the soft sand but park at the bottom of the hill at the start of the isthmus. There are miles of sandy beach on either side of the isthmus and, if you can find it, this is a superb location. From Kattavia, the road rejoins the east coast and between here and APOLAKIA (a modern, uninteresting town with a few pensions) there are about 5 miles of deserted, sandy beach within 200 yards of the unmetalled road. This often windswept beach has rough breakers and slippery pebbles at the water's edge and, in this isolated location, it would be best not to take any chances and keep out of the sea. Nevertheless, a superb area in which to acquire an all-over tan.

Things To Do: In Rhodes – visit the Palace of the Grand Masters. Open 08.30 to 16.00 except for Sundays and holidays when it is open from 10.00 to 15.00, closed Tuesday. There is a tour of the inner walls every Monday and Saturday at 15.00. A 'Sound and Light' presentation takes place here nightly at 22.00. The performance is given in English, French, German and Swedish on different nights. Tickets may be purchased at the gate. In summer there are performances of Greek folk-dancing at the Nelly Dimoglou Dance Theatre at 21.15 (follow the arrows from the main shopping street – Sokratous Street). The Rhodes Museum is housed in the fifteenth century former Hospital of the Knights. Open 07.30 to 19.30, 10.00 to 20.00 on Sundays.

Lindos – the acropolis is open 07.30 to 19.30, 10.00 to 20.00 on Sundays.

The ruins of the ancient city of Kamiros which overlook the sea (21 miles from Rhodes town on the west coast) are interesting. Halfway to Kamiros is a turn-off which leads to Petaloudes, better known as the 'Valley of the Butterflies'. The valley stretches for about a mile through the trees. From June until September thousands of orange and black butterflies flock there attracted by the sweet resin of the trees which is used to make frankincense. Buses go there in summer and there is a small entrance charge.

Kallithea Hot Springs (on the coast road to Faliraki) is mentioned as a place to visit in most guide books. In its heyday it was probably worth visiting. Now the hot springs are no more and the whole place is crumbling and rather tatty (recent reports suggest that some renovation is taking place). Have a look if you're passing but don't make a special effort. Also don't be tempted to make a special trip to see Mount Profitis Ilias. The mountain itself is heavily wooded obstructing the fine view which you would otherwise have and, except for two chalet-style hotels, there is nothing there when you get to the top.

Getting Around: Buses to Lindos leave the 'Sound and Light' Square in Rhodes town at 09.00 and 11.30, 13.00 and 15.00. The last bus back is at 18.00. A regular bus service to Faliraki leaves from the same place. Buses to Kallithea go from Averof Square and here also is a service to Petaloudes ('Valley of the Butterflies') leaving at 09.00 and noon. Caiques leave Mandraki harbour (Rhodes town) in the morning for the following beaches – Kallithea, Faliraki, Ladiko, Kolimbia, Tsambika and Lardos. Car and scooter hire in Rhodes, Faliraki and Lindos.

Tour Operators:

FALIRAKI: Amathus (H); Avra (H); Beach Villas (S); Cook, Thomas – 'Hotels, Coaches and Cruising' Brochure (H); Enterprise (H); Flair (H); Global (H,S);

Grecian (H,P,R,S); Horizon (H); Intasun – 'Plain and Simple' Brochure (H); Manos (H,R,S); Olympic – Main Brochure (H); Olympic – 'A Touch of Greece' Brochure (R); Portland (H); Rhodian Travel (H); Rooks, Martin (H); Sigma (H,S); Sirama (S); Sunmed (H,P,R,S); Thompson – 'Summer Sun' Brochure (H); Ventura (H,R,S).
AFANDOU: Sigma (H,S).
HARAKI: Aegina Club (S); Timsway – 'Original Holidays in Greece' Brochure (S).
LINDOS: Aegina Club (S); Airlink (H,S); Beach Villas (R,S); Club 18-30 (R,S); Ellerman (S); Grecian (P,R,S); Intasun – 'Plain and Simple' Brochure (S,T); Laskarina (R,S); Manos (R,S); Meon (S); Olympic – Main Brochure (P,R,S,T); Olympic – 'A Touch of Greece' Brochure (P,R,S,T); O.S.L. (S); Rhodian (S); Sigma (S); Sirama (R,S); Thomson – 'Villas and Apartments' Brochure (S); Timsway – 'Original Holidays in Greece' Brochure (P,R,S); Twelve Islands (R,S).
PEFKOS: Aegina Club (S); Airlink (S); Olympic – Main Brochure (S); O.S.L. (S); Timsway – 'Original Holidays in Greece' Brochure (S); Twelve Islands (S).
GENNADI: Aegina Club (S); Small World (S); Sunvil (S); Timsway – 'Original Holidays in Greece' Brochure (S).
APOLAKIA: Small World (H).

KARPATHOS

Karpathos, approximately 30 miles long and 8 miles across at its widest points, is a beautiful island with spectacular, mountainous scenery. A 3,500 foot mountain divides the island and travelling around is not easy. Many Karpathians emigrated to America around the turn of the century and the island owes much of its prosperity to the large expatriate community. Karpathos will suit those who enjoy a quiet time, Greek atmosphere and dramatic scenery. Unlike some islands, Karpathos does not need to rely on tourism for its income and tourism is tolerated rather than actively encouraged.

Connections: By air – up to two flights a day from Athens (via Rhodes) and up to four flights a day from Rhodes; on Tuesdays, Thursdays, Saturdays and Sundays with Sitia (Crete). By sea – twice daily with Rhodes (7 hours) and Agios Nikolaos and Sitia on Crete (6 hours), Santorini and Piraeus. Once a week with Folegandros, Naxos, Paros, Syros, Ikaria, Samos, Chios, Lesbos and Kavala.

Centres: PIGATHIA (now more commonly known as KARPATHOS) is the rather functional main town and port. There are rooms to rent here and a few hotels and both often get full in midsummer. Near-by is the enormous, sandy beach at Vrontis Bay. The 'C' class Porfyris (tel. 25294) overlooks the beach and reputedly serves some of the best Greek food on the island. Four miles south is AMOPPI with a number of beaches, rooms to let and a new hotel. You can walk here from Pigathia in about half an hour and there is also an infrequent bus service (see Getting Around). The island's second port is at DIAFANI in the north-west. It is an unremarkable place but there are cheap rooms to rent here.

Beaches: Reports suggest that the locals, although friendly, are rather conservative so that on some beaches even going topless might be inadvisable.

There are reports that the long crescent of sand at VRONTIS BAY is used for nudism (in the vicinity of notices prohibiting it) but, in view of the preceding remarks, sensible discretion should be exercised.

AMOPPI** has three beaches. One of these is used by naturists because of its remoteness from houses but, unfortunately, it is rough and rocky. South of Amoppi are several miles of sandy beach which offer the ultimate in seclusion.

LEFKOS, on the west coast, has three small bays of white sand. One of these is adjacent to some fishermen's houses and nude sunning is probably inadvisable here, although it might be possible in the other bays.

ARKASSA, also on the west coast, is a 'get away from it all' sort of place with a nice harbour. Five minutes' walk to the south, on a promontory, are the remains of ancient Arkessia. Just beyond is the beach at the back of which are dunes and also fields where locals can frequently be seen working. Notices here prohibit nudity. The sea is often very rough on this west coast and the beach is affected by rubbish which has been washed up by high seas.

In view of the apparent sensitiveness of the locals, the best places for nudism are probably along the south-eastern coast. Although the scenery is bleak and almost desert-like here, there are many deserted sand and pebble beaches. Also, to the south of Diafani paths lead to isolated beaches while other beaches along this stretch of coastline are only accessible by boat.

Things To Do: Karpathos is an excellent island for ramblers and nature lovers, especially in spring. A visit to Olympos, the highest village on Karpathos, is worthwhile. The road to Olympos (also called Olimvos) was completed only comparatively recently and the previous isolation of this village is evidenced by the fact that people still wear traditional costumes and have retained a unique dialect which is unintelligible to outsiders. The colourful village (some of the houses are painted blue on the first storey and white on the second) is spectacularly situated overlooking a terraced valley and the coast below.

Getting Around: Bus to Amoppi from Pigathia every day at 10.00 returning at 16.30. Buses from Pigathia to many villages. In season, caiques from Pigathia to the east coast beaches and Diafani. Car, moped and bicycle hire in Pigathia.

Tour Operators:

KARPATHOS TOWN: Aegina Club (H,S); Allsun (H); Laskarina (H); Meon (S);

Sirama (H); Tanntours (H,P); Timsway – 'Original Holidays in Greece' Brochure (H,S); Twelve Islands (H,S).
AMOPPI: Laskarina (R); Timsway – 'Original Holidays in Greece' Brochure (H).

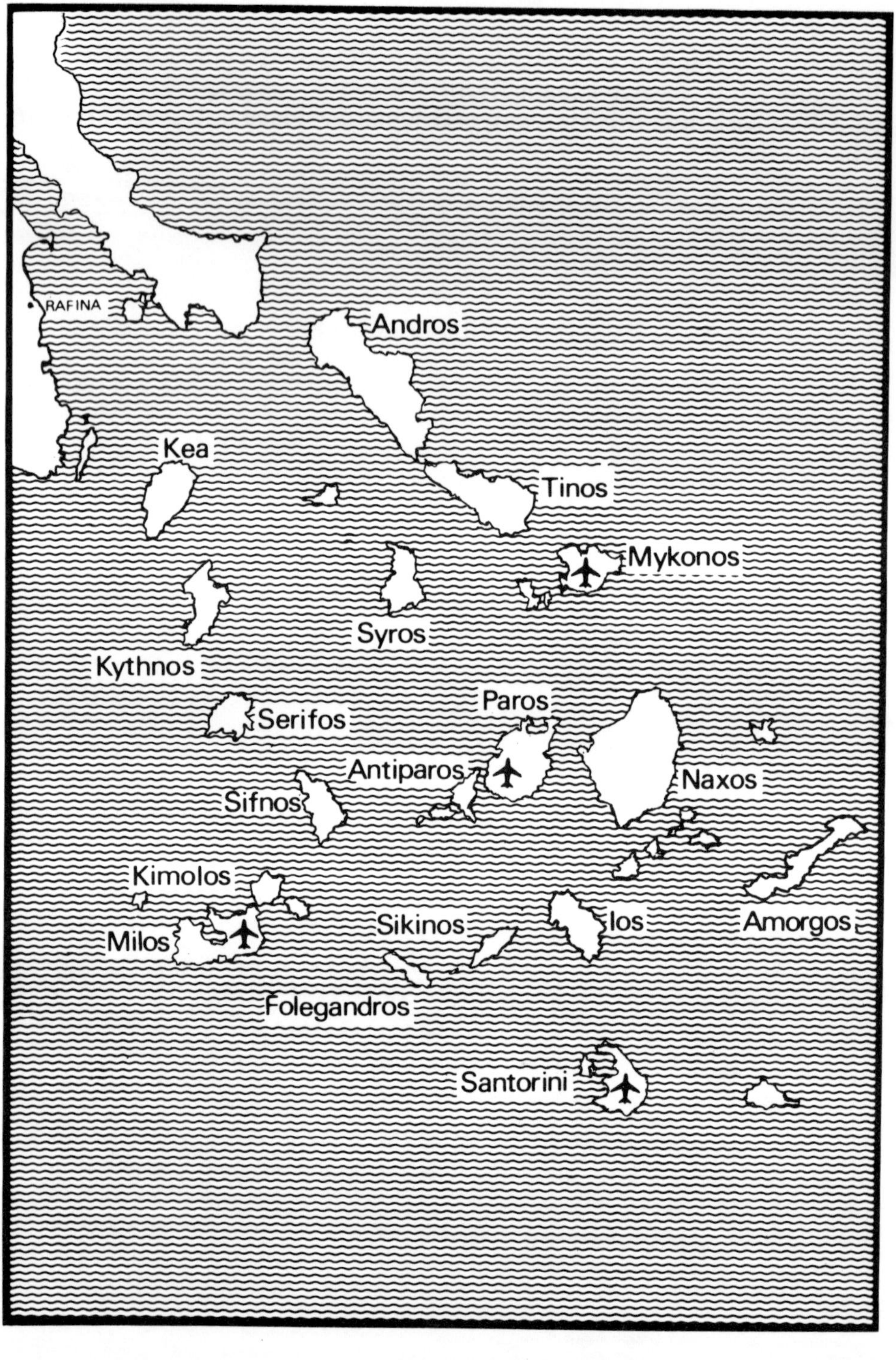
RAFINA
Andros
Kea
Tinos
Mykonos
Syros
Kythnos
Paros
Serifos
Antiparos
Naxos
Sifnos
Kimolos
Sikinos
Ios
Amorgos
Milos
Folegandros
Santorini

THE CYCLADES

The Cyclades are the largest group of islands and are so named because they encircle the tiny island of Delos. Now uninhabited, Delos once achieved influence out of all proportion to its size as a great spiritual and trading centre. The islands which make up this group typify most peoples' conception of a Greek island with whitewashed villages of cubist houses clinging to rocky hillsides. The Cyclades become brown and parched in summer and on some there may be water shortages. They are also more exposed to the prevailing winds than are the other island groups (particularly in early spring and from about mid-July and throughout August when the **meltemi** periodically whips across the Aegean). This can make lying on the beach unpleasant if not impossible and also results in the cancellation of all but the largest inter-island ferries (sometimes for days on end). As the islands are relatively close together it is possible to visit a number of them without losing too much time in transit.

ANDROS

Andros, approximately 21 miles long and 8 miles wide, is the second largest island in the Cyclades group and also the northernmost. In spite of being one of the greener islands, with pine covered hills and lush fertile valleys, it is little visited by foreign tourists. In fact, Andros is relatively prosperous and does not need to rely on tourism for its livelihood. This is because Andriots have, for many years, been abandoning the land in favour of more lucrative careers in the merchant marine. So much so that today Andros is known as an island of shipowners and sailors. Andros is ideal for a relaxing holiday and is not recommended for those who enjoy a lively time.

Connections: Daily ferryboat to Rafina (3 hours) and Tinos (2 hours). Three times a week with Mykonos and Syros.

Centres: The ferryboats arrive at GAVRION, a friendly if uninspiring little village, with a strip of sand at one side of the harbour which serves as a beach. There are tavernas here, one good restaurant, a few rooms to rent and the 'B' class Aphrodite Pension (0282 71209).

ANDROS town, the island's capital, is situated on a promontory and is flanked by sandy beaches. It is a lovely town with numerous neo-classical mansions and winding, traffic-free, stone streets. Unfortunately, most of the available rooms are often taken by holidaying Greeks and finding somewhere to stay can be difficult. Hotels include the Paradissos (0282 22187/9) and the Xenia (0282 22270), both 'B' class and the 'C' class Aegli (0282 22303).

The main tourist centre is BATSI, an attractive village built around a large, sandy bay. There are shops here, quayside tavernas and three discos which operate in season. Places to stay include the 'B' class Lykion Pension (0282 41214), the 'C' class Chryssi Akti (0282 41236/7) and the 'C' class Skouna

Hotel (0282 41315).

Beaches: About 40 minutes' walk from Gavrion is an isolated, sandy beach at AGIOS PETROS* which is usually sufficiently sparsely populated to allow nudity (close by is an excellently preserved 65 feet high Hellenistic tower). There are good beaches to the south of GAVRION bay. These are within walking distance and the more secluded ones may be suitable for nudism. There are two beautiful, deserted sandy beaches at FELOS*, north of Gavrion (a long walk or moped ride).

There is an immense beach at ANDROS town and a smaller one at KORTHION, a few miles down the coast, and some of the island's best beaches are said to be hereabouts.

BATSI has a sandy tree-lined beach and pedeloes, canoes and windsurfers can be hired here. On either side of Batsi there are good sand and shingle bays which can be reached by fisherman's boat or on foot. DELAVOYAS** is south of the village along a rough but drivable track (follow the road past the harbour to the war memorial before bearing right). It takes about 10-15 minutes to walk to the beach which consists of a mixture of fine shingle and sand. There is no natural shade here and there are no facilities, although there is a taverna on the next beach, AGIA MARINA*, about 5 minutes' walk away. Unfortunately, a block of apartments has been built at the back of Delavoyas and it is feared that this may adversely affect the use of the beach for naturism.

Things To Do: Visit the ancient town of Paleopolis (take the bus from Batsi to Andros town and ask to be put down at the appropriate spot – about 5 miles south of Batsi). Hundreds of steps lead down to the sea passing through a lush valley scattered with interesting remains. Also visit Arni, a lovely inland village with wonderful views of the surrounding countryside; you will need to negotiate with a friendly taxi driver.

Getting Around: Mopeds and bicycles for hire in Gavrion; mopeds, motorbikes and a few cars for hire in Batsi. Buses between Gavrion and Andros town (leave shortly after each boat arrival – usually around 07.00, 10.00, 11.00 and 17.00). Three buses a day between Andros and Korthion.

Tour Operators:
GAVRION: Tanntours (H).
BATSI: Aegina Club (H,S); Falcon (H,S); Manos (H); Tanntours (H,S); Timsway – 'Original Holidays in Greece' Brochure (H,S); Zeus (R,S).

KEA (TSIA)

Kea is an undeveloped, beautiful and very Greek island. Although rugged and rocky there are two green valleys which are cultivated with vines.

Connections: Daily ferryboat from Lavrion (2½ hours); once a week with Kythnos.

Centres: CHORA, the island's capital, is an attractive white village located inland high above the sea. KORISSIA, the port, has a couple of tavernas and is connected to Chora by bus. Accommodation is mainly in hotels and basic rooms at these two places. Some package holidays are available to the 'B' class Kea Beach (tel. 21411). Although it is situated on a beach it is in an extremely isolated location.

Beaches: There are many secluded bays where nude sunning can be enjoyed undisturbed. There is a large, secluded, sandy beach 15 minutes' walk to the north of the Kea Beach Hotel which is reported as being used by naturists. Other beaches at Ag. Irene (Vourkari), Otzias (reached by bus), Poiessa and Koundoros.

Things To Do: Nothing to see of real interest.

Getting Around: A few buses each day from Chora to Korissia and Otzias. A few taxis.

Tour Operators:
Manos (S).

TINOS

Tinos became famous throughout the Greek Orthodox world following the discovery in 1822, by a nun from the island's Kehrovouni Convent, of a miraculous healing icon. The Church of Panayia Evangelistra was built over the spot and today it has become the most important pilgrimage destination in Greece and is jam-packed at festival times (25th March and 15th August). For the more secular visitor the island's appeal lies in its tranquillity and in the beauty of its terraced hills, sparkling white villages and pretty dovecotes (of which there are said to be eighteen hundred and forty-eight).

Connections: Ferryboats daily from Piraeus and Rafina via Andros; daily boat from Mykonos and Syros; twice a week with Leros, Patmos, Kalymnos, Rhodes, Kos, Ikaria and Samos; more frequently with Paros and Naxos.

Centres: TINOS town is large and really not all that attractive with large hotels lining the sea-front. A broad street leads from the port to the Church of Panayia Evangelistra. All along the way are dozens of shops selling icons, candles, incense and other religious knick-knacks. A monumental staircase leads to the church and the interior is typically ornate with one hundred silver candelabra. The centre of attraction is, of course, the icon. It is set in a gold and bejewelled frame and is itself surrounded by a dazzling display of gold and silver artefacts.

Outside the periods of pilgrimage rooms are plentiful. Hotels in town include the 'B' class Tinion (0283 22261) and the Avra (0283 22242), Flisvos (0283 22243) and Poseidonion (0283 23123) – all 'C' class. Nightlife is livelier than one might expect in a place like this and there are some good restaurants and tavernas.

Beaches: The closest beach to town, and therefore the most frequented, is the long strand at AGIOS FOKAS, an easy walk east of the harbour. Another beach at KIONIA is about a mile to the west but, to enjoy nudity, you will need to travel further afield. One of the few reasonably accessible good, sandy beaches is at KOLIBITHRA*. This is reached by following the rough road between the villages of Komi and Kalloni and then by path to the beach (about a half an hour's walk).

PORTO KOUVAROS**, on the south-east tip of the island, is a more easily accessible beach and can be reached by bus or by walking from town. The walk will take about an hour (less by taking a short-cut down a wide and easily distinguishable track where the road bends sharp left). Here you will find a small headland with sandy beaches on either side. The area is known to be used by naturists although they are usually outnumbered by clothed bathers.

Things To Do: Visit the Kehrovouni Monastery (really a convent), a picturesque hill-top village in miniature, which is a delight to explore.

Getting Around: A good bus service operates from the harbour and the K.T.E.L. office here has timetables. Moped and bicycle hire in Tinos town.

Tour Operators:
TINOS TOWN: Aegina Club (H); Grecian (H,S); Manos (H); Olympic – Main Brochure (H); Tanntours (H,P); Thomson – 'Summer Sun' Brochure (H).

MYKONOS

The island is about 9 miles from west to east and 6 miles north to south and, although rocky and barren, it has a charm of its own. The main town is one of the most beautiful in the Cyclades and also one of the most sophisticated. The bustling harbour is packed with bars, restaurants and shops. Petros the pelican, the island's mascot, is often to be seen here. The town stretches back from the harbour up the hillside and consists of a myriad of dazzling white, shadow-dappled alleyways in which the visitor can get pleasantly lost. It is said that the town was built in this way to confuse marauding pirates but now the narrow twisting streets serve only to deny access to motor vehicles (with the exception of little three-wheeled motorised trucks which are just narrow enough to pass through). Here you will find quiet back streets inhabited by locals contrasting with a wide variety of bars, discotheques, sophisticated fashion boutiques, gold and jewellery shops and furriers. To one side of the harbour is the area known as Alefkandra. Here the ancient buildings stand shoulder to shoulder crowding the water's edge, their wooden galleries and balconies overhanging the sea below. Overlooking these, on a ridge of higher ground, stand the famous trio of windmills which have become the town's most famous landmark.

Mykonos has been a popular island with the cognoscenti for many years. The beauty of the town, the fine beaches, easy ambience and liberal attitudes have drawn hedonists from all over the world. For the same reasons it also attracted a large number of gays and it may, in part, be due to them that the island developed the unique atmosphere which was its great attraction. The introduction of direct flights was bound to have an effect and those of us who knew the old Mykonos cannot help feeling a twinge of regret. Mykonos, always busy in season, is now in danger of becoming jam-packed and the beautiful people have, for the most part, moved on – most visitors these days look as if they could be visiting any resort anywhere in Europe. Prices tend to be on the high side but, in spite of all this, it is still a super holiday island with fantastic beaches, frenetic nightlife and one of the most picturesque villages to be found anywhere.

Connections: By air – direct flights now available from Gatwick, Birmingham and Manchester; up to thirteen flights a day from Athens; once a day from Santorini; once a day from Iraklion (Crete) – twice on Mondays in season – and once a day from Rhodes. By sea – daily to Piraeus (6½ hours), Tinos (1 hour), Syros (2 hours) and Rafina; five times a week to Paros, Ios, Santorini and Andros; twice a week to Crete.

Centres: It is best to stay either in town or in Plati Yialos which is close to the majority of naturist beaches. Here lies the dilemma. If you opt to stay in the town, getting to and from the beaches can be a problem. Although bus services are regular, everyone seems to leave the beaches at about the same time and in the late afternoon the buses become choc-a-block with hot, perspiring, sun-oiled bodies returning to town. If, on the other hand, you stay near to the beaches you will almost certainly find yourself travelling to town most evenings for the restaurants and nightlife.

PLATI YIALOS has much to recommend it. Here the beaches are within easy reach and by the time you have come off the beach, showered and changed, the buses, although probably still busy, will be less like Turkish baths. The 'C' class Petinos (0289 22127) is here. Regretfully, this particular establishment was guilty of double-booking last year (although if you are booked through a tour operator you are unlikely to experience any difficulty). Also in Plati Yialos is the Seaside Pension (0289 22125) and the excellent Patasos Beach (0289 23437) which is beautifully situated overlooking the bay at Psarrou.

In MYKONOS town there are numerous rooms to rent as well as a good selection of small hotels. The ferryboats are met by locals offering accommodation. If you arrive late without anywhere to stay already arranged you would be well advised to take one of these, particularly in July and August when it can be difficult to find a room at all. The rooms nearest to the harbour get booked up first and they are also the most expensive. The tourist police are to be found by the boat landing stage in town (0289 22482).

SAN STEFANOS, three miles north of town, has a few hotels, rooms to rent and reasonably priced tavernas but it is a little bit 'out on a limb'.

Beaches: A nudist paradise. Beach nudity is widely practised and accepted and nearly all the beaches are sandy which is unusual by Greek island standards. The main nudist beaches are to be found at Piranga, Paradise, Super Paradise, Elia and Panormos. With the exception of Panormos, all of these beaches are on the south coast and involve a ten minute bus journey from town to Plati Yialos followed by a walk or a boat trip. Plati Yialos has a fine sandy beach (not nudist), tavernas and some hotel accommodation. The road from Mykonos town ends at Plati Yialos and if you walk back a little way up the hill you will come to a little path on the left which leads to Psarrou Beach. This is one of the best beaches on the island but, unfortunately, is only topless. Little boats run regularly from Plati Yialos to Paradise, Super Paradise and Elia. You can usually walk the short distance from where the bus stops to the small landing stage and hop straight onto a waiting boat. Alternatively, you can walk to Piranga from Plati Yialos. It takes about fifteen minutes. From the far end of Plati Yialos beach take the track which leads up and around the headland. You will come to a small sandy beach with a taverna called Nicolas. Carry on following the stone wall or cut across the field to Piranga. It is possible to get one of the little ferryboats to drop you off at Piranga although, unless there are a few people wanting to go there, this can sometimes be difficult.

PIRANGA*** is a nice, clean beach of coarse/fine sand. There is no natural shade although two tavernas adjoin the beach. Swimming is safe and good. One of the tavernas has toilets and showers, although both often leave something to be desired.

PARADISE*** can also be reached on foot from Plati Yialos although the going gets rough and you should avoid the trek when the sun is at its hottest. Walking time from Plati Yialos is about thirty minutes. The beach consists of coarse, gritty sand. There is no natural shade although there are a number of rattan shades on the beach as well as a taverna. There are cold showers on the beach. Swimming is safe and good and there is also an official campsite here.

The very brave can try walking to SUPER PARADISE***. Another nice beach of fine sand with no natural shade and a taverna. This beach attracts a large number of gays who head for the left-hand side of the beach when leaving the boat.

ELIA*** is a long beach of mainly coarse sand with finer sand in places. It rarely gets crowded and, although it used to be the least easily accessible of the four nudist beaches along this coast, a new bus service from town has now made getting to Elia easy (see Getting Around). There are two tavernas here. The one nearest to the bus stop has a French proprietor and, not surprisingly, serves the best food. If you walk westward from Elia, along the well-used path which runs along the back of the beach, you will come, after about fifteen minutes, to AGRARI***. This is a nice beach of coarse sand with a few scattered sunshades and a bamboo wind-break at its eastern end. There is also a restaurant here which comes highly recommended. Both Elia and Agrari shelve fairly steeply so that they are not popular with non-swimmers and families with small children.

At SAN STEFANOS*** there are no nudists on the main part of the beach but they are to be found behind a rocky outcrop at the northern end of the beach close to a notice which states 'No Nudism By Order Police.' There are also large numbers in further small coves a little way along.

PANORMOS*** is a beautiful beach of fine sand backed by low dunes. There is no natural shade here and it can be windy on this side of the island. There is one taverna. The beach is reached by means of an appalling track off the Mykonos to Ano Mera road. Unless you are very experienced don't even attempt it on two wheels. At the bottom end of Panormos Bay is FTELIA BEACH*. Nude sunning can be enjoyed here and often the beach is deserted. Unfortunately, the back of the beach is littered with plastic bags, bottles etc. There is one taverna. The bottom is sandy and swimming is good.

Things To Do: Two museums in town (the Folklore Museum and the Archaeological Museum). Tours to the archaeological site on the island of Delos available every morning at 09.00. Visit the Paraportiani Church in town.

Getting Around: Virtually continuous bus service to Plati Yialos in season. Buses leave from the square at the top end of the town (there are arrowed signs at strategic places in town showing the way). The first and last buses are at 08.00 and 02.00 respectively. The trip takes about 10 minutes and costs 25 drs. one way. Buses to Elia leave from outside the entrance to the Hotel Leto (opposite the town beach) at 10.00, 11.00, 12.00, 13.00, 15.30, 16.30, 17.30 and 18.30. Return departures from Elia are 30 minutes later than these times. The trip takes about 20 minutes and costs 40 drs. one way. Previously Elia could only be reached by boat from Plati Yialos and the new bus service is quicker and cheaper. Buses to San Stefanos also leave from the Hotel Leto at 08.15, 09.00, 10.00, 11.00, 12.00, 13.00, 14.00, 15.00, 16.00, 17.00, 18.00, 19.00, 20.00, 21.00, 22.00, 23.00, 01.00 and 02.00. Return buses are 15 minutes later than these times.

Boat fares from Plati Yialos – Paradise, 32 drs.; Super Paradise, 52 drs.; Agrari and Elia, 63 drs.

Taxis available when the buses stop running. Car, jeep and moped hire in town.

Tour Operators:

MYKONOS TOWN: Aegina Club (H,R); Allsun (H); Grecian (H); Greek Sun (H,R); Manos (H,R); Olympic – Main Brochure (H,P,R); Sunmed (H,P,R,S); Thomson – 'Small and Friendly' Brochure (H); Thomson – 'Villas and Apartments' Brochure (S); Zeus (R).

PLATI YIALOS: Aegina Club (H); Freedom (H); Kypros (H); Manos (H,S); Sunvil (H).

PSARROU: Sunmed (P).

PARADISE BEACH: Freedom (Paradise Pension).

SYROS

The island is about 11 miles by 6 miles at its widest points. Southern Syros is not very attractive but the north of the island is rugged and empty with spectacular mountain scenery and isolated beaches. Tourist amenities are minimal.

Connections: Daily ferryboats to Piraeus (4½ hours), Tinos (1 hour), Mykonos (2 hours), Paros and Naxos; four times a week with Santorini, Iraklion (Crete), Andros and Rafina (3½ hours); twice weekly to Sikinos and Folegandros.

Centres: ERMOUPOLIS is the largest town in the Cyclades and is their administrative capital. It is picturesquely situated but has an unattractive port area. The port has lost much of its former importance and the town is now quiet and underpopulated. The nicest hotel in Ermoupolis is the 'B' class Hermes (tel. 0281 28011). Almost opposite the boat landing stage is a tourist office and you can obtain details of rooms to rent here. They also have details of houses which can be rented at various beaches. There are no decent beaches at Ermoupolis. At GALISSAS, a fishing village to the west of Ermoupolis, there is camping and a good, sandy beach.

Beaches: GALISSAS has a fine, sandy beach with an inexpensive taverna. A pristine whitewashed church stands on the hill which overlooks the village and the adjacent cove is used for naturism and unofficial camping. Walk along the main beach in a southerly direction before climbing a steep and rocky slope to the church. Keep left here and then carry on down an equally steep slope to the beach. ARMEOS*** is not a large beach and consists of shingle and sand. There are some trees which provide shade and there is also a valley which opens onto the beach. If you follow this valley for about a quarter of a mile you will come to a natural spring.

More isolated beaches are to be found further north and these are reputed to be the better beaches on the island and are often deserted.

Things To Do: Visit the medieval Venetian town on Ano Syros, one of the two hills at Ermoupolis.

Getting Around: Frequent buses from Ermoupolis round the south coast. Moped and car hire in Ermoupolis.

Tour Operators:
GALISSAS: Greek Sun (H).

KYTHNOS

Hilly Kythnos is one of the most primitive of the Cyclades and accommodation is limited. Fishing and farming are the main occupations and many of the locals weave baskets.

Connections: Five ferries a week with Piraeus (4 hours); four times a week with Serifos, Sifnos, Milos, Syros and Santorini; four or five times a week with Lavrion.

Centres: The capital, called CHORA or KYTHNOS, is a sleepy, picturesque village surrounded by farmland and windmills. Most tourists prefer to stay in Merichas or Loutra. MERICHAS, six miles from Chora, is one of the island's ports. It has the only modern hotel on Kythnos, the 'C' class Possidonion (0281 31244), a few tavernas and a stony beach. LOUTRA is the other port and is even quieter. Most accommodation is in rooms.

Beaches: Easily accessible (but not very sandy) beaches near Merichas, Loutra and Kanala. Other beaches are reached by a long walk and include Kolona, Fikiado, Lefkas and Episcopi.

Things To Do: Nothing to see of real interest.

Getting Around: Buses from Merichas to Loutra. Occasional bus to Kanala. One taxi.

Tour Operators:
MERICHAS: Tanntours (H).

SERIFOS
A small island with few tourist facilities. Fishing and also farming in the two fertile valleys are the main occupations. Beautiful scenery. Good if you are looking for a quiet time and enjoy walking and the simple life.

Connections: Daily with Piraeus, Kythnos, Milos and Sifnos; twice a week with Ios and Santorini.

Centres: LIVADI, the island's port, has a beach, a couple of hotels, the 'B' class Perseus Pension and the 'C' class Maistrali (0281 51220/51298/51381), and rooms to rent. In high season, late arrivals may find it difficult to find a room and it is advisable to make reservations in advance. Many of those who do not do so end up sleeping rough in one of the coves which make up Karavi Beach.

CHORA, the island's capital, is a half an hour's walk from Livadi up cobbled steps which short-cut the road. There is also a bus service. It is a pretty village of alleyways and steps with superb views over the bay. There are some rooms to rent.

Beaches: Less than 15 minutes' walk from Livadi is the fine, sandy beach at KARAVI**. To get there, walk up the steps at the southern end of the harbour (don't try to skirt around the jetty). Many people camp here and the beach is lined with the bamboo huts which they have built. The best beach on the island, however, is at PSILI AMMOS**. It is situated below and to the east of Chora. Alternatively, it can be reached by walking for 50 minutes along the shoreline from Livadi. There is a taverna behind this quiet stretch of sand.

Things To Do: Trip to caves reached by boat. Visit the Monastery of Taxiarchos.

Getting Around: An hourly bus service connects Livadi with Chora and there is a less frequent service to the villages of Megalo Livadi and Galini.

Occasional boat trips around the island in season.

Tour Operators:
LIVADI: Aegina Club (P); Freedom (P); Sunvil (P); Tanntours (P); Timsway – 'Original Holidays in Greece' Brochure (P).

SIFNOS

Sifnos is one of the greenest and most fertile of the Cyclades and its pretty scenery, good beaches and lack of commercialisation have made it a popular stopping-off point for island hoppers. Although some new building is taking place, accommodation can be difficult to find, particularly in high season.

Connections: Daily with Piraeus (5½ hours) and Serifos; four times a week with Kythnos and Milos; three times a week with Ios and Santorini.

Centres: KAMARES, the island's port, stands to one side of a bay which is flanked on either side by high, barren mountains reminiscent of a Norwegian fjord (in fact the whole of this western side of the island is quite rocky and barren). It is not a particularly attractive village. There are some rooms to rent and a few small hotels including the 'B' class Kamari Pension (0284 31641) and the 'C' class Stavros. Unofficial camping takes place under the trees on the beach. Evening entertainment centres around the tavernas and there is one disco. From Kamares a road winds its way through a pleasant valley before climbing to the series of adjacent mountain tops on which stand the villages of Petali, Exabela, Katavati, Apollonia and Artemon.

The journey to APOLLONIA, the island's capital, takes about 15 minutes by bus. It is a picturesque and typically Cycladic town with many churches and small, cobbled streets to explore. Here you will find the bank, tourist police and post office as well as boutiques selling local pottery and woven goods. The Folk Museum, in the square by the bus stop, is open in the mornings and contains furniture, textiles and other examples of local art. There are rooms to rent here, the 'B' class Apollonia Pension (0284 31490) and three small 'C' class hotels, the Anthoussa (0284 31431), the Sifnos (0284 31624) and the Sofia (0284 31238).

Two miles from Apollonia and connected to it by bus is KASTRO, the charming medieval capital of the island, where there are some rooms to rent. The village is built on a rocky outcrop with almost sheer drops to the sea on three sides. Its narrow winding streets are enclosed by the town walls (formed from the backs of houses) which have survived from Venetian times. Venetian coats of arms can still be seen on some of the houses and there are the remains of an ancient acropolis. If you want to swim, it is a 15 minutes' walk to the rocky peninsula below the town.

Also on a bus route is PLATI YIALOS, a growing resort on the south coast, with a long, sandy beach (where you can camp), tavernas, rooms to rent and the 'B' class Platis Gialos (0284 31224).

Beaches: KAMARES has a wide, well-used although clean beach of fine sand with small dunes at the back. There are showers at the town end of the beach (20 drs. charge). The bay is sheltered from the wind and the gently shelving bottom makes it suitable for children. Although mainly topless, it is possible to sunbathe nude in the dunes but you will need to cover up to swim making this a less than satisfactory location.

FAROS***, a 20 minute bus ride from Apollonia, has three small beaches of fine sand. Two of these beaches are overlooked by the harbour and a sign on one of the two tavernas here states that nudism is prohibited. The third beach is nudist. From the harbour walk a short distance back along the road towards Apollonia before climbing the steps which are to be found between two houses on the right. At the top, follow the track until you see the small beach on the right of the track and a taverna to the left (this taverna is, incidentally, very good). This is a beach of fine sand although rocks make access to the water difficult. There is unofficial camping at the back of the beach and, although the sand is mainly clean, some of those camping can't be bothered to remove their rubbish and consequently a small pile of refuse is steadily growing at the end of the campsite.

It is a 10-15 minute walk from Faros to the beach at CHRYSSOPIGI (cross the two non-nudist beaches and follow the track which leads around the cliff face). At one end of the bay stands the Monastery of Chryssopigi built, as legend has it, on a holy rock in 1650. There is also a taverna here and the clean beach of fine sand is backed by small trees which provide shade. Nude sunning is only possible from the rocks on the cliff edges.

The long, sandy beach at PLATI YIALOS is not nudist and is reported to be somewhat scruffy. It can also get very windy here.

VATHI* can only be reached by boat from Kamares. It is a small village on a bay with a couple of tavernas, a peaceful sandy beach and little else. It is one of the nicest beaches on the island and is suitable for naturism at the far end.

Things To Do: Folk Art Museum situated in the bus square in Apollonia. Open 07.00-10.00.

Getting Around: Buses from Kamares to Apollonia every hour or whenever a ferry arrives. The bus timetable is posted on the door of the Olympic Office (which is, rather illogically, at the opposite end of the village to the bus stop). There are two bus stops in Apollonia, one for buses to Kamares (in the square) and the other (around the corner) for buses to Artemon, Kastro, Faros and Plati Yialos (times of buses to these places are posted on the wall).

Boats to Vathi from Kamares three times a day (73 drs. each way). Mopeds for hire in Apollonia and Kamares.

Tour Operators:
KAMARES: Aegina Club (P); Freedom (H); Tanntours (H); Timsway – 'Original Holidays in Greece' Brochure (H).

PAROS

Although Paros, about 9 miles by 11 miles at its widest points, is less barren than Mykonos it lacks the rugged beauty of Naxos, its nearest neighbour. It is hilly rather than mountainous, very fertile, in spite of the shortage of fresh water and is mostly given over to farming (mainly the production of barley and sweet red wine).

Connections: By air – up to eight flights a day from Athens, four flights a week from Rhodes and three a week from Iraklion (Crete). By sea – daily ferry service to Piraeus (7 hours), Syros, Mykonos, Tinos, Naxos (except Sunday) and Ios (except Sunday); to Santorini on Monday, Thursday and Saturday and to Sifnos on Monday, Wednesday and Saturday; once a week to Samos and Rafina.

Centres: PARIKIA, the capital, is a large town by Cyclades standards with a very busy port. Directly opposite the landing pier is the windmill which houses the tourist police. There used to be a 'Nudity is Forbidden' sign here but this has now been replaced by one which states that 'nude bathing is permitted only on Parasporos (Parikia) and Agios Ioannis (Naousa)'. In fact, beach nudity is practised on many other beaches apparently without hindrance but this new notice is, nevertheless, a welcome sign of changing attitudes. As you face the windmill, the main road to the left leads to the hotels and beaches which border the bay north of the town while to the right the road runs south-westerly passing the restaurants that line the waterfront here. Two roads run into the town. On the left a short road passes the Post Office on the one side and a small park on the other. At the top of this road stands one of the oldest remaining churches in Greece, the lovely Ekatontapyliani (the Church of One Hundred Doors). The other of these two roads passes between two small cafes and through a square before becoming the main shopping street. This part of the town is very reminiscent of Mykonos with picturesque narrow winding streets, some pretty churches and many shops. There are numerous hotels and rooms to choose from although the town gets crowded in season and it can be difficult to find anywhere to stay. In any case, for easy access to naturist beaches, you would probably do better to stay elsewhere. There are plenty of eating places as well as discos. The most popular discos are Sirocos and Hesperides (along the waterfront) and the Magic Disco (follow the signs). There is an official campsite at Parasporos, south-west of the town (take the Pounda bus and ask to be put down at Parasporos).

NAOUSA, an attractive fishing village turned tourist resort, is about 7 miles from Parikia. It has much to recommend it as a place to stay including a good choice of accommodation (in both hotels and rooms), tavernas, a few music bars and three lively discos. There are also some superb nudist beaches as well as an official campsite (on the road to Kolimbithres).

PISO LIVADI (13 miles south of Parikia) is a small fishing village with a pretty harbour and a sandy beach. There are some rooms to rent here and a number of small hotels including the Corali (0284 41289). There is a choice of four or five places to eat, a couple of music bars and, surprisingly, a disco (Poly's Pub) which can get very lively. However, tourism is relatively low-key and Piso Livadi will appeal to those who like to get away from the bustle. Near-by is the official campsite, Camping Captain Kafkis, which is hardly used because most people camp on Pounda or other beaches close by.

After Piso Livadi, the road runs for another 2½ miles before losing its tarmacadam at DRIOS. There are a half-a-dozen hotels in Drios as well as summer houses belonging to well-off Athenians. However, other than the magnificent Chrysi Akti (Golden Beach) there is little else to recommend a stay here.

Beaches: In Parikia the beaches closest to town get crowded and are not nudist. Across the bay is KRIOS and a small boat, which leaves from the harbour near to the windmill, ferries people backwards and forwards to this beach for 100 drs. return. West of the main beach are smaller bays where peaceful co-existence between nudists and non-nudists should be possible. Approximately 2 miles west of the town is PARASPOROS*** which is signposted off the main road and which has been designated an official naturist beach. This beach has a taverna and a distinctive palm tree at one end. On windy days huge breakers build up in this bay making it possible to body surf. Close by is an official campsite, Parasporos Camping. Unfortunately, Parasporos is somewhat isolated and getting into Parikia is difficult.

The best choice of nudist beaches is to be found at Naousa. Naousa is situated at the bottom of a huge bay and from the quayside boats ply to the beaches of Kolimbithres, Agios Ioannis (better known as Monastiri), Langeri and Santa Maria. KOLIMBITHRES (which means basins in Greek) is a mass of strange rock formations interspersed with small, sandy coves. Although there is occasional nudism here, the largest bay is used by Greek families and is not suitable. Further around the bay is the island's other official naturist beach, MONASTIRI***. It is an easy scramble over the rocks from where the boats land to this narrow beach of fine sand. It is situated in a well-sheltered bay which offers protection when the prevailing north-westerly wind is blowing. The bottom is sandy and the water remains waist deep for some distance offshore making it safe for children. There is no natural shade although there is a taverna at one end of the beach. The beach is well used and is mainly nudist. On either side of Monastiri are other sandy beaches which can be used for nudism. One is reached by walking in the opposite direction from the boat landing stage (to the right) passing the taverna (which is, incidentally, very good). To reach the other, walk across Monastiri and follow the track passing a boatyard. The beach is just a little further on. The cost of the 20 minute boat trip to Monastiri is 120 drs. return. Boats for Kolimbithres and Monastiri leave the quayside in Naousa every half an hour between 10.30 and 14.00 and then every hour until 18.00. Alternatively it is possible to drive around the bay to both Kolimbithres and Monastiri. On the opposite side of the bay is LANGERI**. This is a longer boat trip from Naousa or, if you are feeling energetic, you can walk here in an hour. Boats leave at 10.30, 11.30 and 12.30 and return at 15.00 and 17.00. The cost of the round trip is 150 drs. Langeri will appeal to those who dream about being cast away on a desert island. There are no facilities of any kind – just a long stretch of sandy beach. Nudists use the far end and here dunes of fine sand surround secluded little coves of crystal-clear water where pine trees provide welcome shade from the heat of the day. On the other side of the same peninsula is the beach known as SANTA MARIA. This can be reached by boat from Naousa (leaves at 11.00 and returns at 17.00) or by bus which leaves town every day at 10.15 and 11.15 (tickets are available from the Caterina Simidji Tourist Agency in the village square). This long beach has a taverna and signs stating that bathing in the nude and camping are strictly prohibited. A dirt road runs along the back of the beach and if you turn right onto it and walk for about a half a mile you will see a track on the right (drivable) which leads to the pretty beach of fine sand known as PLATIS AMMOS*. While this beach cannot be claimed to be nudist, it should be possible to enjoy nudity at the far end (the end furthest away from the track which leads onto the beach) provided that you are prepared to have the courage of your convictions. There is a taverna at the back of the beach which is hidden among the trees.

PISO LIVADI has a sandy beach (not nudist). A quarter of a mile to the south is LOGARAS, a nice sandy beach although a rocky shelf just below the waterline makes entry into the sea difficult in some places. There are a couple of tavernas here and some camping sauvage at the back of the beach. At the far end, a track leads up over the hillside and down to POUNDA*** (20 minutes' walk from Piso Livadi). This is a smaller bay of fine sand with a gently shelving bottom. Entrance to the sea is made difficult by rocks under the waterline at one end but at the other (closest to the path leading onto the beach) the bottom is completely sandy. A row of trees in front of one of the two tavernas provides shade and there is nudity for the whole length of this beach (even in front of the taverna). In spite of the fact that many people camp on the beach, the sand is very clean. The beach is visited by the police from time-to-time (probably at the behest of Captain Kafkis, who owns the official campsite down the road and who must be feeling pretty 'miffed' that the tourist boom is passing him by). The constabulary arrive heralded by much banging of doors and even tooting of horns. This gives the whole beach just enough time to cover up their 'naughty bits'. The law then have stern words with the campers (some, who are not in the 'know', even begin to take their tents down) before departing. The tents stay in situ and the beach gets on with 'business as usual' until the next performance of this charade. Pounda can also be reached by means of a track (drivable) off the main road from Piso Livadi to Drios. From Pounda a footpath follows the shore to the very long beach at MEZADHA (about 10 minutes' walk) and on to TZIRDAKIA (another 10 minutes) before reaching the magnificent, long, sandy beach at CHRYSI AKTI (Golden Beach)***. Alternatively, the Drios bus stops close by (ask for Chrysi Akti – the beach is a short walk down a track from the bus stop). There are a couple of small hotels and a taverna at one end of the beach and another taverna part way along. The beach is used for nudism a little way after passing this second taverna. The sandy bottom shelves gently and swimming is safe. Windsurfers can be hired and there is some unofficial camping at the back of this very wide beach. There is no natural shade. If, when you walk down onto the beach, you turn right and continue walking to the end, you will see that it is possible to walk along the water's edge beneath some low cliffs. There are a series of sandy inlets here where, when the main beach is too windy, you may be sufficiently protected to enjoy nude sunning.

Things To Do: Visit the Ekatontapyliani Church (but make sure that your shoulders are well covered or incur the wrath of the nun who stands sentinel). Open 07.00-12.00 and 16.00-20.00 daily. Unfortunately, the church is surrounded on three sides by less attractive additions and the best view is to be had from the grounds of the High School which is behind and to the left of the top of the square from which you gain entrance to the church. Visit Lefkes, located high above the sea and one of the loveliest villages on Paros and its capital in medieval times. Also worthy of a visit and near to Piso Livadi are the close trio of villages of Marmara, Marpissa and Prodhromos where village life continues largely unaffected by tourism and where visitors are still something of a novelty. Excursions to Antiparos and to Petaloudes (no self-respecting Greek island can be without its Valley of the Butterflies).

Getting Around: The island has a good road network although road surfaces can be bad in places. Bus schedules are posted in front of the tourist police's windmill on the harbour-front in Parikia. A list of hotels is also displayed here. Buses from Parikia to Pounda (for the ferry to Antiparos) run at 08.00, 10.00, 12.00, 14.00, 16.00 and 19.00. Buses in the opposite direction run at the same times. Buses from Parikia to Naousa run at 08.00, 09.00, 10.00, 10.30, 11.30, 12.00 and every hour on the hour until 20.00. Return trips at 07.30, 08.30, 09.30, 10.30, 11.00, 11.30, 12.00, 12.30, 13.30 and every hour on the half hour until 20.30. The trip takes half an hour. Buses to Marmara, Prodhromos, Piso Livadi and Drios leave Parikia at 08.00 and then every hour on the hour until 18.00. Return trips at 07.30, 09.00 and then every hour on the hour until 19.00. The trip to Piso Livadi takes about one hour. Bicycle and moped hire in Parikia, Naousa and Drios. Cars and jeeps for hire in Parikia and Naousa.

Tour Operators:
NAOUSSA: Aegina Club (H); Club 18-30 (R); Grecian (H,S); Sunmed (H,P,R,S); Sunvil (S); Tanntours (P).

PISO LIVADI: Freedom (H); Greek Sun (P); Sunvil (H); Ventura (H,R,S).
DRIOS: Tanntours (H).

ANTIPAROS

The satellite island of Antiparos, about 3 miles by 7 miles at its widest points, lies off the west coast of Paros. The island is rugged and undeveloped and most of the 540 inhabitants live in the village where the ferry docks (also known as Antiparos).

Connections: Antiparos can be reached by caique from Parikia on Paros. These boats run regularly between 08.00 and 17.00 (check the schedules posted on the boats themselves) and the trip takes about 40 minutes. Alternatively, you can take the bus to Pounda where there is a frequent ferry service across the channel to Antiparos.

Centres: The village of ANTIPAROS has several small hotels including the 'C' class Chrysi Akti (0284 61286) and two 'D' class hotels, the Anarghyros (0284 61206) and the Madalena (0284 61227). There are also some rooms to rent. Nightlife centres around a few bars, tavernas and several open air discos. There is an official campsite 10 minutes' walk to the north and signposts mark the path from the village. There is a small cafe here and good sanitary facilities as well as a naturist beach close by.

Beaches: There is a modest beach near to where the boats dock in the village. SIFNAIKOS YIALOS** is close to the official campsite (see above) and is one of the best beaches on the island. Other beaches accessible on foot include LIVADHI BAY* (a 40 minute walk west of the village) and AGIOS GEORGIOS* (a walk of over 5 miles to the south-west).

Things To Do: Visit the island's famous cave. Excursion boats leave from the village at 09.30, 10.30 and 11.30 or you can walk there (two hours). The easiest way of ascending the 540 feet from sea-level to the entrance of the cave is by donkey (at a cost of about 200 drs.). From the top there are splendid views to the near-by islands of Ios, Sikinos and Folegandros. The 300 foot descent into the cave used to be made with the aid of ropes and candles but now 400 concrete steps and electric lights have made the descent safer, if more prosaic. The stalactites and stalagmites, which are the cave's main attraction, have been covered with graffiti and even Lord Byron is supposed to have left his mark.

Getting Around: There is no public transport on the island and all excursions are on foot or by boat.

Tour Operators:
ANTIPAROS VILLAGE: Manos (H,S); Olympic – Main Brochure (H,S).

NAXOS

Naxos is the largest island in the Cyclades group being about 19 miles by 15 miles at its widest points. It is also one of the most beautiful. A great deal of farming takes place in its rich valleys, particularly the cultivation of lemon trees. Unlike many islands, Naxos does not need to rely on tourists for its survival and virtually no concessions are made to the tourist trade. It will appeal to those who are content with the simple pleasures of life – sunning, swimming, walking and enjoying the beautiful scenery.

Connections: Daily to Piraeus (8 hours), Paros (1 hour), Syros, Ios and Santorini; less frequently to Folegandros, Iraklion (Crete), Astipalea, Kalymnos and Rhodes; once a week to Rafina; tourist boat every day to Mykonos.

Centres: There are two main centres, Naxos town and Apollon. NAXOS town waterfront is unappealing but don't be put off by this. Behind are colourful streets winding up to the Venetian fortress. It is extremely hard to find single rooms in Naxos town (without paying for a double) and often the only place to find a room at all is in the newer part of town behind the harbour. There are a number of hotels, the most attractively situated being the 'B' class Ariadne (0285 22452). The 'C' class Aegeon (0285 22852) is also worthy of mention because single rooms are available here.

There are rooms to rent at APOLLON, a small fishing village with two beaches and several tavernas.

Beaches: AGIA ANNA*** is well used by naturists in spite of signs on the beach stating 'Nudism Forbidden'. Turn left and walk along the sand past the church and around the point. Here the sandy beach stretches for miles and few people wear clothes. If you turn in the opposite direction and walk for 15 minutes you will come to AGIOS PROKOPIS***, the tiny port of Agia Anna. The sandy beach here is also predominantly nudist.

The beach at PIRGAKI*** can be reached by walking the 9 miles from Agia Anna but it's easier by bus. There's a taverna near to where the bus stops. The sandy beach is interspersed with rocky coves and stretches for about 4 miles to Panagia Gialous and most people don't bother with clothes.

There is a small beach at APOLLON**. Part is too near to the village for nudism although people do use the far end. Unfortunately, it is very stony here and is not a good choice in view of the other excellent beaches.

Some of Naxos's most secluded beaches are on the east coast and are accessible only by car or on two wheels (great care required). Try MOUTSOUNA*, AGIOS ARTEMIOS* and PSILI AMMOS*.

Things To Do: It would be a pity to visit Naxos without seeing some of the interior of this lovely island. This is best achieved by hiring a car, motorcycle or moped (but you should be an experienced rider in the case of the latter two). Alternatively, you can take the bus and, as there are five buses a day, it is possible to break your journey and linger awhile before catching the next one. During the first hour of the ride the road climbs from the coastal plain through richly cultivated mountainsides before reaching one of Naxos's prettiest villages, Chalki. It is here that the Tragea begins – a magnificent olive grove spreading along the terraced valley. The next stop is Filoti, the largest town in the region, which is overshadowed by Mount Zas (or Zeus). The mountain rises to 3,200 feet and is the highest peak in the Cyclades. 15 minutes further on is Apiranthos, another small village with a traditional arts museum and from here to Komiaki, an hour's drive away, the land, terraced and planted with fruit and olive trees, falls away dramatically with magnificent views of the valleys far below. Past Koronos the road descends via a series of spectacular hair-pin bends to the charming fishing village of Apollon. In a near-by marble quarry you can see the famous kouros – a huge, recumbent, marble statue of Apollo, which was abandoned unfinished by the sculptor, probably following the discovery of a flaw. To reach it from the village, walk back along the main road (in the opposite direction to the beach) and turn right by a small sign which states 'kouros'. It is a 20 minute hike to the statue from here.

A boat trip from Naxos town to Apollon (stopping for three hours at a beach en route) leaves daily at 08.00.

Getting Around: Four or fives buses daily to Agia Anna. The first leaves at 10.00 and the last one back is at 17.00. The trip takes about 30 minutes and costs 28 drs., one way. The bus journey to Pirgaki takes about an hour and costs 45 drs. The last bus back to town is a bit early at 16.00. The first bus to Apollon leaves at 08.00 and the last one is at 14.00. Caiques to Agia Anna leave from the harbour hourly between 08.30 and 19.30. Car, moped and bicycle hire in Naxos town.

Tour Operators:
NAXOS TOWN: Aegina Club (H,P); Freedom (H,P,S); Greek Sun (H,P,R,S); Manos (H,S); Olympic – Main Brochure (H,P); Sunvil (H,P,S); Tanntours (H); Timsway – 'Original Holidays in Greece' Brochure (H,S); Ventura (H,R,S).

AMORGOS

Amorgos is an island of impressive mountains and sheer cliffs. Roads are so bad (or non-existent) that it is, effectively, almost two islands and the easiest way to get from north to south is by boat. Surprisingly, it is well visited, being especially popular with the Germans, so that it can often get very crowded.

Connections: By boat – daily with Naxos; twice a week with Piraeus (11 hours), Astipalea, Symi and Rhodes (9 hours); once a week with Rafina (10 hours), Paros, Tinos, Kos and Kalymnos.

Centres: KATAPOLA, the main port, is charming with rooms to rent and the Pension Amorgos (0285 71214). Unofficial camping takes place on the town beach but for long-term stays, head up to Panteleimon Beach (a cove to the left of the town).

CHORA, a bus ride away (or 40 minutes' walk), is a typical, white Cycladic town with a line of windmills stretching out to the cliffs which tower more than 1,000 feet above the sea. In summer the town gets so busy that the two restaurants are permanently packed and people sleep in the streets. A road has been built to the Monastery of Hosoviotissa, a startling white fortress of a place at the bottom of a 200 foot high orange cliff. Inside are fifty rooms and just three monks.

EGIALI, the island's second port, is in the north of the island. It is pleasant here with rooms to rent and one ten room hotel, the 'C' class Mike (0285 71247).

Beaches: It is a 20 minute scramble (head down the hill to the right of the path which leads to the monastery and cut across the road where it doubles back on itself) to AGIA ANNA**, a spectacular beach of white pebbles. To the right is a much bigger beach than the first cove and here nudity and unofficial camping are commonplace. There is also unofficial camping at EGIALI*, on the northern tip of Amorgos and it should be possible to go unclothed on this long, sandy beach. Near-by is the harbour town of ORMOS and a short hike along the cliffs opposite brings you to isolated, sandy coves which offer opportunities for acquiring an all-over tan in complete solitude. Other beaches are at AGIOS PANTELEIMON, KATO AKROTIRI and AGIA PARASKEVI.

Things To Do: See the Hosoviotissa Monastery (see above).

Getting Around: An aged bus runs between Katapola and Chora; boats to other places on the island.

IOS

Although Ios, about 11½ miles long and 5 miles wide, is a barren, arid island, it has much to recommend it including many sandy beaches where nudity is commonplace. In recent years the island's character has undergone something of a metamorphosis. In the 1960's it was known as a hippy island – living was cheap but accommodation was spartan and food was generally poor. After the demise of 'flower power' the island continued to be popular with a cosmopolitan and mainly young set attracted by the easy ambience and low prices. In the last few years Ios has entered the mainstream of mass tourism and package tour operators have tended to swamp the island with a predominance of British and, surprisingly, Irish tourists. This has brought the advantages of better accommodation and a huge improvement in the standard of food. Unfortunately, the last few years have also seen problems with noise, theft, litter and other anti-social behaviour. Nevertheless, Ios is cheaper than many other islands with beautiful beaches, a charming town and swinging nightlife and, for many, the island possesses a magical quality which attracts them back year after year.

Connections: Daily to Piraeus (10 hours), Santorini (2 hours), Naxos (3 hours), Paros (5 hours) and Syros. Almost daily boats to Mykonos. Three times a week to Iraklion (Crete); less frequently to Folegandros, Milos, Kimolos, Sifnos and Serifos.

Centres: Visitors' first sight of Ios is from GIALOS (the port). Gialos is somewhat characterless as well as being more expensive than the town. However, almost all the hotel accommodation is at sea-level and in Gialos you will find two 'C' class hotels – the Armadoros (0286 91201) and the Flisvos (0286 91315). Part-way up the hill, between the harbour and the town, is the 'C' class Homer's Inn (0286 91365).

IOS town is picturesquely situated on a hillside overlooking the sea. It is connected to Gialos by road although the village itself is pedestrian, being a myriad of passageways only wide enough to allow donkeys to pass. In these whitewashed alleyways you will find restaurants, tavernas and boutiques as well as scores of bars and discos. Hotels include the 'C' class Phillippou (0286 91290) and there are also rooms to rent including those belonging to Anna Metou (0286 91445). They are situated above the Deja Vu Cafe (immediately behind the post office). There is no shortage of bars and discos and nightlife is frenetic. Part way down the hill is the Ios Club. This is an open-air disco which plays classical music from 19.00 until sunset. You can enjoy a magnificent view of the bay and maybe a spectacular sunset while listening to perhaps Brahms or Debussy.

During the day most people head for Mylopotas Beach (25 minutes' walk from town or by frequent bus service) and you could consider staying here. The 'C' class Hotel Delfini (0286 91341) stands nearly on the beach and close by is the Pension Galaxy. There are two campsites on the beach, Camping Stars (0286 91302) and the Soulis Campground (the more attractive of the two). People also camp unofficially on Mylopotas in spite of periodic police action. To the east of the harbour in Gialos is one of the best campsites to be found on any Greek island. Ios Camping (0286 91329) charges 100 drs. per person per night including hot water for showers and washing clothes. There is a self-service cafeteria, restaurant and bar with a small disco. Tents can be rented for an extra 100 drs. per person.

Ios tends to get crowded in summer and if you experience difficulty in finding accommodation you should try the tourist police in the town or the 'Akteio' travel agents in Gialos.

Beaches: There are numerous beaches on the island ranging from huge bays to tiny coves and beach nudity is widely practised and accepted. MYLOPOTAS***, the biggest beach, is a beautiful bay of coarse, yellow sand. After the first 50 yards or so nudity is commonplace, although the beach becomes 'clothed' again at the end (50-75 yards before the Dracos Taverna). A number of large tavernas front the beach (and play pop music all day) and there is also a windsurfing school with pedeloes and canoes for hire.

If you walk along the rocky headland path (north-west of the town) you will pass a number of small coves before reaching COUMBARA BEACH***.

Reports suggest that this pleasant, sandy cove is about 50% nudist and 50% clothed and that it tends to be affected by litter. There is a taverna here.

Caiques run to MANGANARI BAY**, on the south coast, where you can find your own idyllic sandy cove.

Other beaches are accessible to hardy walkers including the superb and usually deserted beaches at THEODOTIS BAY** (3½ hours' walk from town) and KALAMOS BAY**. These beaches are both on the east coast.

Things To Do: No places to visit of real interest. At 10.00 on Wednesdays a boat leaves the harbour to circumnavigate the island, stopping at various beaches on the way. Excursion to the islands of Sikinos and Folegandros.

Getting Around: Buses leave the port for Mylopotas (stopping at Ios town on the way) at intervals of approximately 15 minutes (or when the bus is full). Cost – 30 drs., one way. Boat every day at 10.00 from the port to Manganari Bay returning at 18.00, 400 drs. return. A jeep trip to Theodotis Bay sets out at 10.00 every day and returns in the afternoon (you will need to book 1-2 days in advance).

Tour Operators:
GIALOS: Aegina Club (H); Freedom (H,P); Grecian (H,P); Intasun – 'Plain and Simple' Brochure (H); Manos (H); Olympic – Main Brochure (H); Sunmed (H,P,R); Sunvil (H,P); Tanntours (P,R); Timsway – 'Original Holidays in Greece' Brochure (H,P).
MYLOPOTAS: Intasun – 'Plain and Simple' Brochure (H); Sunmed (P,R).

SIKINOS

Sikinos is less desolate than it first appears and will appeal to those seeking genuine island life and solitude.

Connections: By boat – once a week to Piraeus (10½ hours) via Syros; daily to Ios and Folegandros.

Centres: SIKINOS is the only village of any size. It is a charming place with a few rooms and a couple of tavernas.

Beaches: No reports of naturism although there are some peaceful beaches including a fine one at SPILIA.

Things To Do: Very little. There is a monastery and a ruined castle but no other places to visit.

Getting Around: No public transport. Mule ride from the harbour to the village, walk elsewhere.

KIMOLOS

Kimolos is a rugged, barren island. Most of the population live on the south coast where it is greener. Unsophisticated and undeveloped, Kimolos will appeal to those who are seeking peace and tranquillity and who are prepared to rough it a little.

Connections: By boat – twice a week with Piraeus (6 hours) via Sifnos, Serifos and Kythnos; twice daily caique to Pollonia on Milos.

Centres: Visitors have to be ferried by caique from the larger ships into the harbour at Psathi. Most of the island's accommodation is in the small village of CHORA, 15 minutes' walk up from Psathi. There are only about fifty beds for visitors on the whole island.

Beaches: No reports – although the island has fine, sandy beaches. There are shady, peaceful beaches near to Chora and other beaches at ALIKI, BOUNATSA, MAVRO SPILIA and KLIMA.

Things To Do: Very little, except relax.

Getting Around: No public transport.

MILOS

Milos, about 9 miles by 14 miles at its widest points, is one of the more prosperous of the Cyclades islands. It is rich in mineral deposits of all kinds and the mining, processing and exporting of minerals including obsidian (a glassy volcanic rock which was first exported from Milos in prehistoric times) is the basis of this relative prosperity. Although barren, Milos has some dramatic scenery which is also a legacy from its volcanic past. There are weirdly shaped rock formations of different hues like the Arkoudes (on the left of the huge bay as you arrive by boat) which rear up from the sea like two wrestling bears and the Glaronissia (Gull Islands) with lava formations which look like massed organ pipes. Another geological novelty is the pure white lunar landscape of Sarakiniko which was formed by volcanic pumice fragments some two or three million years ago. Milos is nearly bisected by a huge bay on the eastern side of which, completely hidden from the open sea, stands Adamas, the island's port. The western half of the island is dominated by Mount Profitis Elias (2,461 feet high) and poor roads make access to this part of the island difficult.

Connections: Two flights a day from Athens (three on Tuesdays and Saturdays). By boat – daily with Piraeus (5½ hours); four times a week with Sifnos (2 hours), Serifos and Kythnos; three times a week with Ios and Santorina; twice weekly with Iraklion on Crete (8 hours), Siros and Folegandros.

Centres: The port of ADAMAS is a small, unremarkable town with a concrete jetty at which freighters wait to be loaded with tons of rock from lorries. These lorries use the main road along the harbour front and, in the mornings, the road is sprayed with water to counteract the dust. Most of the accommodation is here in rooms and some hotels including the 'B' class Hotel Venus Village (0287 41770) and the 'B' class Chronis Bungalows (0287 41625). There are about eight tavernas offering the usual Greek dishes as well as one or two fast food establishments serving pizzas, burgers, etc. Nightlife is centred around the tavernas although there are three or four music bars and two discos. One disco is on the road to Plaka (a 10 minute walk uphill) and the other is at the back of Lagada Beach (in front of the Venus Village Hotel on the outskirts of town).

The villages of Pera Triovassalos, Triovassalos, Plakes, Plaka and Trypiti are all grouped together on a hilltop north of Adamas (10 minutes by bus). The nicest of these is PLAKA which is also the island's capital. There are two museums here, the Archaeological Museum (near the bus stop) and the Folklore Museum. Both are closed on Tuesday, Wednesday and Sunday and, of the two, the Folklore Museum is much more interesting. The greatest attraction, however, is the magnificent view (especially at sunset) from the Venetian Kastro which stands above the village. There are a few rooms to rent in Plaka although there is hardly anywhere to eat and most tourists stay in Adamas. Between Plaka and Trypiti, a small winding road descends to the charming fishing village of Klima. The road down passes the modern entrance to some early Christian catacombs. A path from the catacombs leads to the place where the Venus de Milo was found and on to a small Roman amphitheatre which has the sea for a back-cloth.

The only other place of note is POLLONIA, a quiet fishing village on the north-eastern tip of the island. Pollonia has one main street which follows the curve of a very pretty half-moon shaped bay. There are rooms to rent and two tavernas. The beach consists of fine sand and to the west people camp among the trees (in spite of signs prohibiting this).

Beaches: LAGADA is the nearest beach to Adamas. It is located on the western edge of town (to the right as you face the sea) in front of the extensive Venus Village Hotel. The beach consists of dirty-looking sand (although it is not dirty) and trees at the back provide shade. There is no taverna here although watersports, including waterskiing, are available and there is a rather smelly toilet at one end of the beach. This beach is not suitable for nudism. However, immediately behind the toilet is a path and if you follow this along the side of the cliff you will come to a small pebble beach at BOMBARDA** which is used for unofficial camping and where nudity seems to be the norm. Although the beach is not very comfortable to lie on it does have the advantages of being very quiet and secluded and is within easy walking distance from Adamas (10-15 minutes). Close by is a marble monument to the French soldiers and sailors who lost their lives on Milos during the Crimean War (1854-56).

From Plaka it is a pleasant walk to the sandy bay at PLATHIENA* where some people do not bother to wear clothes.

PALEOCHORI** is situated on the south coast, a 30 minute bus ride from Adamas. The road is tarmacadamed only as far as the small village of Zefiria after which a bumpy track winds its way to the coast. There are some nasty bends and near vertical drops and it would seem that a bus could never negotiate this route although it does – three times a day! This journey is not recommended for two-wheeled transport. The magnificent beach at Paleochori is backed by tall cliffs which offer protection from the prevailing northerly winds thus ensuring that the sea remains calm even on windy days. The beach is a mixture of fine shingle and pebbles and is very clean and free from rocks. There are two tavernas close to the bus stop and there are toilets here. The beach close to the tavernas is mainly topless. Walk along the beach to the right until you reach a tunnel which leads through the cliff-face. Wade through here (the water is knee-deep in places) to a less populous cove where nudity can be enjoyed. The beach consists of the same fine shingle as the main beach. The far end of the main beach is also suitable for nudism although it can be a tiring walk on the loose shingle. There is no shade or watersport facilities on either of these beaches.

PROVATAS*** is also on the south coast but can only be reached by hired transport. Follow the main road from Adamas around the bay and past the airport. Before reaching Hivadolimni, a dirt track branches off on the left to Provatas (easier for two-wheeled transport than the one to Paleochori). The easiest and most comfortable way to get to Provatas is by taxi. The driver will arrange to pick you up again later in the day and, as you don't pay for the trip until the return journey, you can be certain that he will reappear. The trip takes 20 minutes and costs 700 drs. return. The track emerges onto a fertile plain before reaching a small clearing at the top of a cliff. A path on the left leads down from here to a beach which is used by locals and which is only topless. The track continues along the cliff-top and there is a taverna part way along which serves drinks and simple food. From the track paths lead down the cliffs (exercise care, some of these paths are very steep) to three smaller coves all of which have beautiful fine sand and safe swimming although there is no natural shade. The protective cliffs enable you to enjoy nudity here even on windy days.

Other sandy beaches in the Bay of Milos are to be found at HIVADOLIMNI, RIVARI (a lagoon with a long, sandy beach which divides it from the sea) and to the east of Rivari, PHATOURENA. No reports of naturism at any of these locations.

Things To Do: Archaeological and Folklore Museums in Plaka (closed Tuesday, Wednesday and Sunday). Catacombs at Klima (a short walk from Plaka or ask for Trypiti if you go by bus), open 09.00 to 13.00 and 16.00 to 18.00. Roman amphitheatre near-by. From Pollonia by boat to Glaronissia (Gull Islands).

Getting Around: Buses to Plaka every hour. Journey takes 15-20 minutes, fare 20 drs. Buses to Pollonia three times a day. Journey takes 20-30 minutes, fare 40 drs. Buses to Paleochori three times a day. Journey takes 30 minutes, fare 30 drs. Bus timetables and taxi tariffs are posted in Adamas town square. Car, moped and bicycle hire in Adamas (the mountainous western end of the island is designated 'out of bounds' by hire companies because of the dangerous roads). Boat trips from Pollonia to Glaronissia, Kimolos and the Papafrangas Caves. Boat from Adamas to Rivari (prior arrangement with the boatman required) or by boat to Empourios and walk to Rivari (20 minutes). From Adamas to Klima, Arkoudes and Plathiena by boat. Return by same boat or walk from Plathiena to Plaka and from there by bus or taxi to Adamas.

Tour Operators:
ADAMAS: Aegina Club (H,S); Amathus (H); Freedom (H); Greek Sun (H); Sunvil (H); Tanntours (H,R); Timsway – 'Original Holidays in Greece' Brochure (H).

FOLEGANDROS

The cliffs of Folegandros rise sheer from the sea and are up to 1,000 feet high in places. The interior is rugged and barren and there are few tourists. A good place for escapists.

Connections: By boat – twice weekly with Piraeus (12 hours) and Syros; daily with Sikinos and Ios (45 minutes); several times a week with Santorini.

Centres: CHORA, the capital, is a pretty village set high above the sea. Here is the 'E' class Danassis. There are also a few rooms to rent and, on the outskirts of the village (on the side furthest from the harbour) another hotel, the Fani-Vevis.

Beaches: Some nudism at both Livadi and Angali. LIVADI** is in the next bay to the harbour at Karavostassis. It is sandy although rubbish dumped among the trees detracts from what would otherwise be a very nice beach. ANGALI** is down a clearly marked track to the left of the road from Chora to Mera and Agios Georgios. It has a taverna and some rooms to rent as well as donkeys for the fairly stiff climb back to the road.

Things To Do: Very little.

Getting Around: There are buses between the island's port Karovostassis and Chora. Some of these go beyond Chora to Mera.

SANTORINI (THIRA)

The island is about 10 miles by 7 miles at its widest points. The approach by sea is breathtakingly spectacular. Fira, the island's picturesque capital, perches on top of 900 foot high cliffs at the bottom of which most of the ferryboats dock (some ferries, especially the Saturday evening boat from Ios, dock at Athinios further down the coast. An inconvenient place when more passengers disembark than can fit into the solitary bus or the few taxis to town). The town is reached by climbing a zigzagging staircase of five hundred and eighty-seven steps cut into the rock. The ascent can be made either on foot (if you are travelling light), by donkey or chairlift.

Santorini as it appears today is the result of a cataclysmic earthquake which occurred three thousand five hundred years ago. In about 1520 B.C. the original island was blown apart by a massive volcanic eruption. This not only wiped out every single living thing on Santorini but the explosion also caused a tidal wave estimated to be three hundred feet high which wiped out the Minoan civilisation on Crete, seventy miles to the south. There is a theory that Santorini was the site of the legendary lost city of Atlantis.

Santorini is a must on every cruise ship's itinerary and the fact that it is so spectacular makes it well worth a visit. However, once you have experienced the spectacular views there is little else to do. The nudist beaches at Kamari and Perissa are away from the main town and involve a lengthy bus ride. Both of these resorts are small and uninspiring. You should try to see Santorini but will probably find that a two or three day stay is sufficient.

Connections: By air – direct flights available from the U.K., up to three flights a day from Athens, daily flights from Mykonos, four flights a week from Iraklion (Crete) and three a week from Rhodes. By sea – daily with Piraeus (10-12 hours), Paros, Ios and Naxos; four times a week with Iraklion, Crete (5 hours); frequently by small boat to Sikinos and Folegandros; once a week with Agios Nikolaos and Sitia (Crete), Karpathos and Rhodes.

Centres: FIRA is the main town with stupendous views, tourist shops, tavernas, restaurants and some nightlife. There are numerous rooms to rent – turn to the right just before you reach the top of the steps from the boat landing stage and follow the path along the edge of the cliffs to the southern end of the town. The majority of rooms are here. Most are pretty spartan and some have no washing facilities in the rooms at all. Hotels can be expensive by island standards – budget choices are the Lygnus (0286 22045) and the Antonio Roussou (0286 22502). Both are to the east of the town's main square. There is a youth hostel about two hundred yards north on the road to Ia. The police (who are situated near to the Olympic Airways office) and Damingos Tours (in the square) are helpful. Before leaving the subject of Fira, a word of warning about the five hundred and eighty-seven steps! Even the descent can be tiring in the heat of the day and the smell of donkey droppings can be nauseating (the steps are swept but the cobbles make this a difficult task and, in any case, the sweepings are simply chucked over the walls). If you must try the steps – walk down and get the chairlift back – it is expensive at 180 drs. one way but it's worth every drachma!

IA is a small town clinging to the rocky cliffs a half-hour bus ride north of Fira. The town was partly destroyed and abandoned after the 1956 earthquake although many of the oldest houses have since been restored by the Greek National Tourist Organisation. The town is picture-postcard pretty and is a perfect example of a Cycladic village in its purest form. The cliffs are honeycombed with ancient caves in which people used to live and precarious steps lead down to the rocky beach at Amoudi where you can swim in a lagoon surrounded by floating pumice stones. Ia is a little off the beaten tourist track making accommodation both cheap and plentiful. Hotels include the 'D' class

Hotel Fregada (0286 71221), which is situated right on the cliff-face, and the 'E' class Hotel Anemones (0286 71220). The Greek National Tourist Organisation has an office in the main street and you can rent houses here.

KAMARI is a small, modern resort favoured by package tour operators. Nightlife consists of three music bars. The Kamari Beach Pension is situated right on the beach and is a good 'C' class hotel (0286 31243).

PERISSA is also small with a few rooms but abundant space for camping. Camping also takes place at the remote MONOLITHOS BEACH and here are the pleasant Kostas Bungalows (0286 22211).

Beaches: All the beaches on Santorini consist of black volcanic grit. Nudists are to be found at Kamari, situated approximately four miles from Fira, at Perissa and at Monolithos.

At KAMARI** the best stretch of beach is close to the village and is not frequented by nudists. They are to be found further along, past the last taverna, but here the beach consists of large pebbles and is uncomfortable. Not recommended.

PERISSA*** is a better beach of fine volcanic grit which is really just like sand to lie on. This is a long stretch of beach and nudists are to be found all the way along except for that part of the beach which is bordered by the road.

MONOLITHOS** on the east coast has a long, empty beach which is used by both nudists and campers.

Things To Do: Archaeological Museum in Fira, open 09.00-15.00 (Sunday, 09.00-13.00), closed Tuesdays. The excavations at Akrotiri (open 09.00-19.00, Sundays 09.00-14.00) are impressive. Like Pompeii, Akrotiri had been preserved under layers of volcanic ash and when it was excavated in 1967 a flourishing Bronze Age city, with a population estimated to be 30,000 or more, was revealed. The whole site has been covered with a protective roof which gives one the peculiar impression of being in a huge warehouse. Here you can see paved streets lined with one-, two-, and three-storey houses, their wooden framed doors and windows still intact. Most of the relics which have been found, including some brilliantly coloured frescoes, have been removed to the National Archaeological Museum in Athens (although a new museum is being built to house them on Santorini and they will shortly be returned).

Trips to the splendidly situated monastery on top of Profitis Elias (the island's highest mountain at 1,600 feet). There are magnificent views from up here (especially at sunset) but you will have to try to ignore the radar station which also shares the peak. Visitors are free to wander around the chapels, workshops and cells of the monks and cover-ups are thoughtfully provided for those who are considered to be inappropriately dressed. The museum (open 08.00 to 13.00 and 15.00 to 18.00, Monday to Saturday) contains a fascinating exhibition of old paintings and monastic crafts and manuscripts.

From Kamari there are daily mule excursions to Ancient Thira, situated on a mountain-top peninsula, or you can walk there in 30 minutes by following the track from either Perissa or Kamari. Although the ruins are impressively large they are difficult to recognise without a guide book (on sale in Fira). Site open 09.00-15.00 Monday to Saturday, Sunday 09.00-13.00.

Daily boat trips around the island and excursions to the smoking volcano (it last erupted in 1956) on near-by Nea Kameni island. Many people will enjoy this trip – but take a stout pair of shoes. You will be left to make your own way from the boat landing stage up to the top. The path is steep and rough in places and it's hot. The old and infirm would be well advised to give this trip a miss. There are some good views but don't expect to see molten lava leaping into the air. You'll have to settle for wisps of sulphurous smoke seeping from the rocks.

Getting Around: Buses leave Fira from the little square on the opposite side of town to the cliffs. Schedules are posted here although buses usually leave when they are full irrespective of advertised times. Buses run eight times a day to Akrotiri and nine times a day (between 09.30 and 22.30) to Ia. In season, there are two or three buses every hour to Kamari and one an hour to Perissa (first 07.00, last 22.00). Less frequent bus service to Monolithos. Roads on the island are good. Jeep and moped hire in Fira.

Tour Operators:
KAMARI: Aegina Club (P); Avra (P,R,S); Freedom (H); Grecian (H,P,R,S); Intasun – 'Plain and Simple' Brochure (P,S,T); Manos (P,S,T); Olympic – Main Brochure (H,P,S); Sunmed (H,P,R,S); Sunvil (H); Tanntours (H); Timsway – 'Original Holidays in Greece' Brochure (H,P).
PERISSA: Allsun (H).

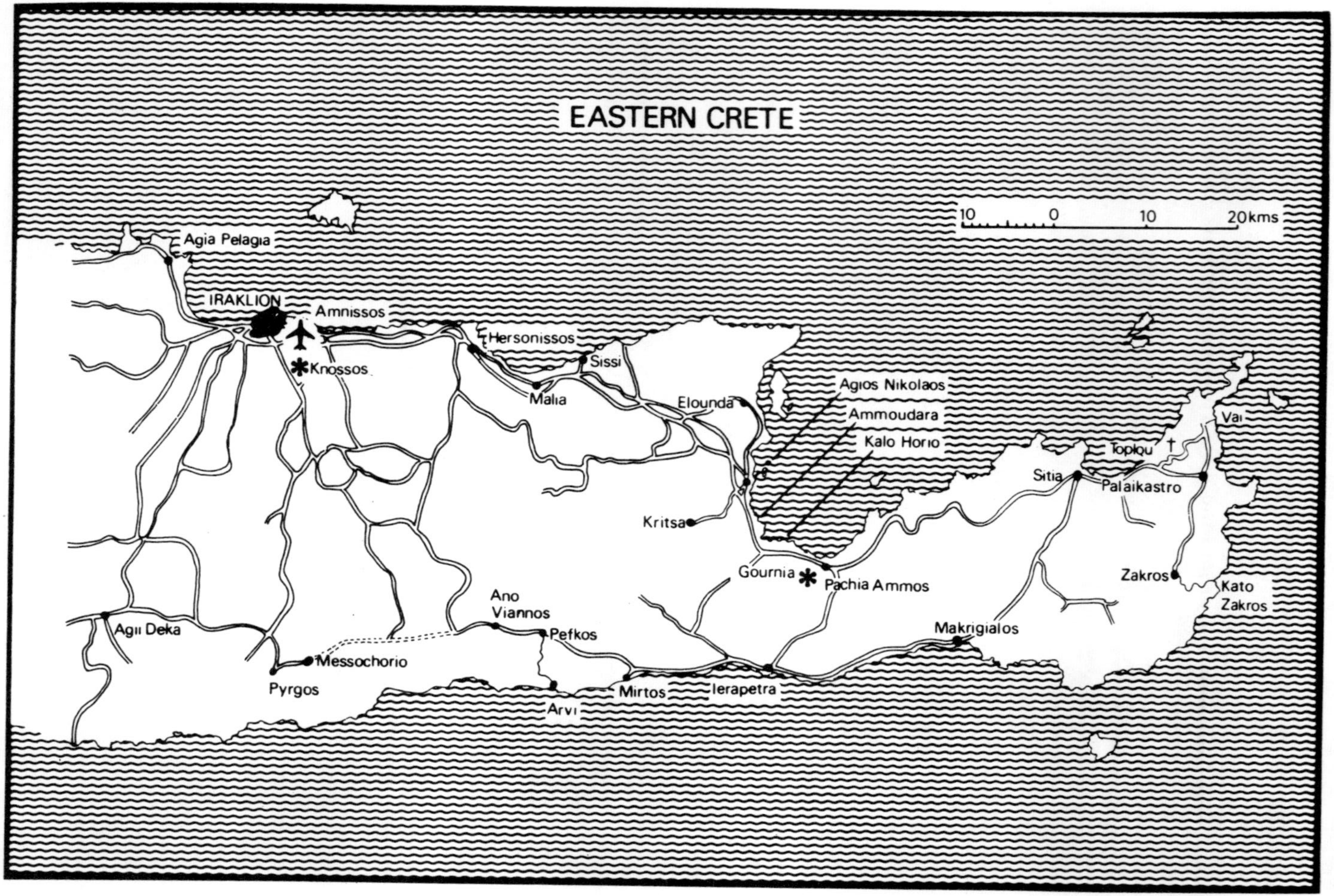
EASTERN CRETE
10 0 10 20kms
Agia Pelagia
IRAKLION
Amnissos
Knossos
Hersonissos
Sissi
Malia
Elounda
Agios Nikolaos
Ammoudara
Kalo Horio
Kritsa
Gournia
Pachia Ammos
Sitia
Toplou
Vai
Palaikastro
Zakros
Kato
Zakros
Makrigialos
Ierapetra
Mirtos
Arvi
Pefkos
Ano
Viannos
Messochorio
Pyrgos
Agii Deka

CRETE

Crete, approximately 150 miles long and 35 miles across at its widest points, is the largest of the Greek Islands. It is rugged with mountain ranges which soar up to 8,000 feet contrasting with intensively cultivated valleys and plains where vine, olive, orange and lemon trees grow in profusion. In some parts of the island the plains are covered with myriads of huge and unsightly polythene-covered greenhouses. Crete also produces large quantities of raisins and in September you will see green, gold and brown carpets of grapes as they dry in the sun on the roofs of houses, in the fields or even by the roadside. As they dry the stalks have to be removed and they also have to be turned periodically – a laborious and time-consuming task which is performed by hand by both men and women.

Distances are deceptive on Crete – roads are often steep and tortuous. The more rural roads frequently have poor surfaces and this, coupled with plunging ravines and not infrequent strong winds, makes it advisable to hire four-wheeled transport if you are planning to travel anything other than short distances.

Crete is especially susceptible to strong winds and when the writer visited the island, it blew more or less continuously for three weeks. On many of the beaches people have constructed wind-breaks from stones and on some the sand is buried under piles of shingle which has been washed ashore by high seas whipped-up by the wind. Although still hot, it can get a little wearing to be buffeted day after day by almost gale force winds which whip up both the sand and the sea and which can make sunbathing less than an enjoyable experience.

A word now about the beaches. Good sandy beaches are often difficult to find (depending on where you are staying) and naturist beaches are even more difficult to find. It is surprising, considering the millions of people who holiday in places like Agios Nikolaos and Elounda, that one rarely hears a complaint about the lack of decent beaches. The fact is that there are no worthwhile sandy beaches in either of these very popular resorts and consequently people are obliged to lie on rocks or pebbles in often less than idyllic surroundings. The paucity of nudist beaches could be due to the fact that the Cretan authorities gained a reputation for harsh treatment of nudists in the past thus frightening off many people who would otherwise visit the island. In addition, what sandy beaches there are tend to be overrun by British holidaymakers (who have all but swamped the more popular parts of the island) and who are notoriously conservative in these matters. The inaccessibility of many of the naturist beaches makes some form of transport desirable if not essential.

Pollution is also a problem. It is difficult to recall visiting any other island in Greece where the beaches and sometimes the sea itself, are so badly affected by pollution. Oil, plastic bottles, aerosols, polythene and other non-biodegradable refuse are much in evidence. Here again the wind is a contributory factor, whipping refuse dumped at sea along the surface of the ocean until it finally comes to rest at the back of the beaches – a sad comment on mans' selfish and unthinking attitude to his own environment. An example of this is that the prevailing wind sometimes drives rubbish dumped at sea off Crete's northern coast down into the Gulf of Marabello, on which stands Agios Nikolaos, and traps it there. The writer has seen the sea along this stretch of coast awash with polythene, tissue paper and other rubbish. In some places the litter problem has been compounded by backpackers who camp on the beaches and who leave behind bottles, tin cans and other mementoes of their stay.

In spite of all this Crete is undeniably a beautiful island with some spectacular scenery, good beaches and, away from the main tourist drags (which could just as easily be on the Costa Brava), much to charm those who enjoy experiencing the simplicity of Greek village life, the spontaneous friendliness of the people and the tranquillity of a landscape untouched by urban sprawl and the other trappings of twentieth century living.

Crete will probably appeal to those seasoned island travellers who are prepared to make the not inconsiderable effort required to explore the island.

Connections: By air – direct flights from most U.K. airports; up to nine flights a day from Athens to Iraklion and five flights daily from Athens to Chania; daily flights to Iraklion from Rhodes and once a day from Mykonos (twice on Mondays); from Santorini to Iraklion on Mondays, Wednesdays, Fridays and Sundays and from Paros on Tuesdays, Thursdays and Saturdays; from Rhodes to Sitia twice daily on Tuesdays, Thursdays and Saturdays and once on Sundays and from Karpathos to Sitia once daily on Tuesdays, Thursdays, Saturdays and Sundays; from Thessaloniki (mainland) to Iraklion on Mondays and Fridays.

By ship from Piraeus every evening at 18.30 or 19.00 to both Chania and Iraklion (12 hours). On Mondays a boat leaves Piraeus at 09.00, arriving in Chania at 20.00. On Sunday there is also a late-evening boat to Chania. Boats daily from Santorini to Iraklion (5 hours). Boats to Iraklion four times a week from Ios, Naxos and Paros; twice a week from Mykonos, Sifnos and Serifos. A boat leaves Rhodes on Tuesday midnight for Sitia and Agios Nikolaos via Karpathos. There is also a once weekly ferry service from Kavala (mainland) to Sitia and Agios Nikolaos via Limnos, Lesbos, Chios, Samos, Ikaria, Kalymnos, Kos, Rhodes and Karpathos. Boats from Piraeus to Agios Nikolaos twice weekly – once via Ios and Santorini and once via Milos, Folegandros and Santorini.

IRAKLION

Iraklion is the largest city in Crete and the fifth largest in Greece. It is a colourful, attractive city with more than a little Venetian influence and also a Turkish quarter. Some will feel that it is over large for a holiday stay while others will enjoy its noisily cheerful and cosmopolitan atmosphere. There is a wide choice of hotels in town as well as rooms. The 'C' class Hotel Poseidon, 46 Possidonos Poros (081 285859/222545) comes highly recommended. There is also a youth hostel at 24 Handakos Street (081 286281). A branch of the National Tourist Organisation is next door to the archaeological museum on Xanthididou Street and the tourist police are to be found on Vas. Konstantinou (081 283190).

Things To Do: Iraklion has the second most important archaeological museum in Greece. Open 08.00 to 19.00 except for Mondays (08.00 to 11.00) and Sundays and holidays (09.00 to 18.00). Admission 100 drs. The museum is famous for its relics of the Minoan culture, many of which were found at Knossos, and is well worth a visit.

The ancient archaeological site at KNOSSOS, three miles from Iraklion, is a must to visit. It originally dates back to 1950 B.C. but was destroyed (probably by an earthquake) in 1700 B.C. It was rebuilt only to be damaged again (this time by fire) in 1400 B.C. It is widely accepted as being the Palace of King Minos and the centre of the Minoan civilisation. It is here that the famous mythological story of the labyrinth and the minotaur originated. As you wander through the partially reconstructed palace along a maze of passageways and staircases, passing the blood red columns and the colourful frescoes which epitomise Knossos, you can but wonder at the sophistication of this civilisation which flourished fifteen hundred years before the birth of Christ. Knossos is, without doubt, one of the greatest archaeological finds of all time. Although you can buy a guide book and make your own way, you will get a better idea of what the palace was like if you join one of the guided tours available at the site. You can often negotiate a price with the guide (especially if there are a few of you) and there are special rates for students. The site is open 08.00 to 19.00 except for Sundays and holidays when it is open from 09.00 to 18.00. Admission is 100 drs. There is a half-hourly bus service from Iraklion (No. 2 from the harbour or the El Greco Hotel).

Beaches: 14 miles west of Iraklion is the village of AGIA PELAGIA. The 'A' class Capsis Beach Hotel is situated here and there are unconfirmed reports that the hotel has two sandy beaches one of which is used by nudists.

The cleanest and closest beach to Iraklion is AMNISSOS. Buses leave for here every half an hour from the bus station by the harbour (bus No. 1). It is a long beach and, when not too busy, it is possible that nudism could be enjoyed at one end.

From Iraklion the main road eastwards passes through uninspiring countryside straddled for most of the way by tavernas, hotels and apartments in various stages of construction (you may be excused for believing that there is no such thing as planning permission on Crete). Approximately 14 miles from Iraklion is HERSONISSOS**, now a fully-fledged tourist resort, with dozens of large hotels and little evidence of what was once a peaceful fishing village. The main beaches are busy and crowded. However, if you walk in a north-westerly direction for half a mile or so (passing the Creta Maris Hotel) and then follow the cliff-top track for about the same distance you will come to an old watchtower on a headland. Beyond lies a long and little frequented beach which, after the first 300 yards, is used for nudism. There is no taverna or other facilities on this beach.

From Hersonissos onwards to Agios Nikolaos the scenery improves. MALIA is the site of a Minoan palace, many hotels, a youth hostel, tourist shops, discos and even floodlit tennis courts. The long, sandy beach can get very crowded but there are dunes at one end where people sleep out and it is possible that this end could be suitable for nudism. 5 miles east of Malia is the little seaside fishing village of SISSI** with an attractive, although rocky, bay. A 15 minutes' walk (along a tiny track) leads to a good beach which consists mainly of sand with fine shingle by the sea. The beach is seldom crowded. An outcrop of rock separates this bay from two small, sandy beaches which are ideal for naturism.

Getting Around: Buses to Malia via Hersonissos run every 30 minutes from 06.30 to 21.00 (same on Sundays). Buses to Agios Nikolaos run at 06.30, 07.30, 08.30, 09.00, 09.30, 10.00, 10.30, 11.00, 11.30, 12.30, 13.00, 14.00, 14.30, 15.30, 16.00, 17.00, 17.30, 18.30, 19.30 and 20.30 (same on Sundays). Buses to Ierapetra run at 07.30, 08.30, 09.30, 10.30, 11.30, 13.00, 14.00, 15.30, 17.00 and 18.30 (same on Sundays). Buses to Sitia run at 07.30, 08.30, 09.30, 10.30, 12.30, 14.30 and 17.30 (same on Sundays). All the above buses leave from the bus station by the port (081 282637).

Buses to Agia Galini run at 06.30, 07.30, 08.45, 10.00, 11.00, 12.15, 14.00, 16.00 and 17.30. Buses to Matala leave at 07.30, 08.45, 10.00, 12.15, 13.00, 15.00 and 16.30. These buses leave from the bus station situated outside the Chania Gate (081 283037).

All the above bus times may be different on Sundays unless stated otherwise.

Car and scooter hire in Iraklion as well as numerous day trips to other parts of the island.

Tour Operators:
HERSONISSOS: Aegina Club (H); Allsun (H); Arrowsmith (H – Creta Maris); Aspro (H); Blue Sky (S); Broadway (H); Cook, Thomas – 'Hotels, Coaches and Cruising' Brochure (H – Creta Maris); Ellerman (H); Global (S); Grecian (H); Horizon (H); Intasun – Main Brochure (H); Intasun – 'Plain and Simple' Brochure (H,S); Kypros (H); Lunarscape (H,R,S); Manos (H); Martyn (S); Meridian (H,S); O.S.L. (S); Rooks, Martin (H); Sigma (H,S); Simply Crete (S); Stuyvesant, Peter (H,S); Sunquest (H); Timsway – General Brochure (H).

SISSI: Grecian (S); Manos (R,S); Timsway – 'Original Holidays in Greece' Brochure (P,S).

AGIOS NIKOLAOS

Agios Nikolaos was once a fishing village. Now, thanks in large part to the television series 'The Lotus Eaters', it is the most popular resort in Crete complete with boutiques, expensive jewellery shops and dozens of restaurants, bars, pubs and discos. It is not typically Greek but is a typical tourist resort. However, as such, it is not unattractive, situated as it is around a supposedly bottomless lake which is connected to the outer harbour by a channel crossed by a bridge. It gets jam-packed in season and its overwhelming popularity is probably more to do with the image which was created for it by the television series than is justified by the reality. There is a stony beach by the bus station.

Food in the restaurants and tavernas is generally of a high standard but can be expensive (avoid the Rififi, overlooking the main harbour – the Avra further around the harbour on the road to Elounda is just as good and a lot less expensive). Accommodation is mainly in hotels of which there is a large selection. The tourist police are to be found in a building by the lake (0841 22321).

About 7 miles north of Agios Nikolaos is ELOUNDA, yet another fishing village turned tourist resort made famous by a television series ('Who Pays the Ferryman?'). It is much smaller than Agios Nikolaos and a lot less commercialised – pleasant but unremarkable. There are no sandy beaches at Elounda. A walk along the coast road is Plaka, a large pebble beach (not nudist). There are hotels in Elounda and some self-catering accommodation (available through tour operators). The tavernas generally serve a good standard of food and there are two or three discos.

Things To Do: Caique trips, including one to the near-by island of Spinalonga. Here stands a Venetian fortress built in 1579 which withstood the Turkish invaders for forty-five years after the mainland had fallen. Later it was used as a leper colony (the last victim died in 1952). Coach trips are also available to various places including Knossos and Vai. Visit the mountain village of Kritsa (about 7 miles from Agios Nikolaos). Although a tourist centre packed with shops selling clothing, leather goods and other locally produced items it still manages to retain its identity (by contrast with Agios Nikolaos). Walk off the main street and explore the back alleyways. Here you can see old women spinning in darkened rooms or tatting on doorsteps while the menfolk sit on the church steps or in kafeneons playing with worry beads and discussing weighty matters.

Beaches: Just over a mile from Agios Nikolaos along the Sitia road is a sandy beach known as the REED BEACH (it has tall reeds growing at the back). The main road runs behind the beach and it is easily found. It is a bit scrubby and not nudist but is remarkable because it is sandy. A little further long is the area known as AMMOUDARA. There are a couple of tavernas on one side of the road here and, on the other side, a small sandy beach which is backed by bushes. It is usually crowded. The main road circles around the back of the beach and it is not suitable for nudism. From here on, the coastline is rocky and there are no sandy beaches until KALO HORIO** which is approximately 8 miles from Agios Nikolaos (about a quarter of an hour by car). Travelling along the Sitia road you will come to a bridge which crosses a river (usually dry). The bridge is narrow, allowing only one car to pass at a time, although a second bridge is being built adjacent to the first. Immediately after crossing the bridge you will see a road on the right signposted Pirgos and followed shortly afterwards by another road on the same side signposted Kalo Horio and Kalamafka. Continue to follow the main road looking out for a track on the left. There is a small signpost here which says 'Beach – Kantina'. If you miss this track you will see another a little further along signposted 'Beach', just before the Mini Market and the Taverna Bar 'Y Pankalos'. This is a pretty bay and the long, sandy beach is not badly affected by litter. There is a sort of portable taverna set among the trees here – it may sound odd but it is very clean and serves excellent souvlaki and home-made beefburgers. In August the beach was very busy for the whole of its length and the writer was reluctant to strip-off but by the second week in September the far end of the beach (to the left as you face the sea) was quiet enough for a number of us to go nude. As so often happens, we were quickly joined by others. This is a large beach and there is enough room for it to be enjoyed by both nudists and non-nudists without problems. However, if no one else is nude and you feel reluctant to take the initiative, follow the path which leads through the trees at the end of the beach. It leads over a headland to another nice bay consisting of pebbles and larger stones which is also known as Kalo Horio. The beach is backed by trees for some of its length and behind the trees are polythene-covered greenhouses. Locals sometimes walk onto the beach from the fields but they keep to themselves and won't disturb you. Except for the far end it is hardly used, save for the occasional naturist. There is oil on the beach in places and access to the sea can be difficult over the pebbles (it is worth investing in a pair of the plastic sandals which can be bought in many shops on Crete) but once through these the bottom is sandy and shelves gently. There are often large breakers when the wind is blowing. The stony beach can get uncomfortable to lie on after a time and, while the beach is less than idyllic, the absence of naturist beaches in this part of Crete justifies its inclusion in this guide.

If you return to the main road and continue to head in the direction of Sitia you will see, after a few hundred yards, two tavernas on the right. The first of these is called the 'Kavos Taverna' and the second is the 'Vrokastro Tavern'. Park here. A path leads down to another sandy beach which is backed by cliffs and which is used by nudists at the far end. Unfortunately, the beach is narrower here with just a small strip of sand. It is also badly affected by rubbish and the large stones make access to the sea difficult.

Although the three beaches described here are quite separate, they all appear to go under the collective name of Kalo Horio.

Continuing along the main road you will pass the Istron Bay Hotel (situated on a horse-shoe bay with a sandy beach) and the archaeological site of Gournia (the most completely preserved Minoan town) before dropping down into PACHIA AMMOS with its beach of dark sand (not nudist). From here the road climbs and twists its way through the Ornon Mountains before descending at Sitia.

Getting Around: Buses to Iraklion run at 06.30, 07.30, 08.00, 08.30, 09.00, 09.30, 10.30, 11.00, 11.30, 12.30, 13.30, 14.00, 14.30, 15.00, 15.30, 16.00, 16.30, 17.30, 18.00, 18.45, 20.00 and 21.00 (same on Sundays). Buses to Elounda run at 07.15, 09.00, 10.00, 11.00, 12.00, 13.00, 14.00, 15.00, 16.00, 17.00, 18.00 and 19.30. Buses to Kritsa run at 06.15, 07.00, 08.10, 09.00, 09.30, 10.00, 10.30, 11.00, 12.00, 13.00, 14.00, 15.00, 16.00, 17.00, 18.00 and 19.30. Buses to Ierapetra run at 06.30, 09.00, 10.00, 11.00, 12.00, 13.00, 14.30, 15.30, 17.00, 18.30 and 20.00 (same on Sundays). Buses to Sitia run at 06.30, 09.00, 10.00, 11.00, 12.00, 14.00, 15.30 and 19.00 (same on Sundays).

All the above bus times may be different on Sundays unless stated otherwise.

Numerous car, jeep, motorbike and scooter hire companies.

Tour Operators:
KALO HORIO: Airlink (H,S); Beach Villas (S); Grecian (H,S); Thomson – 'Summer Sun' Brochure (H); Thomson – 'Small and Friendly' Brochure (H); Ventura (S).

SITIA

Sitia, 45 miles to the east of Agios Nikolaos, is a pleasant town built in a semicircle around a bay. There is a plethora of waterfront tavernas, a couple or so discos, hotels and a youth hostel at 24 Agelaki Street (0843 22693). The beach, which consists of coarse sand, stretches eastwards for over a mile. The beach is backed for the whole of its length by the main road which makes it unsuitable for nudism. The hulks of two rusting ships just a little way offshore are something of an eyesore but at least they provide amusement for divers and snorkellers.

Things To Do: Visit the fourteenth century Monastery of Toplou. It stands in splendid isolation about 11 miles east of Sitia and contains the eighteenth century 'Lord Thou Art Great' icon, considered to be one of the greatest masterpieces of Cretan art. Visit the palm-fringed beach at Vai.

Beaches: East of Sitia the coastline is mainly rocky and there are no beaches worthy of comment. After some way you will reach a fork in the road which leads to the sandy beach at VAI*** by way of the Monastery of Toplou (the shortest route from here). Alternatively, you can carry straight on to reach Vai by passing through the village of Palaikastro. Both of these roads cross barren hillsides inhabited only by goats and this desolation lends even greater impact to your first glimpse of Vai for, amazing as it may seem, the fine sandy beach is backed by a luxurious grove of palm trees more reminiscent of the Caribbean than a Greek Island. It is said that the palms grew as a result of date stones left behind by Saracen or Egyptian landing parties. Amazingly, in view of its isolated position, the main beach at Vai gets jam-packed in season. Holidaymakers come in droves attracted by Vai's exotic aspect and there is a regular bus service from Sitia, daily coach tours from all over eastern Crete as well as backpackers who sleep rough under the palms. It would be uncomfortable if not impossible to go naked on the main beach in high season. It may be possible at the northern end of the beach (the opposite end to where the two tavernas are situated) earlier in the year and after, say, the second week in September when things have quietened down a bit.

However, there are two beaches on either side of the main beach which are used by nudists. The one to the left (as you face the sea) is best reached by following the path which leads up over the rocky hillside. You will see the small sandy cove after climbing a short distance but the way down is steep and you should be extremely careful. The beach is sandy and reasonably clean and the swimming is good, although the sandy bottom shelves steeply and this, coupled with the steep descent, makes it unsuitable for children. There is no natural shade and the beach loses the sun early due to the cliffs which surround it. The other naturist beach is to the right of the main beach and is also reached by a steep climb (the path starts near the steps which lead up to the taverna). It is bigger than the one already described and is mainly composed of coarse sand. It is well used by nudists. It is also more exposed and people have built stone wind-breaks which afford some protection on windy days. The bottom is sandy (although it shelves steeply) and the swimming is good. There are no facilities although bushes at the back of the beach provide a little shade. A nice beach which could easily be ruined by the inconsiderate few who can't be bothered to take their litter away with them. Vai is a 30 minute car drive from Sitia and there is a regular bus service (see Getting Around) which takes about an hour and costs 80 drs.

As an alternative to Sitia you could consider staying in PALAIKASTRO* which is the nearest village to Vai. The bus from Sitia stops here on its way to Vai so you wouldn't even have to hire transport. It's an unremarkable place, except for the rather grand church in the village square. The 'in' place in the evenings is the 'Why Not Pub' – cocktails and good music – which is used more by locals than by tourists. There are one or two other examples of attempts to cash-in on the tourist boom which, in the event, never got quite as far as Palaikastro (and hopefully never will). Except for the arrival of motorised transport and electricity, Palaikastro probably hasn't changed much in the last hundred years. You can stay in rooms here for about 500-600 drs. for a double and there are a couple of hotels including the 'E' class Itanos (0843 22508/22227). Another good reason for staying here is the deserted sandy beaches a little way out of the village. From the town square follow the road which runs to the right of the Hotel Itanos. There is a signpost here which points the way to the 'Marina Village'. Continue to follow these signs leaving the made-up road after a short distance for one which is unsurfaced. A little further on you will come to a crossroads and up ahead you will see a small village (which is, incidentally, called Agathia). Turn left here and continue along this road, passing the Marina Village on the left. The road runs along the back of the long beach which consists of sand – some fine and some coarse. There are two tavernas. One of the tavernas overlooks the sea at one end of the beach. The other is at the back of the beach and serves mainly fresh fish including expensive and unappetising fish soup. The soup consists of a huge tureen of green liquid (which tastes like olive oil and lemon juice) and, on a separate plate, the fish (including the heads) and boiled pototoes – so be warned! How these tavernas survive is a mystery for even in August the beach was hardly used, allowing nude sunning to go undisturbed at the end furthest away from the tavernas.

If you continue along the road a short distance you will come to another beautifully situated beach which is backed for most of its length by small weather-beaten cliffs. This beach also consists of fine sand with coarser sand and small pebbles in places. It is less open and exposed than the first and is suitable for nudism. There are no facilities but shade can be found in niches in the rocks.

From Palaikastro the road continues to Zakros and thence to the site of a Minoan palace at KATO ZAKROS* (the bus from Sitia, however, travels only as far as Zakros so you will have to walk or get a taxi for the last part of the journey). It is 5 miles from Zakros to the coast along a rough road which winds its way amid banana plantations. Here, in addition to the palace, which is surrounded by the extensive remains of a Minoan town, there is a gorgeous, sandy beach where you can camp as well as sunbathe and swim without clothes. The hamlet has three tavernas as well as two pensions. From Kato Zakros you can travel no further and it is best to retrace your steps to Sitia.

The road to the south coast from Sitia winds its way through pleasant countryside before reaching the coast at MAKRIGIALOS**. The naturist beach can be reached by walking back up the hill out of the village. Pass the road on the left, which is signposted Pefki, and continue for about 350 yards until you see a track on the right (opposite a new house near a bend in the road). Follow the track for about a half a mile to a beautiful sandy beach where nudism can be enjoyed in idyllic surroundings. Shade is provided by a number of tamarisk trees and swimming is excellent here. The beach extends for a quarter of a mile and at the far-end is an easily climbed rocky headland and beyond this is an even longer sandy beach.

The coastline between here and Ierapetra is unexceptional and the beaches are mainly rocky.

Getting Around: Buses to Agios Nikolaos run at 06.45, 09.15, 11.30, 12.15, 13.30, 14.15, 16.15 and 19.30 (same on Sundays). Buses to Vai run at 09.00, 11.00, 12.00, 14.00, 16.00 and 17.30 returning at 10.00, 12.00, 13.00, 15.00, 17.30 (17.00 on Sundays) and 18.30. Buses to Iraklion run at 06.45, 09.15, 11.30, 12.15, 13.30, 14.15, 16.15 and 19.30 (same on Sundays). Buses to Ierapetra run at 09.00, 12.15 (12.00 on Sundays), 14.00, 18.00 and 19.30 (20.30 on Sundays).

Car and scooter hire in Sitia.

Tour Operators:
PALAIKASTRO: Sunvil (H).
MAKRIGIALOS: Inter Island (S); Timsway – 'Original Holidays in Greece' Brochure (P,S).

IERAPETRA

Ierapetra is a large, unremarkable town and is the centre of the region's agricultural industry. In recent years it has attempted to cash in on the tourist boom and there is now a string of pleasant waterfront tavernas as well as some hotels and discos. In spite of this it doesn't give the impression of being a particularly attractive place in which to spend a holiday.

Things To Do: The usual trips to other parts of the island.

Beaches: There is a long beach of coarse grey sand in IERAPETRA. Unfortunately, the best part is in the town and this is also the most crowded section and is not suitable for nudism.

Westwards from Ierapetra the road passes yet more ghastly polythene-covered greenhouses before reaching the quiet village of MIRTOS* (signposted left off the main road). Mirtos has one hotel, the 'C' class Mirtos (0842 51215), as well as some inexpensive rooms to rent and a number of tavernas. There is also a gorgeous beach of black sand which stretches westwards for 3 miles to the village of Tertsa. The beach is popular with campers and is long and secluded enough for nudism to go undisturbed. Buses stop at Mirtos seven times a day from Ierapetra and twice daily from Iraklion. From Mirtos the main road climbs inland. After passing through the village of Pefkos you will see a turn-off on the left signposted 'Amiras and Arvi Beach'. The unmade road runs for about 9 miles before reaching ARVI. In spite of its inaccessibility the village is usually packed with German and

Greek tourists and, although there is a pleasant beach, there are no reports of naturism.

Getting Around: Buses to Iraklion run at 06.30, 08.30, 10.30, 11.30, 13.30, 14.30, 15.30, 16.30, 17.30, 19.00 and 20.00 (same on Sundays). Buses to Agios Nikolaos run at 06.30, 08.30, 10.30, 11.30, 13.30, 14.30, 15.30, 16.30, 17.30 and 19.20 (same on Sundays). Buses to Sitia run at 06.30 (not Sundays), 08.30 (08.00 on Sundays), 10.00, 12.00, 14.00 and 16.30.

Tour Operators:
MIRTOS: Sunvil (H).

MATALA

If you continue to follow the main road after leaving Arvi, you will come to Ano Viannos (picturesquely situated on a hillside). Enjoy the next 4 miles or so from here for this is the last surfaced road that you will see for 17 miles (at a rough estimate) until you reach Messochorio. The road bumps its way up hill and down dale through picturesque scenery and remote mountain villages where it becomes so narrow that you will think that you have lost your way. It is slow progress – but worth every minute. From Messochorio follow the road through Pyrgos and Agii Deka to Mires. In Mires you can turn left in the town for Matala.

Matala is famous for the caves carved into the cliff-face which overlooks one side of the pretty bay. These caves were probably first occupied by early Christians. They were also used by the Germans for military purposes and in the 1960's hippy communes claimed squatters' rights before the authorities clamped down and fenced the caves off making access more difficult. Matala has a good, wide beach consisting mainly of fine sand and some shingle at one end. It is backed for much of its length by attractive tavernas/restaurants. Behind these is the village which originally consisted of a few fishermens' cottages built around a square. Recent years have seen the addition of tavernas, tourist shops, hotels, discos and a campsite near the beach. There is, however, still not a great deal to Matala and it remains relatively unsophisticated.

Beaches: The main beach at MATALA often gets crowded with people bussed in for the day and it is not suitable for nudism. RED BEACH*** is the closest naturist beach. Some 60 yards before the road into the village ends at the Plaka Taverna, turn left up a rough path almost opposite Zorbas Bar. Ignore the first path on the left but take the next one which runs diagonally uphill between some dwellings. This path ascends fairly steeply and is reasonably well defined. Keep with the path for three-quarters of a mile until you are parallel with a fence on your left. Soon the summit is reached and here you can fork right for a few yards to gain a view of the beach. Return to the main path which begins to descend. Soon afterwards you will pass through a gate before reaching the small beach of fine sand which is predominantly nudist. The whole walk will have taken 20-25 minutes. There are no facilities and hardly any shade on this beach.

KOMOS BEACH*** is about 3 miles north of Matala (about 50 minutes' walking time). Follow the road which leads back up the hill out of the village and take the second dirt road on the left (signposted 'Komos'). Alternatively, you can catch the bus and ask to be put down here (this reduces the time it takes to walk to the beach to 20 minutes). After following the track for a short distance you will see a small house on the left with a 'rooms to rent' sign. The track deteriorates further along and some people park here. If you continue, you will see that the track divides a little further on. One track leads down the hillside towards the sea and it is, in fact, possible to drive almost onto the beach. Getting down isn't a problem but coming back can be. Towards the bottom of the hill the track runs across fine sand and it's easy to get stuck – even in a four-wheel drive jeep! It is far safer to park nearer the top and walk down. Alternatively you can continue to follow the main track keeping left around the hillside. There is a magnificent view from up here down onto the sandy beach which stretches as far as the eye can see towards Agia Galini (7½ miles away, as the crow flies, across the bay). Almost immediately below are the remains of a Minoan settlement which stand virtually on the beach surrounded by sand. There is limited parking further along the track near a little white church and from here a path leads down to the beach. This must be one of the best beaches on the whole island and it is predominantly nudist. The wide beach stretches for miles and is free from both oil and litter. Swimming is good and the bottom is mainly sandy and shelves gently. The beach, although well used, is so large that it never gets crowded even in high season. There is no natural shade and no tavernas on this part of the beach so you are advised to at least take something to drink. The beach extends for about 3 miles and at its northern end is the village of Kalamaki (reached from Matala via Pitsidia and Kamilari – about 8 miles). The beach here is sandy with some pebbles and rocks along the waterline which make it unsafe to swim in windy weather. There is one (good) taverna on this part of the beach and there are rooms to rent in the village.

Getting Around: Buses to Iraklion run at 07.00, 09.30, 12.15, 14.30, 17.00 and 18.30. On Sundays at 08.00, 10.00, 12.00, 13.00, 14.30 and 17.00.

Tour Operators:
MATALA: Aegina Club (H); Falcon (H,P).

AGIA GALINI

From Matala it is necessary to retrace your steps to rejoin the main coastal road before passing through Timbaki. The road from here runs along a flat coastal plain for much of its length and is not particularly attractive. Here again,

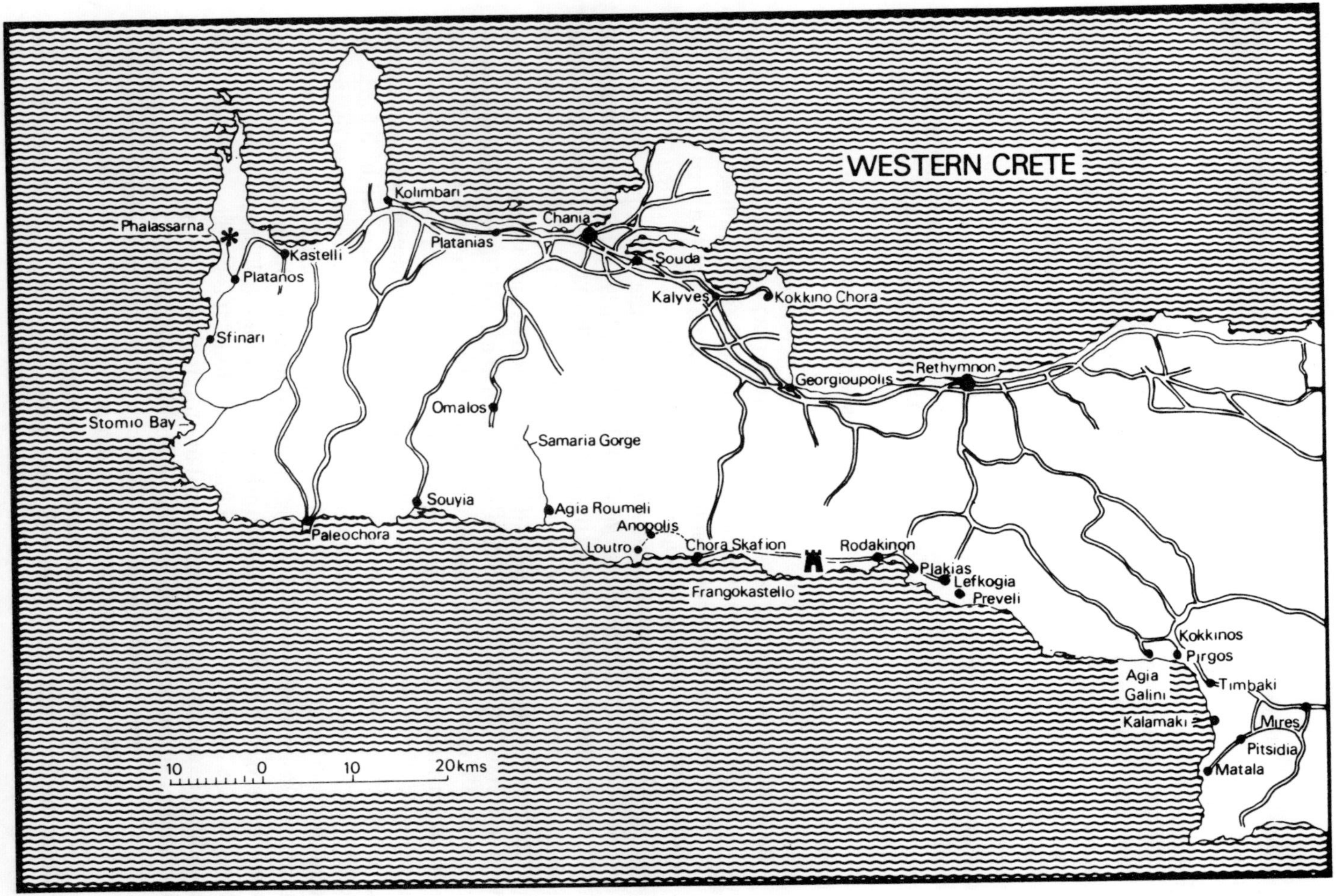
WESTERN CRETE
Phalassarna
Kastelli
Platanos
Sfinari
Stomio Bay
Kolimbari
Platanias
Chania
Souda
Kalyves
Kokkino Chora
Georgioupolis
Rethymnon
Omalos
Samaria Gorge
Souyia
Paleochora
Agia Roumeli
Anopolis
Loutro
Chora Skafion
Frangokastello
Rodakinon
Plakias
Lefkogia
Preveli
Kokkinos
Pirgos
Agia Galini
Timbaki
Kalamaki
Mires
Pitsidia
Matala
10 0 10 20kms

polythene frequently dominates the scene covering both the greenhouses and the sides of the road where it often accumulates after being discarded. The road climbs again before dropping down into Agia Galini. It takes about 50 minutes by car to travel the 28 miles between Matala and Agia Galini.

Agia Galini was once a small fishing village. It is still small but fishing has given way to tourism as the main source of employment. The village is very picturesquely situated on a steep hillside around a pretty harbour. The main street is known as Taverna Street and is pedestrian. At night it comes alive and is so packed with tables and chairs from the tavernas which line both sides of the street that pedestrians have to squeeze through a narrow passage-way. You can get a reasonably priced meal in most of the establishments here and the food is generally of a good standard. Besides the tavernas Agia Galini boasts a number of cocktail bars and two discos (down by the beach).

There is plenty of accommodation in rooms and small hotels and the accommodation in some of the newer establishments is of a surprisingly high standard for a place of this size.

Things To Do: Trips to the Samaria Gorge, Knossos, etc.

Beaches: Although a nice place to stay AGIA GALINI** is defective in one major respect – its beaches. On one side of the harbour a path leads around the base of the cliffs to the main beach. A sign on the cliffs at the start of the path proclaims 'Is Forbidding the Nudism and the Camping'. The path cuts across a small pebble beach (usually jam-packed) beneath the cliffs and then passes fortified gun emplacements, built into the cliffs during the German occupation, before leading onto the main beach. This beach consists of a little sand but is mainly dirty-looking grey grit strewn with pebbles and stones (some of which are quite large) and is so unattractive that, in the opinion of the writer, it hardly qualifies to be called a beach at all. It is narrow and gets very crowded. There are large, slippery boulders at the water's edge which make getting into the sea difficult if not dangerous (this is probably evidenced by the unusually large number of people hobbling around town with sprained ankles). After a hundred yards or so, the beach is divided in two by a fordable waist-deep creek. Beyond here the sea is edged by a narrow strip of stones which stretches for as far as the eye can see. The main beach gets so crowded that people are almost forced to cross over and here they have made hollows in the stones which they have surrounded with stone wind-breaks. This part of the beach is used by the occasional nudist. Frankly, it is hard to see why these beaches are so busy. The likeliest explanation is that Agia Galini's somewhat isolated position makes access to other beaches too difficult for many people and so it is, presumably, a question of making the best of what's available.

About 7 miles from Agia Galini and about 20 minutes by car is a nice beach at KOKKINOS PIRGOS* where naturism can be enjoyed. Leaving Agia Galini follow the Timbaki road. You will pass a military camp on the right before descending a steep hill at the bottom of which are more, of the by now familiar, polythene greenhouses. Look out for a track on the right which is signposted 'The Brothers Hotel' and 'Hotel Libyan Sea'. Follow this track for a short distance before rejoining a surfaced road. Turn right and almost immediately take the next track on the right (there is a taverna standing in the fork made by the main road and the track which you are about to follow). The track is bumpy and passes through tall reeds which grow on either side. After a little way you will see the beach on the left. The best part for nudism is to the right (facing the sea). Here you will find good stretches of fine sand (further along the beach becomes shingly) interspersed with boulders which have become detached from the low cliffs at the back of the beach. There is no natural shade and there are no facilities although the beach is clean and free from rubbish. In some places you will have to cross a narrow strip of pebbles and stones as you enter the sea but after this the bottom is sandy and shelves gently. While this cannot be claimed to be a naturist beach (so that sometimes you may be on your own) it is long and little used and, except for the occasional passer-by, you should not be disturbed. Locals sometimes use the beach, probably after they have been working in the fields, but they seem unconcerned by nudity.

There is also another very long, sandy beach at the other side of Kokkinos Pirgos (access from the village) which stretches in a south-easterly direction towards Matala in the far distance. Here again the sheer size of the beach and the fact that it is hardly used make it suitable for nudism. Kokkinos Pirgos is really just a collection of small hotels and tavernas strung along a road. It is a drab place which, in spite of its magnificent beaches, has been by-passed by the tourist boom. It is on the bus route between Iraklion and Agia Galini.

Getting Around: Buses to Iraklion run at 08.00, 09.30, 10.30, 12.15, 13.15, 15.00, 16.30, 18.30 and at 08.00, 10.30, 12.30, 15.00, 17.30 and 19.30 on Sundays

Tour Operators:
AGIA GALINI: Aegina Club (P); Falcon (H,R,S); Inter Island (H); Small World (H); Sunmed (H,P,R,T); Sunvil (H); Zeus (H).
KOKKINOS PIRGOS: Sunvil (H).

RETHYMNON

Rethymnon is situated on the north coast and is halfway between Chania and Iraklion. It is a town of narrow streets, over-hanging wooden balconies and crumbling Venetian houses. The ancient atmosphere, picturesque harbour and huge stretch of sandy beach make it an attractive place to stay. Nightlife centres around the tavernas on the harbour and there are also discotheques in this area. There is a wide choice of hotels and rooms. The tourist police are to be found next to the museum on Arkadiou Street (0831 28156).

Things To Do: The Cretan Wine Festival (last week in July and first in

August) takes place in the park at Rethymnon. For 100 drs. or so you can drink as much as you like. The Fortezza is open Monday-Saturday 09.00 to 19.30, Sunday 09.00 to 16.00. Nias Tours at Arkadiou 116 (0831 23146) operate one day tours to the Samaria Gorge. On Thursdays they have a tour of remote mountain villages, the monastery at Vrodissi and the beach at Agia Galini.

Beaches: A wide, but somewhat dirty, sandy beach extends for about 6 miles east of Rethymnon. Reports suggest that part of this beach is used for nudism. Follow the coast road eastwards (passing the Orion and Rethymnon Hotels) and, before the road joins the National Highway, look out for a track on the left (signposted 'Tavern Bar') which leads to the beach. Turn right at the bottom and walk along the sand to a series of coves where it should be possible to strip-off.

6 miles to the west of Rethymnon is the Gulf of Georgioupolis and here the coastal highway runs along the back of one of the longest stretches of sandy beach on Crete. Unfortunately, the road is so close to the water that the beach is unsuitable for nudism. Between Georgioupolis and Chania is the little village of Kokkino Chora which was the location for the film 'Zorba the Greek'. Near-by is KALYVES* and west of the village is a quiet beach, littered with driftwood, which is reputed to be a good place for nude sun and sea bathing. However, sensible discretion should be used when locals are around.

On the Libyan Sea coast, about 20 miles south of Rethymnon, is the village of PLAKIAS* with a long beach of coarse sand. Although Plakias has recently been discovered by one or two tour operators it is not yet overcrowded. There is a campsite and rooms to rent and people also sleep out on the beach here. It is a long beach and it ought to be possible to enjoy nude sunning at the far end. For those who are prepared to walk there are several empty, sandy beaches east and west of Plakias. Naturists are said to frequent DAMNONI** and AMMOUDI BEACHES**. The closest is Damnoni and can be reached by walking for about a half a mile or so along the road to Lefkogia before turning right along a dirt road. There is unofficial camping here, two tavernas and a pension. From Plakias you can also visit the Preveli Monastery (cover-up well). PREVELI BEACH* is about 4 miles down a dirt road (reached off the Preveli road). People camp on this dirty but secluded beach and there is also a taverna close by (follow the dirt road from where it begins for about a mile or so before crossing a bridge – the taverna is signposted from here).

West of Plakias is the tiny village of RODAKINON* with a lovely beach and caves. Still further westwards are the awesome remains of the Venetian fort of FRANGOKASTELLO**. An eerie place, it was the site of a massacre during the War of Independence. On the 17th May, the anniversary of the massacre, it is said that the Cretan dead rise up, fully armed, and march into the sea. There is unofficial camping on this broad beach of clean sand as well as nude bathing. One of the two tavernas has rooms to rent. From Frangokastello it is seven or eight miles by road to the town of Chora Skafion.

CHORA SKAFION** is a crowded but pleasant resort town with a small beach. Here is the 'B' class Xenia Pension (0825 91202) and there are also rooms to rent. If you walk west along the main road for about 10 minutes you will come to a beach of good, clean sand which is used for nudism. The caves here are used by some to shelter from the midday sun. From Chora Skafion a path follows the coastline via Loutro (2½ hours' walking time) to Agia Roumeli (6 hours or more). The path starts near to the village of Anopolis (a 20 minute walk from Chora Skafion along a made-up road) and allows you to explore some of the best and least visited beaches in Crete. Midway between Chora Skafion and Loutro is SWEETWATER BEACH**, so called because several fresh-water springs surface among the pebbles of this mainly nudist beach. The beach is also popular with campers. The quiet, old fishing village of Loutro is situated halfway between Chora Skafion and Agia Roumeli and is also accessible by regular caique services from both of these places. You can stay in one of five pensions here. Just over the hill is the archaeological site of Fenix and close by is the small settlement of Livaniana. A 40 minute walk west of Fenix is MARBLE BEACH**, its black pebbles contrasting with the striking whiteness of the marble rock formations which give the beach its name. Here again, nudity is the order of the day.

Getting Around: Regular bus service from Rethymnon to both Chania and Iraklion. One bus a day from both Chania (14.00) and Chora Skafion (16.00) to Frangokastello. Boats to Loutro and Agia Roumeli leave Chora Skafion at 10.30 and 11.30 and return from Agia Roumeli at 09.00, 14.00 and 16.00.

Tour Operators:
PLAKIAS: Aegina Club (P); Freedom (H); Inter Island (H); Small World (H); Sunmed (H,P,R); Sunvil (H,T).
CHORA SKAFION: Sunvil (H).

CHANIA (HANIA)

Chania, the capital of Crete, is a picturesque city with its old fishing harbour, crumbling sandstone walls and narrow, animated, winding streets. These give what is, for the most part, a modern city an air of eighteenth century grandeur. Most boats dock in the huge Souda naval base in preference to the harbour in Chania itself. Buses meet the boats for the 3 mile or so trip into town. Chania has plenty of accommodation in hotels and rooms. The harbour area is a pleasant place to stay but if you are unable to get accommodation here you will have to walk the short distance up the hill into town. In case of difficulty try the tourist police at 44 Karaiskaki Street (0821 24477) or the Chania Tourist Office which can be found by a mosque on the waterfront. The youth hostel is at 33 Drakonianou (0821 53565) and is a 5 minute ride on the Ag. Ioannes bus which leaves from the marketplace in town. Night-times are lively with tavernas, restaurants and discotheques. Beaches are some distance outside the town but Chania makes a good base for touring western Crete.

Things To Do: Visit the spectacular Samaria Gorge which runs for 11 miles and is the longest gorge in Europe. You can either go on an excursion or make your own way by catching the bus from Chania to Omalos, a small village on a high mountain plain at the head of the gorge. The gorge runs down from Omalos to the coast at Agia Roumeli. The walk down will take about 6 hours and good walking shoes are essential. There is plenty of fresh water along the way so you don't need to take anything to drink. From Agia Roumeli take the caique to Chora Skafion (at 09.00, 14.00 and 16.00) from where there are buses back to Chania. To avoid getting stranded you would be wise to make an early start from Chania. Also, before you go, check the bus times at the bus station behind Plateia 1866. If you do get stuck you can spend the night in rooms at Agia Roumeli and there are hotels and pensions at Chora Skafion.

The Chania Travel Bureau, 46 Karaiskaki Street (0821 24780) operates trips to Samaria Gorge, Iraklion, Phalassarna, Paleochora and other places. On Thursday evenings they have an excursion to the coastal village of Kalyves with dinner, wine and Cretan folk dancing.

Beaches: After trekking through the Samaria Gorge, the sea beckons at AGIA ROUMELI**. Agia Roumeli is surrounded by good pebble beaches and a few minutes' walk east of the village brings you to a 4 mile long stretch which is used by both nudists and campers. The village has one hotel, the Roumeli, and there are also rooms to rent here.

Back in Chania there are no worthwhile beaches in the town itself although there is a decent beach (not nudist) at GALATAS, a short bus ride to the west. A few miles further west is PLATANIAS with a sandy beach and bamboo forest. Between Platanias and Kolimbari the beach is virtually continuous and, although by no means always sandy, is deserted for long stretches between villages – could be suitable for nudism. About 14 miles further on is the town of Kastelli (also known as Kissamos). The beach here is rocky and dirty and the town is modern and uninteresting. However, from here you can visit PHALASSARNA**, once the site of an ancient city, with a superb, wide sandy beach (although recent reports suggest that it has suffered badly from oil pollution) which is used by naturists. There is a bus service as far as Platanos (three times a day from Kastelli) and the beach is 3 miles away down a rough track. There are two tavernas with rooms to rent here as well as unofficial camping on the beach. The last bus back to Platanos leaves at 17.30 (but only on schooldays). Still travelling south, the road is surfaced only as far as Sfinari. There is a quiet pebble beach here and a few rooms for rent. Further south still is Stomio Bay where you will find the monastery of Chrysokalitissa and beautiful isolated beaches. From here a long detour is required to get to the south coast and the village of PALEOCHORA*. The village is situated on a promontory with a long, sandy beach on the western side and a seemingly endless pebble beach on the eastern side. Both of these beaches are long enough and empty enough to be used for nudism and unofficial camping takes place among the pine trees which fringe the sand. Here is the 'C' class Lissos and the 'D' class Livykon (0823 41250) as well as a number of inexpensive pensions. About 6 miles to the east is the remote and beautiful hamlet of SOUYIA** which stands on a wide bay of grey sand and pebbles. Naturists use one end of the bay (reached by clambering over the rocks). There is a small hotel here, the seven-roomed Pikilasos, as well as rooms to rent.

Getting Around: Buses to the beaches west of town (Kalamaki, Aptera, Glaros) depart from Plateia 1866. Buses run to the port at Souda at 20 minute intervals from in front of the central market. Buses to Chora Skafion leave from N. Episkon Street at 09.00 and 14.00. Buses back at 06.30 and 18.30. Buses to Omalos leave from Smirnis Street at 05.15, 09.00 and 16.00 returning at 06.45, 10.30 and 14.00. Regular buses to Kastelli leave from Smirnis Street (hourly or so). There are regular bus services (hourly or so) to Rethymnon and Iraklion. They leave from El Venizelou Street. Buses to Souyia leave Chania, Monday-Saturday at 09.00 and 14.00 and on Sunday at 08.00.

Boats from Agia Roumeli to Loutro and Chora Skafion leave at 09.00, 14.00 and 16.00. Boats from Agia Roumeli to Souyia and Paleochora leave at noon on Mondays, Thursdays and Saturdays (after 1st July, every day).

Car and scooter hire.

Tour Operators:
PALEOCHORA: Cretansun (H,R,S,T); Small World (R); Sunmed (H,P,R,T); Sunvil (H).
SOUYIA: Cretansun (H).

TOUR OPERATORS

Name	*Address*	*Tel. No.*
Aegina Club	25A Hills Road, Cambridge.	0223 63256
Airlink	9 Wilton Road, Victoria, London, SW1V 1LL	01-828 7682
Allsun Holidays	141 New Bond Street, London, W1Y 0BB.	01-493 3975
Amathus Holidays	51 Tottenham Court Road, London, W1P 0HS.	01-580 7597/8
Arrowsmith Holidays	Royal Buildings, 2 Mosley Street, Piccadilly, Manchester, M2 3AB	061-236 2361
Aspro Holidays	42 Bute Street, Cardiff.	0222 481721
Avra Holidays	110 Argyle Street, London, WC1H 8QZ.	01-278 3111
Beach Villas Limited	8 Market Passage, Cambridge, CB2 3QR.	0223 311113
Blue Sky Holidays Limited	Blue Sky House, 46 Gordon Street, Glasgow, G1 3PE.	041-221 6142
Broadway Holidays	41 Old Bond Street, London W1X 3AF.	01-409 0668
Club 18-30 Holidays	Academic House, 24/28 Oval Road, London, NW1 7DE.	01-485 4141
Club Mark Warner	20 Kensington Church Street, London, W8 4EP.	01-938 1851
Thomas Cook Holidays	P.O. Box 36, Thorpe Wood, Peterborough, PE3 6SB.	0733 502200
Corfiot Holidays Ltd	6 High Street, Datchet, Slough, SL3 9EA.	0753 48811
Corfu à la Carte	8 Deanwood House, Stockcross, Newbury, RG16 8JP.	0635 30621
Corfu Trust	616 Kingston Road, London, SW20 8DN	01-543 2587
Cosmos	1 Bromley Common, Bromley, Kent, BR2 9LX.	01-464 3444
Cretansun	Wendcrete Limited, 54 Elizabeth Road, Waterlooville, Hampshire, PO7 7DN.	0705 258540
CV Travel	43 Cheval Place, London SW7 1ER.	01-589 0132
Ellerman Sunflight	Travel House, Broxbourne, Hertfordshire, EN10 7JD.	0992 87233
Enterprise/Sovereign Holidays	British Airways, P.O. Box 10, London (Heathrow) Airport, Hounslow, Middlesex, TW6 2JA.	01-897 4545
Falcon Holidays	190 Campden Hill Road, London, W8 7TH.	01-221 6298
Flair Holidays	1 Wardour Street, London, W1V 3HE.	01-734 4070
Freedom Holidays	224 King Street, London, W6 0RA.	01-741 4751/5
Global	Glen House, 200 Tottenham Court Road, London, W1P 0JP.	01-323 3266
Grecian Holidays	31 Topsfield Parade, Crouch End, London N8.	01-341 7171
Greek Connection Travel Limited	Just Looking Showrooms, Bryslan House, Upper Street, Fleet, Hampshire.	02514 29231
Greek Islands Club	66 High Street, Walton-on-Thames, Surrey, KT12 1BU.	0932 220477
Greek Sun Holidays	23 Haymarket, London, SW1Y 4DG.	01-839 6055/6
Gryphon Travel Club	Grafton House, 2-3 Golden Square, London, W1R 3AD.	01-434 4598
Horizon	Broadway, Edgbaston Five Ways, Birmingham, B15 1BB.	021-632 6282
Ilios Island Holidays	18a Market Square, Horsham, West Sussex, RH12 1EU.	0403 59788

Name	*Address*	*Tel. No.*
Intasun	Intasun House, Cromwell Avenue, Bromley, Kent, BR2 2AQ.	01-290 1900
Inter Island	152 Shirland Road, London, W9 2PT.	01-286 9185
Kosmar Villa Holidays Limited	'Data House', 85/86 Tottenham Court Road, London, W1P 9HD.	01-323 4705/6
Kypros Holidays	Kypros House, 190 Camden High Street, London, NW1 8QP	01-267 9211
Lancaster Holidays	Tetley Street, Bradford, Yorkshire, BD1 2SA.	0274 736644
Laskarina Holidays	St. Mary's Gate, Wirksworth, Derbyshire, DE4 4DQ.	062-982 4881
Leisure Villas Limited	363 West Wycombe Road, High Wycombe, Buckinghamshire, HP12 4AE.	0494 31554
Loggos Tourist Co.	St. Florence, Tenby, Dyfed, SA70 8LJ.	083482 589
Lunarscape	56 Bedford Avenue, High Barnet, Hertfordshire, EN5 2ER.	01-441 0122
Manos Holidays	65 South Molton Street, London, W1Y 1HH.	01-408 2175
Martyn Holidays	224 Great West Road, Heston, Middlesex, TW5 9AW.	01-577 0090
Meon Villa Holidays	Meon House, Petersfield, Hampshire, GU32 3JN.	0730 66561
Meridian Holidays	12/16 Dering Street, London W1.	01-493 2777
Olympic Holidays	17 Old Court Place, Kensington High Street, London, W8 4PL.	01-229 2411
OSL	Travel House, Broxbourne, Hertfordshire, EN10 7JD.	0992 87233
Pan Holidays	Ashley House, 1A Ashley Road, Walton-on-Thames, Surrey, KT12 1HY.	0932 247617
Portland Holidays	218 Great Portland Street, London, W1N 5HG.	01-388 5111
Rhodian Travel Ltd	18 James Street, London, W1M 5HN.	01-491 2749
Martin Rooks Holidays	204 Ebury Street, London, SW1W 8UU.	01-730 0808
Sigma Holidays	P.O. Box 1, Sheringham, Norfolk, NR26 8HB.	0263 822142
Simply Crete	480 Chiswick High Road, Chiswick, London, W4 5TT.	01-994 4462
Sirama Limited	Suite 108, Victory Business Centre, Somers Road North, Portsmouth, PO1 1PJ.	0705 862814
Skiathos Travel Ltd	4 Holmesdale Road, Kew, Richmond, Surrey, TW9 3JZ.	01-940 5157
Small World	Old Stone House, Judges Terrace, East Grinstead, Sussex, RH19 1AQ.	0342 27272
Peter Stuyvesant Travel Limited	35 Alfred Place, London, WC1E 7DY.	01-631 3278
Sun Club Holidays	3 Replingham Road, London, SW18 5LT.	01-871 2622
Sunmed Holidays	Sunmed House, 4-6 Manor Mount, London, SE23 3PZ.	01-699 7666
Sunquest Holidays Limited	Aldine House, 9/15 Aldine Street, London, W12 8AW.	01-749 9933
Sunstart Holidays	186 Campden Hill Road, London, W8 7TH.	01-221 8204
Sunvil Travel	Upper Square, Isleworth, Middlesex.	01-568 4499
Tanntours	Central House, 34/36 Oxford Street, London W1.	01-636 2835

Name	*Address*	*Tel. No.*
Thomson Holidays	Greater London House, Hampstead Road, London, NW1 7SD.	01-387 8484
Timsway Holidays	Penn Place, Rickmansworth, Hertfordshire, WD3 1RE.	0923 771266
Twelve Islands	219 South Street, Romford, Essex RM1 1QL.	0708 752653
Twentys Holidays	15 St. Peter's Street, Hereford, HR1 2LQ.	0432 277377
Ventura Holidays	279 South Road, Sheffield, S6 3TA.	0742 331100
Villa Seekers	296-300 St. John Street, London, EC1V 4PA.	01-837 5605
Zeus Holidays	Suites 93 & 94, Kent House, 87 Regent Street, London W1.	01-434 1647

HELP WANTED

Although great care is taken to ensure accuracy things can change quickly and we would be grateful for comments based on your own experiences. If you think that we've got something wrong or you have any additional information please let us know.

This third edition has been extensively revised and improved following the tremendous response which we received to our last request for help. Please help us to make the next edition even better. We will again be acknowledging readers' contributions which are used.

You may wish to use all, or any one, of the following headings:

General: background information on a particular island, the nature of the scenery, noteworthy characteristics of the island or its people, etc.

Connections: details of air and sea connections.

Centres: details of towns/villages to stay, availability of accommodation, nightlife, etc.

Nudist Beaches: location and how to get there, description (sand, shingle, etc.), amenities including details of tavernas and toilet facilities.

Things To Do: places of interest which you feel are worth visiting.

Getting Around: availability of public transport, taxis, car/moped hire, etc.

Please send your contributions to John Dunn, Sunseeker Publications, FREEPOST, Congleton, CW12 3BR (no stamp required).

INDEX TO ISLANDS

* Pserimos is included in details for Kos.

IT COSTS JUST £1.00 TO BE A SUNSEEKER!

The exclusive Sunseeker T-shirt pictured here comes in white and features the Sunseeker logo in black. These extra large T-shirts are one size and are suitable for all chest sizes up to 42".They have been selected for their durability and washing properties and represent excellent value for money. They are offered exclusively to Sunseekers at the very special price of £3.60.

Other benefits of being a Sunseeker include:

- ★ a free Sunseeker car window sticker
- ★ an occasional newsletter giving details of special offers and discounts exclusive to Sunseekers
- ★ advance details of future Sunseeker guides.

You can become a Sunseeker by completing part A of the form below. If you also require a T-shirt, you should complete both part A and part B.

(This advertisement is only applicable to residents of the United Kingdom).

PART A SUNSEEKER REGISTRATION
Name (in full) Mr/Mrs/Miss
Address:
Postcode:
Please register me as a Sunseeker. My cheque/P.O. for £1.00 is enclosed

PART B T-SHIRT ORDER FORM	
Please send me .... Sunseeker T-shirts at £3.60 each. Total Cash Price	£
Postage & Packing	£0.35
Sunseeker Membership	£1.00
GRAND TOTAL	£
I ENCLOSE A CHEQUE/P.O. IN THE SUM OF	£

Please ensure that you have filled in all the details correctly. Send the completed form together with your payment to Sunseekers, FREEPOST, Congleton, CW12 3BR (no stamp required).
Cheques and postal orders should be crossed "A/c Payee".

OFFICE USE ONLY	Mem. No.	Date Issued:	Goods Desp. Date:

Central Council for British Naturism

The C.C.B.N. is the national nudist organisation for Great Britain and Northern Ireland. Membership details can be obtained from C.C.B.N., Freepost, Assurance House, 35-41 Hazelwood Road, Northampton, NN1 1BR.

Further Reading

Free Sun by Phil Vallack. Published by John Waite Ltd. A guide to over 1,000 beaches in Britain and Europe where you can sunbathe and swim without clothes. Available from W.H. Smith's and all good bookshops or by mail order from Mercury, 70-72 High Street, Malmesbury, Wilts.

NOTES

NOTES

NOTES

NOTES